*The Desacralization of the French Monarchy
in the Eighteenth Century*

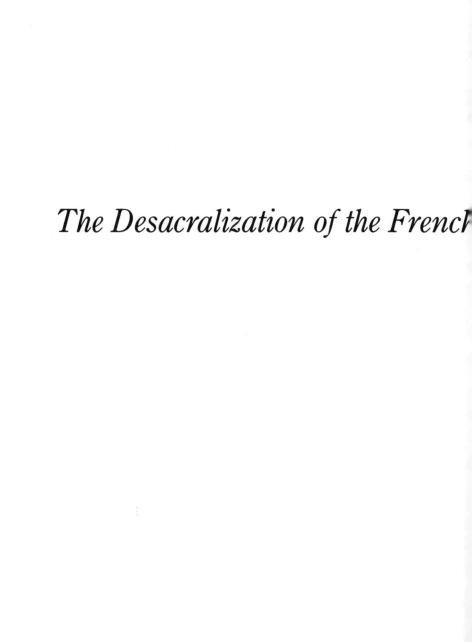

The Desacralization of the Frencl

onarchy in the Eighteenth Century

JEFFREY W. MERRICK

LOUISIANA STATE UNIVERSITY PRESS   BATON ROUGE and LONDON

99 98 97 96 95 94 93 92 91 90   5 4 3 2 1

Designer: Amanda McDonald Key
Typeface: Century Old Style
Typesetter: G&S Typesetters, Inc.
Printer and binder: Thomson-Shore, Inc.

Library of Congress Cataloging-in-Publication Data
Merrick, Jeffrey.
    The desacralization of the French monarchy in the eighteenth
century/Jeffrey W. Merrick.
        p.   cm.
    Includes bibliographical references.
    ISBN 0-8071-1537-1 (alk. paper)
    1. France—History—Revolution, 1789–1799—Causes.   2. Monarchy—
France—History—18th century.   3. Divine right of kings—France—History—
18th century.   4. Religion and politics—France—History—18th century.
    5. Protestantism—Influence.   I. Title.
    DC138.M46   1990
    944.04—dc20   89-13491
                                                                      CIP

The author is grateful to the editors of the following publications for permission to use material from his previously published articles that have appeared under these titles: "'Disputes over Words' and Constitutional Conflict in France, 1730–1732," *French Historical Studies,* XIV (1986), 497–520; "Conscience and Citizenship in Eighteenth-Century France," *Eighteenth-Century Studies,* XXI (1987), 48–71; "Politics in the Pulpit: Ecclesiastical Discourse on the Death of Louis XV," *History of European Ideas,* VII (1986), 149–60; "The Coronation of Louis XVI: The Waning of Royal Ritual," *Proceedings of the Eighth Annual Meeting of the Western Society for French History* (1981), 191–204; "Patterns and Prosecution of Suicide in Eighteenth-Century Paris," *Historical Reflections/Réflexions historiques,* XVI (1989), 1–53; and "Royal Bees: The Gender Politics of the Beehive in Early Modern Europe," *Studies in Eighteenth-Century Culture,* XVIII (1988), 7–37.

For Steve

Contents

Preface

Intellectual historians working on the Enlightenment have traditionally ignored social history, and social historians working on the ancien régime have commonly ignored intellectual history. Intellectual and social historians alike have generally ignored the political history of France in the eighteenth century. In recent years Michel Antoine, Keith Baker, William Doyle, François Furet, Robert Kreiser, Bailey Stone, Dale Van Kley, and others have rehabilitated the study of this neglected subject. These historians have ransacked the archives and reconceptualized the issues. Their work demonstrates that we must reconstruct the political culture of France in the reigns of Louis XV and Louis XVI in order to understand the origins of the Revolution. Having just celebrated the two-hundredth anniversary of the storming of the Bastille, we can no longer accept simplistic Whiggish descriptions of the Revolution as the result of a battle of the books starring the philosophes or simplistic Marxist characterizations of the Revolution as an inevitable class struggle between a feudal aristocracy and a capitalist bourgeoisie. Whiggish interpretations, which reduce politics to intellectual conflicts, exaggerate the revolutionary character of the Enlightenment and underestimate the extent of its assimilation by the traditional order. Marxist interpretations, which reduce politics to social conflicts, exaggerate the revolutionary character of the "bourgeoisie" and underestimate the extent of its incorporation into the traditional order. Both types of interpretations assume that the ancien régime was more monolithic and more moribund than it really was. They suggest that outsiders allegedly excluded from the structures of authority and privilege (the philosophes and the bourgeoisie) naturally subverted the traditional order and eventually caused its destruction. This book, like the work of the historians mentioned above, rejects the Whiggish and Marxist trivializations of politics and emphasizes the importance of conflicts within the traditional order in the background of the Revolution.

When I identified the subject of my research as the desacralization of the French monarchy during a job interview some years ago, one of the interviewers snorted, "What the hell does that mean?" It means the breakdown of the conjunction of religion and politics that characterized traditional conceptions of kingship and kingdom. My sources do not allow for systematic investigation of the fate of the mystique of kingship "by the grace of God" in popular mentalities. They reveal much more about the fortunes of the construct of divine right in the conflicting discourses of the crown, the clergy, and the parlements, who choreographed the political life of the country. Their disputes, which probably influenced the literate public more than did the Enlightenment, desacralized the monarchy by discrediting the juridical principle of the divine ordination of royal authority, which exempted the king from accountability to his subjects. The politico-religious strife spanning much of the eighteenth century not only undermined the religious character of kingship but also circumscribed its religious obligations. Protracted controversies concerning Jansenism and toleration encouraged the expansion of secular at the expense of ecclesiastical jurisdiction and the disengagement of citizenship from religious conformity. These controversies desacralized the monarchy by redefining the responsibilities of the king and the bonds that unified the kingdom. Kings, royal councillors, bishops, parlementaires, Jansenists, Protestants, and pamphleteers claimed to defend the traditions of the ancien régime against the philosophes, but their contestations, in the last analysis, weakened these traditions more effectively than the philosophes themselves.

Chapters 1 and 2 explain the problematic conjunction of religion and politics disrupted by these contestations. Chapter 1 outlines the canonical history, constitutional principles, conventional rhetoric, and traditional rituals that embodied the religious character of kingship. Chapter 2 describes the relationship between spiritual and temporal authority and examines the crown's obligations to enforce sacramental conformity, censor unorthodox opinions, and punish irreligious and immoral conduct. Chapters 3, 4, and 5 discuss the decades of ecclesiastical and constitutional disputes engendered by the papal condemnation of Jansenism in the bull *Unigenitus* (1713). These chapters do not provide a comprehensive narrative of the disputes in question; they concentrate largely on developments in Paris. They show how conflicts about the interpretation of the principles of the politico-religious order challenged the unaccountability of the divinely ordained king and strained the linking of citizenship and Catholicity. Chapter 3 analyzes the events of the years 1730–1732 in considerable detail because the issues and maneuvers involved in this episode set the pattern for the more well-known quarrels of the 1750s. The chapters on the Jansenist controversies do not deal systematically with the contemporaneous fiscal controversies, which raised many of the same constitutional questions, but Chapter 3 concludes with a coda on the *vingtième* of 1749. Because of the clergy's vociferous defense of its fiscal exemptions, this tax, like *Unigenitus*, provoked polemics about ecclesiastical privileges, royal obligations, and the role of religion in the public order.

Chapter 4 examines the acrimonious conflicts occasioned by the withholding of sacraments from Jansenists in the 1750s. These conflicts led the crown to abandon its customary support of the clergy against the magistrates and prompted Damiens to strike Louis XV in 1757. The attempted assassination of the king dramatically illustrates the corrosive effects of decades of well-publicized dissension on the traditions that sanctified his person as well as his authority. Chapter 5 discusses the conclusion of the religious disputes in the debates surrounding the assembly of the clergy of 1765 and the culmination of the political disputes in the contentions that marked the last years of the reign of Louis XV and the first years of the reign of Louis XVI. Chapter 6, finally, considers the role of the controversies concerning the Protestants in the desacralization of the monarchy. Protestants, unlike the "patriotic" pamphleteers of the 1770s, did not repudiate the principle of divine ordination. They did urge the king to abdicate his traditional religious obligations more decisively than did the Jansenists, who joined the campaign for toleration in the second half of the century. Arguments formulated by magistrates and royal councillors—many of them involved in the other conflicts about the conjunction of religion and politics—shaped the edict of 1787 by which the king eventually divorced citizenship from Catholicity and redefined the character of his kingdom.

This book, in one form or another, has been my most constant companion for the last ten years. For sharing their eighteenth-century resources with me during these years, I am grateful to the libraries of Yale, Columbia, and Princeton Universities and the State University of New York at Albany, the New York Public Library, Library of Congress, Bibliothèque Nationale, Archives Nationales, Bibliothèque de Port Royal, Bibliothèque de la Société de l'Histoire du Protestantisme Français, Bibliothèque de l'Arsénal, and Bibliothèque du Sénat. Peter Gay and R. R. Palmer supervised the writing of the first version of this study and have encouraged me in my work ever since. Keith Baker, Carol Blum, Sarah Hanley, Thomas Kaiser, Darline Levy, Lloyd Moote, Norman Ravitch, Eugene Rice, Lionel Rothkrug, Alexander Sedgwick, Bonnie Smith, Dale Van Kley, and John Woodbridge generously took time to read and comment on the manuscript in various stages. The editors of *Eighteenth-Century Studies, French Historical Studies, Historical Reflections/Réflexions historiques, History of European Ideas, Proceedings of the Western Society for French History,* and *Studies in Eighteenth-Century Culture* granted permission to use material included in articles published along the way. Steven Atkinson, Marjorie Benedict, William Moore, and Robert Schumann helped with the chore of proofreading the computer printout submitted to LSU Press. Margaret Dalrymple, Catherine Barton, Julie Schorfheide, John Easterly, and Betty Waterhouse guided *The Desacralization of the French Monarchy* through the process of publication. My thanks, finally, to Penelope Johnson, Paul and Deane Stepansky, and Ann Withington for helping me survive what I often thought was an incurable case of "firstbookitis."

Abbreviations and Short Titles

AN	Archives Nationales
Arsénal	Bibliothèque de l'Arsénal
BSHPF	*Bulletin de la Société de l'histoire du protestantisme français*
Collection intégrale	Jacques-Paul Migne (ed.), *Collection intégrale et universelle des orateurs sacrés* . . . (99 vols.; Paris, 1844–1892).
FF	Fonds Français, Bibliothèque Nationale
JF	Joly de Fleury collection, Bibliothèque Nationale
Mémoires sur la cour	Charles-Philippe d'Albert de Luynes, *Mémoires sur la cour de Louis XV, 1735–1758*, ed. Louis-Etienne Dussieux and Eudoxe Soulié (17 vols.; Paris, 1860–1865).
NAF	Nouvelles Acquisitions Françaises, Bibliothèque Nationale
PF	Bibliothèque de la Société de l'histoire du protestantisme français

PR   Bibliothèque de Port-Royal, LePaige collection

PV   *Collection des procès-verbaux des assemblées générales du clergé de France depuis l'année 1560 jusqu'à présent* (8 vols. in 9; Paris, 1767–1780).

Recueil général   François-André Isambert *et al.* (eds.), *Recueil général des anciennes lois françaises depuis l'an 420 jusqu'à la Révolution de 1789* (29 vols.; Paris, 1821–1833).

Les Remontrances   Jules Flammermont (ed.), *Les Remontrances du Parlement de Paris au XVIIIe siècle* (3 vols.; Paris, 1888–1898).

Sénat   Bibliothèque du Sénat

*The Desacralization of the French Monarchy
in the Eighteenth Century*

1

The Religious Character of the Monarchy and the Traditions of Christian Kingship

"The Catholic faith is national in France. This is not a question; it is a fact."[1] The experience of generations of French subjects and the traditions of the French monarchy confirmed the abbé Fauchet's confident characterization of his country as a Catholic kingdom on the eve of the Revolution. Transcending the multitude of social distinctions and regional differences that divided them, Catholicism united French men and women of all ranks and provinces in the faith that had guided French history for more than a millennium. Permeating the popular mentality and the public order, religion informed the collective sense of space, time, identity, and authority in the ancien régime. It defined the familiar geography of the parish, marked the rhythms of the calendar, measured the stages of life from baptism to burial, and consecrated both the daily bread of ordinary subjects and the venerable crown that commanded their allegiance. The Most Christian King, who reigned as the father of his people and the earthly image of the Divinity, concerned himself with their spiritual welfare as well as their material sustenance. Priests throughout France led their congregations in prayers for the sovereign and exhorted them to obey his edicts, which, like the annals of his predecessors and the coins of the realm, bore the hallowed formula "King by the grace of God."

1. Claude Fauchet, "De la religion nationale," in *Collection intégrale*, LXVI, 32.

In the France of the ancien régime, God sanctified the king, and the king defended the ancestral faith of the country as well as the worldly privileges of its ministers. French history illustrates the permanence and the problematic character of this symbiotic relationship of religion and politics. The territoriality of the Church not only provided Christianity with earthly foundations but also involved the clergy in controversies about property and citizenship. Government "by the grace of God" not only invested monarchy with divine legitimacy but also entangled the crown in disputes about the sacraments and toleration. The linking of religion and politics unified the Christian kingdom in theory but occasioned as much contention as cooperation in practice. The disparate commitments and divergent interests of altar and throne provoked perennial conflicts about the differentiation of spiritual and secular concerns and jurisdictions. Well before the end of the eighteenth century these conflicts raised questions about the religious obligations of kingship and the confessional traditions of the kingdom, questions that Fauchet deliberately ignored in 1789.

The French dated the Christian character of their country from the baptism of the Merovingian king Clovis on Christmas Day in the year 498 (or 499). With this blessed event, as one eighteenth-century historian declared, "commenced the reign of God over the fairest and most powerful monarchy in Europe, and the time of such an auspicious event was that of the very foundation of this monarchy, as if, in the designs of Providence, the Christian faith was to be so linked with the constitution of the French realm that the latter could not, without the former, endure with glory and with stability."[2] Legend claimed that Saint Rémy consecrated Clovis with oil transported from heaven by a dove and subsequently preserved in the Holy Ampulla of Reims, but the custom of royal anointment among the Franks actually originated in the eighth century. Pepin, the first of the Carolingian monarchs, was anointed in 751 with the blessing of Pope Zacharias and again in 754 by Pope Stephen II himself, who needed Frankish assistance against the Lombards and support against the Holy Roman Empire. The Old Testament practice of consecration, combined with

2. Etienne Oroux, *Histoire ecclésiastique de la cour de France* . . . (2 vols.; Paris, 1776), I, xxix.

the Germanic and Byzantine traditions of election and coronation, gave religious sanction to the dispossession of the Merovingians. The crowning of Pepin's son Charlemagne by Pope Leo III on Christmas Day, 800, renewed the spiritual and military alliance between Rome and the Carolingians. This ceremony symbolically consummated Charlemagne's efforts to Christianize his kingdom by converting heathens, convening councils, reforming the clergy, and enforcing the canons of the Church. The development of the practice of thaumaturgic royal touching for scrofula provided divine legitimization for the Capetian usurpation of the throne in the tenth century. Among the sovereigns of the third dynasty, Louis IX, who crusaded against infidels abroad and strove to establish the reign of God within his realm, epitomized the ideal of Christian kingship. Eighteenth-century panegyrists appointed by the French Academy annually glorified this saintly king, who set an example for his successors by protecting the Church, ruling justly, and exterminating heretics.

By the fifteenth century, when Joan of Arc completed her mission with the consecration of Charles VII at Reims, the French monarch had acquired the titles that distinguished his crown: the Most Christian King and the Eldest Son of the Church. He ruled "by the grace of God" as the Anointed of the Lord and, in his quasi-sacerdotal capacity as External Bishop, participated in the affairs of the Church in France. The legacy of medieval monarchy, however, was recorded not only in pious epithets, crusading epics, and the statuary of Gothic cathedrals, but also in the hostilities between Philip Augustus and Pope Innocent III, Philip the Fair and Pope Boniface VIII, which exposed the political ambivalence of the religious character of kingship. On the one hand, divine ordination allowed the sovereign to justify meddling in ecclesiastical matters, to defy ultramontane assertions of papal supremacy, and to counter "feudal" assumptions about contractual restraints upon his prerogatives. At the same time, it left the monarchy vulnerable to foreign and domestic challenges. Popes claimed the power to release kingdoms from obedience to kings who betrayed their sacred calling, and vassals appropriated arguments for royal accountability in order to legitimize resistance to rulers who transgressed the customary limits of their authority.

The medieval mix of religious and political challenges to the independence of the crown exploded in the civil wars of the sixteenth century. Confessional antagonisms, aristocratic factionalism, and foreign intervention prolonged these conflicts and destabilized the throne for decades. Both Protestant Monarchomachs, outraged by the Saint Bartholomew's Day Massacre, and Catholic Ligueurs, appalled by the assassinations of the Guises and the accession of Henry of Navarre, challenged the monarchy on religious as well as constitutional grounds. Their indictments of ungodly and tyrannical rulers, based on subversive interpretations of Scripture and the traditions of the kingdom, invoked popular sovereignty and justified regicide. When strife eventually subsided, the *politique* principle of the priority of order over orthodoxy prevailed. Henry IV, whose conversion to Catholicism preserved the Catholicity of the throne, forced the clergy and the parlements to accept the Edict of Nantes. This last and most lasting of the edicts of pacification granted limited liberty of worship and military privileges to the Huguenots and effectively denied the Catholicity of the realm.

The civil wars not only provoked attacks on the authority of the crown but also prompted the formulation of classic theories of royal sovereignty by Jean Bodin and Charles Loyseau. The assassinations of Henry III (1589) and Henry IV (1610) by the fanatics Jacques Clément and François Ravaillac accelerated the absolutist expropriation of the principle of divine ordination. When the Estates-General assembled in 1614, the Third Estate called for the adoption as a fundamental law of the realm, "conforming to the word of God," of the axiom that "no power on earth whatever, spiritual or temporal," could "take away the sacred nature of our kings," who held their crown "from God alone," or "dispense their subjects of the fidelity and obedience which they owe them for any cause·or pretext whatever."[3] The Parlement of Paris, which had nullified the papal excommunication of Henry IV, supported the article, but the clergy, asserting their monopoly on the interpretation of "the word of God," convinced the Regency government to block its ratification. During the ministry of cardinal Richelieu the monarchy subsequently rescinded the military

3. Quoted in J. Michael Hayden, *France and the Estates-General of 1614* (Cambridge, England, 1974), 131.

privileges of the rebellious Huguenots but also allied itself with the Protestant powers against the Habsburgs in the Thirty Years' War. In response to criticism from devout circles, apologists for Richelieu's foreign policy appealed both to divine right, insisting upon the immunity of the monarch from accountability to his subjects, and to reason of state, insisting upon the autonomy of political imperatives from religious considerations.

Richelieu's successor, Mazarin, who prolonged the war against Spain for another ten years after the signing of the Treaty of Westphalia, reconfirmed the religious liberties of the Protestants in return for their loyalty during the Fronde. In this civil war, unlike those of the sixteenth century, religious issues did not play a significant role, although Jansenism had much to do with the agitation of the Parisian clergy in the wake of the Fronde. Parlementaires and princes rebelled against the cardinal's wartime fiscal expedients and the "despotism" of royal intendants in the provinces. Pamphleteers did not attack divine right in principle, but they maintained that the Most Christian King had to reign lawfully and respect the customs of the realm. They argued that he must submit his edicts, especially fiscal edicts, to the parlements for registration and that he could not circumvent parlementary jurisdiction by appointing new officers or evoking cases to the royal council. Frondeurs, unlike Monarchomachs and Ligueurs, did not threaten the king with deposition, but they did enlist God on their side in justifying opposition to the unjust commands of his agents.

The Fronde, like the civil wars of the preceding century, discredited resistance and hastened the development of absolutism. Louis XIV muzzled the parlements and never summoned the Estates-General. He domesticated the nobility and repressed the peasant revolts. Like his predecessors he also expanded royal power in ecclesiastical affairs in the name of Gallicanism, which entailed not only the independence of the French Church from Rome but also its subordination to the crown in some regards. The monarchy had already exercised the prerogative of nominating bishops for a century and a half by the time Louis XIV antagonized the Holy See by extending his regalian rights over revenues and appointments in vacant bishoprics throughout the kingdom. Papal opposition prompted the convocation of the extraordinary assembly of the clergy of 1682, which reaffirmed the conciliar doctrine of the supremacy of councils over popes. The clergy not only defended the prerogatives of the French Church but also upheld the sovereignty of the king by belatedly ratifying the principle that he was not subject to ecclesiastical authority in temporal matters and could not be deposed under any circumstances. Louis XIV eventually backed down and soft-pedalled the Gallican resolutions of the assembly, but the Parlement of Paris, which had registered the Four Articles of 1682 at his behest, enshrined them among the fundamental laws of the realm.

Louis XIV undermined the independence of the institutional Church, as well as other corporate bodies, but he also reinforced the linking of religion and politics in the public order. He enlisted the clergy, along with the academies and the press, in the glorification of the monarchy. In the hands of Bossuet and other apologists of absolutism, divine ordination shed its menacing ambivalence and left the sovereign accountable only to God. Anxious to serve God and placate the papacy, Louis XIV abrogated the privileges of the Protestants one by one and finally revoked the Edict of Nantes outright in 1685. He continued the cardinals' campaign against the Jansenists and solicited what was intended to be the definitive condemnation of their heresy from Rome in the bull *Unigenitus* of 1713. French Protestants and Jansenists denounced the Glorious Revolution across the Channel and insisted upon their own loyalty to the crown, but Louis XIV equated confessional nonconformity with subversive "republicanism." His efforts to rid the realm of both groups of dissidents, so as to ensure its stability as well as its orthodoxy, earned him a place in the pantheon of Christian kingship along with Clovis, Charlemagne, and Saint Louis.

Political realities, of course, never conformed to the rhetoric of divine-right absolutism that flourished in the seventeenth century and survived until the Revolution. The corporate structures of the kingdom, not to mention its size and lack of uniformity, imposed de facto limitations on royal power. Louis XIV made the most of the spectacle of kingship and immortalized himself in public monuments as the resplendent Apollo, the victorious Alexander, and the pious David, but defeat, misery, and criticism darkened the last decades of his reign. Disgruntled aristocrats like Saint-Simon, dissatisfied reformers like Vauban, and disillusioned bishops like Fénelon documented the shortcomings of the Sun King's absolutism. The resolution of Louis XIV's differences with the papacy laid to rest the Roman threat that had haunted the realm for centuries. The jeremiads of Protestant exiles like Pierre Jurieu and the chiliastic insurrection of the Camisards in the Midi closed the book on confessional rebellions against ungodly rulers in France. Accusations of ultramontanism and "republicanism," however, reverberated well into the eighteenth century because they served partisan purposes, but more serious challenges to royal sovereignty lurked within the politico-religious traditions shaped by a millennium of kingship "by the grace of God."

According to the royal historiographer Moreau, the study of the past was of interest not for the discovery of new principles, but for the confirmation of ancient truths.[4] Clerics, jurists, and antiphilosophes reaffirmed the religious character of the French monarchy by restating these truths in sermons, treatises, and polemics during the reigns of Louis XV and Louis XVI. The language of Bossuet had become utterly trite by Moreau's time, but its persistence underlined unchanging assumptions as well as defensive apprehensions about the role of religion in the ancien régime. "Christianity," declared the bishop of Langres, "is bound up with our constitution," in the loose sense of that word. As a private and public imperative, Catholicism unified the country and legitimized the social and political order. "Without getting lost in vague questions about the origin and formation of societies," the bishop of Troyes explained, "it brings the entire social system back to a great and single center, God, the principle and origin of all things, the sacred source from which derive both the prerogatives of authority and the duties of dependence."[5] The ancestral faith of the kingdom left no doubt about the divine purposes at work in the course of French history and the constitution of the traditional order.

Moreau and the bishops assumed that God Himself had designed society in the abstract and the society of the ancien régime in particu-

4. Jacob-Nicolas Moreau, *Leçons de morale, de politique, et de droit public puisées dans l'histoire de notre monarchie . . .* (Versailles, 1773), xi.

5. César-Guillaume de La Luzerne, "Sur l'harmonie entre les deux puissances et l'intérêt qu'elles ont réciproquement à la maintenir," in *Collection intégrale*, LXXIII, 906; Etienne-Antoine de Boulogne, "Sur la religion," *ibid.*, LXXIV, 112.

lar. Providence created humans unequal so as to unite them, like the parts of the body, through the diversity of their functions, but their sinfulness perpetually threatened the harmony of the whole. Religion, which instructed all humans in their common dependence on the Creator and their moral obligations toward one another, preserved the concord of earthly communities. By restraining the passions and consecrating the responsibilities of every station, religion, according to the abbé Chaudon, made "the ruler humane, the subject submissive, the magistrate honest, the master lenient, the servant faithful, the husband virtuous, the wife chaste, the father affectionate, the son obedient." Since the Fourth Commandment prescribed obedience to all superiors in the social and political order, Moreau traced "to the throne of God Himself the chain of all the duties which unite us."[6] Because Christianity checked selfishness and sanctified obedience, the entire network of authority and subordination rested upon the foundation of the ancestral faith of the realm.

Apologists for the traditional order considered dependence the "natural condition" of the human species. They identified the wife, children, and servants as minors within the microcosmic kingdom of the family. The father derived his authority over them, described by the bishop of Senez as "the oldest and most sacred authority there is among humans," from God Himself. The father had absolute authority (though not the power of life and death) over his household, and yet, as the royal councillor Joly de Fleury noted, "he has obligations to fulfill" toward those entrusted to his care.[7] At least one ecclesiastical commentator acknowledged that the Fourth Commandment deliberately omitted any mention of this reciprocity of obligations, so as not

6. Louis-Mayeul Chaudon, *Dictionnaire antiphilosophique* . . . (2 vols. in 1; Avignon, 1769), xi; Moreau, *Les Devoirs du prince réduits à un seul principe ou discours sur la justice dédié au roi* (Versailles, 1775), 197. Different denominations have traditionally numbered the Ten Commandments (Exod. 20:2–17) in different ways. According to the Catholic system of numbering used here and throughout the text, the Fourth Commandment enjoins humans to honor their parents.

7. Anonymous discourse on inequality, in Roger Tisserand (ed.), *Les Concurrents de J.-J. Rousseau à l'académie de Dijon pour le prix de 1754* (Paris, 1936), 200; Jean-Baptiste-Charles-Marie de Beauvais, "Sur la piété filiale," in *Collection intégrale*, LXXI, 354; Jean-François Joly de Fleury, "Mémoire sur les évocations" (1766), in JF, Vol. 1051, fol. 66.

to encourage minors to pass judgment on their superiors in an unnatural and sacrilegious manner.[8] Even moralists who reminded the father that Saint Paul (Ephesians 5:21–6:9) required him to love his wife, educate his children, and treat his servants well inevitably reminded these subjects of the domestic monarch that they were permitted to disobey him only if his orders explicitly contravened the word of God.

The descendants of Adam, the first father and the first king, came into this world dependent not only on their own fathers but also on the kings ordained by God to maintain peace in the macrocosmic family of the kingdom. Invested with "supreme, independent, and absolute power," not by human convention, as the abbé Richard added, but by divine institution, the Most Christian Kings of France reigned as "the visible images of the Divinity." Modeled on what the bishop of Senez called "paternal sovereignty," their government replicated "that which the Holy Scripture describes." The king, as the marquis de Saint-Aubin explained, "is appointed by the Lord; royal authority derives from God and not from the people. The king is accountable for his administration only to God, who gave him this absolute authority for the good of the people."[9] The people did not choose their ruler, any more than children chose their fathers, and he was therefore not answerable to them. Because monarchy embodied a commission from the Almighty, not a contract with the nation, subjects had no grounds for disobeying the monarch unless his commands flatly violated the word of God. Traditionalists like Moreau usually consigned this qualification to the footnotes, but they never tired of citing the Pauline equation of disobedience to authorities ordained by God with rebellion against God Himself (Romans 13:1–2).

The sacred character of kingship exempted the French kings from earthly accountability, but it also required them to rule as the lieutenants of the Deity, who instituted them, as Richard maintained, "to represent Him and take His place in the government of men." As

8. Bertrand de Latour, "Discours sur l'éducation des enfants," in *Collection intégrale*, LXI, 131.

9. Charles-Louis Richard, "Sur les devoirs des sujets envers le souverain," in *Collection intégrale*, LXVII, 612; Beauvais, "Sur la piété filiale," *ibid.*, LXXI, 355; Gilbert-Charles Legendre de Saint-Aubin, *Traité de l'opinion ou mémoires pour servir à l'histoire de l'esprit humain* (6 vols.; Paris, 1735), V, 120.

God's representatives, they were expected to protect the Church, promote the spiritual welfare of the realm, and defend the faith that ensured the salvation, as well as the obedience, of their people. Divine ordination obliged the people to obey their sovereign, but it also obliged the sovereign to rule them justly, treating them as children rather than slaves: "a sacred contract not concluded by men," the bishop of Troyes specified, "but written by the hand of God Himself." The monarch alone legislated, like the omnipotent Lord, but he promulgated laws for the benefit of his subjects, and he respected those laws himself, just as God abided by the laws of the cosmos He had created. "The power of the king," as Saint-Aubin put it, "is absolute but paternal, tempered by laws which can emanate only from his own authority and for the observance of which he is responsible only to God, whose providence established monarchy over the people for the advantage of the people itself." [10] God Himself made the sovereign responsible for the welfare of his subjects, who lacked the competence to select their own rulers and the ability to look after their own needs.

Religion, "the sacred bond which unites the monarch with the people and all men with God," made the people "loyal and devoted" and the monarch "just, good, and generous." Divine ordination not only legitimized monarchy, by founding it upon providential purposes rather than selfish human interests, but also prescribed standards for monarchical rule that transcended faulty human conventions. Inasmuch as it required the sovereign to imitate God in the dispensation of justice— described by the abbé Géry as "the most august function of kings, that which most likens them to the Divinity"—it underlined the crucial distinction between absolute and arbitrary authority in the vocabulary of the ancien régime. Royal authority was absolute because it was not subject to constitutional restrictions in the form of institutionalized checks and balances. At the same time, it was not arbitrary, according to Moreau, "because it is subject to laws which humans did not frame," as well as customary restraints in the form of the fundamental laws of the realm. The French kings did not exercise their absolute authority in an arbitrary manner, he explained, because Providence

10. Richard, "Sur les devoirs des sujets," in *Collection intégrale*, LXVII, 612; Boulogne, "Sur la religion," *ibid.*, LXXIV, 114; Legendre de Saint-Aubin, *Traité de l'opinion*, V, 116–17.

intended them to use this authority "to maintain their subjects in all the benefits which they derive from nature" and "all the civil and political benefits of the society in which God has made them born."[11]

The Most Christian King conformed to the mandate of God and the expectations of his subjects by respecting the so-called fundamental laws of the realm. These laws, never recorded in the form of a definitive charter, preserved the hereditary succession to the throne according to the rule of primogeniture in the legitimate male line, the inalienability of royal authority and of the royal domain, the Catholicity of the crown, the Gallican liberties of the Church, the hierarchy of the three estates, and the lives, privileges, and property of French subjects. The fundamental laws did not represent limitations upon the monarchy, because these principles of the unwritten constitution distinguished it from despotism as a form of government. Louis XIV's tampering with several of these traditions in the last years of his reign—by renouncing his grandson's claims to the French throne in order to secure the Spanish succession for him as Philip V and by elevating his illegitimate sons (the duc de Maine and comte de Toulouse) to the rank of princes of the blood in the order of succession—contributed to criticism of his "despotism" after his death. In revoking the rights of the illegitimate princes in 1717, the Regency government explicitly recognized the "fortunate powerlessness" of the crown to alter the fundamental laws in this manner.[12]

The lawful patriarchalism of kingship "by the grace of God" suited the refractory particularism of the kingdom, which lacked linguistic, fiscal, and legal uniformity. French subjects were, as the solicitor general Séguier put it, "divided into as many different corporate bodies as there are different stations in the realm," like so many links in a chain. Their privileges, liberties, and rights (synonymous terms in the traditional vocabulary) depended upon the configuration of their memberships in the conglomeration of families, guilds, professions, estates, towns, and provinces subject to the crown. Differences in parentage,

---

11. Brochier, *Oraison funèbre de . . . Louis XV . . .* (Vienne, 1774), 21; Isaac-Alexis Dessauret, "Oraison funèbre de Louis XV," in *Collection intégrale*, LXIX, 501; André-Guillaume Géry, "Panégyrique de Saint Louis," *ibid.*, LXIII, 751; Moreau, *Devoirs du prince*, v–vi, 18, 188.

12. *Déclaration du roi*, August, 1717, in *Recueil général*, XXI, 147.

rank, occupation, and residence translated into differences in legal status. In a juridical sense the unity of the monarchy resided only in the monarch, for he alone commanded the obedience of all of his people, regardless of the corporate groupings and diverse privileges that divided them. "All of the bonds of society," the abbé Guidi declared, converged "in the hands of the ruler, who, in spite of the diversity of ranks, privileges, sexes, characters, opinions, habits, educations must tighten the bonds of the body politic, preserve harmony throughout, dispense justice with impartiality." Like the Divinity in the creation, like the sun in the heavens, like the father in the family, like the heart in the body, the sovereign was, in the abbé Clement's words, "the center of the society which he governs," and order emanated from his throne.[13]

Reigning over the intractable disorder of the ancien régime, the king was the only public personage in the kingdom, in the sense that he alone wielded authority over the entire realm and represented all of his subjects, whose interests he identified with his own. "The whole nation," as the royal councillor Gilbert de Voisins pointed out, "is so to speak confounded with the king, in whose hands and under whose sovereignty it rests." Like a father, according to Guidi, "who takes in at a glance everything that is happening in his vast household," the monarch looked beyond the selfish demands of rapacious individuals and jealous corporate bodies. Given this royal perspective, he alone could assess the needs of his people as a whole and promote the collective welfare of the country. Absolutism accordingly vested authority "in the person of the monarch," Joly de Fleury specified, "without dependence, division, condition." He made the laws, and he alone, as one royalist pamphleteer insisted, "has the right to interpret them."[14] He accepted advice from his appointed councillors and various corpo-

13. *Les Remontrances*, III, 345; [Louis Guidi], *Suite du dialogue sur les mariages des protestants* . . . (N.p., 1776), 25–26; Denis-Xavier Clément, "Sermon pour l'inauguration de la statue du roi érigée par le roi de Pologne," in *Collection intégrale*, LIV, 1755.

14. Pierre Gilbert de Voisins, Draft for *arrêt du conseil* (1765), in Ser. U, Vol. 872, unpaginated, AN; [Guidi], *Dialogue sur l'état civil des protestants en France* (N.p., 1778), 5; Joly de Fleury, "Mémoire sur les évocations," in JF, Vol. 1051, fol. 65 v.; [Auguste-Pierre Damiens de Gomicourt], *Observations sur la nature des biens ecclésiastiques* (London, 1751), 5.

rate bodies, but he did not recognize the voice of "the public." Absolutism disallowed public participation in the government of the realm, which remained the private concern of the sovereign and the agents to whom he delegated his authority.

As the judge of the public interest and the source of justice in the kingdom, the king adjudicated differences between his subjects and preserved peace among them, in spite of what Moreau described as "the opposition of their tempers, the clash of their passions, and the dissonance of their interests." While supporting patriarchal authority within the family by punishing unruly wives, children, and servants, he defended his own sovereignty by settling conflicts between corporate bodies that disturbed the harmony of the realm. Checking the ambitions of the mighty and providing for the needs of the humble, he rectified the injustices committed by the contentious people entrusted to him and maintained them in the stations assigned to them by God. "It is through him," the future Keeper of the Seals Miromesnil contended, "through his care, through his protection that everyone ought to enjoy possession of his status in peace." Because the monarchy guaranteed the public welfare by protecting the private privileges of all subjects, as the royal councillor Gin declared, "this government, for which God has shown us the model in paternal authority, is the most favorable to the liberty of each of the individuals who make up the society."[15]

The authority of the king, in the last analysis, had to be absolute, so as "to keep all the orders of the state in line, but this absolute authority," Miromesnil warned, "should have as its object to reconcile everything, to conserve everything, and never to destroy anything." The Fourth Commandment seemed to sanctify the venerable principles of the unwritten constitution in the collective mentality and juridical practices of the ancien régime. Patriarchalism dictated subservience to the customs of the forefathers as well as submission to the fatherly monarch, charged with the responsibility of preserving the privileges of his subjects and the traditions of the realm. Apologists of absolutism realized that the sovereign "must change the laws when

15. Moreau, *Leçons de morale,* 23; Armand-Thomas Hue de Miromesnil, "Lettres sur l'état de la magistrature en l'année 1772," in FF, Vol. 10986, fol. 8; Pierre-Louis-Claude Gin, *Les Vrais principes du gouvernement français . . .* (Geneva, 1780), 13.

the welfare of the state seems to him to require it," as Joly de Fleury maintained.[16] At the same time, they recognized that he had to "tolerate" abuses, inequities, and contradictions that had become part and parcel of the customary order. Reform, therefore, often meant the introduction of new ordinances, offices, and jurisdictions without the abolition of the old, and these institutional superimpositions compounded the administrative confusion of the ancien régime.

"Let us take the constitution as it has been handed down to us," counselled Moreau, "and let us beware of making any innovations in it."[17] "Innovation" had pejorative connotations in the vocabulary of Moreau and his contemporaries, because it involved dangerous meddling with the familiar principles of the past. Fidelity to these principles preserved the monarchy from the fearful excesses of "despotism" and "republicanism," which suggested unrestrained tyranny on the one hand and unbridled individualism on the other. Traditionalists abhorred both the lawlessness of the Turks and the "independence" of the English, who had killed one king in 1649 and deposed another forty years later. "Independence," as the Parlement of Paris declared, "is a flaw in the political order because the individual is always tempted to abuse his liberty." Catholicism distinguished the legitimate "liberty" of French subjects from pernicious "license," just as it prevented the degeneration of "absolute" into "arbitrary" government. "All other religions tend toward the republican system," according to opponents of toleration, but the faith of the Bourbons and their people consecrated the authority of the crown and the customary order of the kingdom. "All the civil institutions are linked to Catholicism," as one magistrate warned. "To disturb the Catholic religion is therefore to risk making the state collapse."[18]

"One faith, one king, one law." The proverbial linking of religious

16. Miromesnil, "Lettres sur l'état de la magistrature," in FF, Vol. 10986, fol. 5; Joly de Fleury, "Mémoire sur les évocations," in JF, Vol. 1051, fol. 65 v.

17. Moreau, *Devoirs du prince*, 199. On the political uses of history by Moreau and others, see Keith Michael Baker, "Memory and Practice: Politics and the Representation of the Past in Eighteenth-Century France," *Representations*, XI (1985), 134–65.

18. *Les Remontrances*, III, 346; Joly de Fleury, "Réflexions sur les mariages des Protestants" (1775), in JF, Vol. 1681, fol. 7 v.; Achille-Pierre Dionis du Séjour, Comments on Chrétien-Guillaume de Lamoignon de Malesherbes, "Mémoires sur le mariage des Protestants" (1785–86), in FF, Vol. 10619, fol. 5.

orthodoxy, royal sovereignty, and public order embodied the experience of centuries of French history as well as the injunctions of the Lord. Just as Catholicism governed the circuit of the year and the cycle of mortal life, the holy circle of the crown imposed unity, if not uniformity, upon the corporate confusion of the ancien régime. As the personification of the realm and the image of the Almighty, the monarch was regarded as a mediator of sorts between God and the kingdom. Blessings and adversity in his private life and on the battlefield manifested the benevolence and the displeasure of God toward the French people, who celebrated births and marriages and lamented illnesses and deaths in the royal family as divine judgments that touched their own lives. The pious chancellor d'Aguesseau confessed that Louis XV's sickness at Metz in 1744 "has so disturbed me and troubled my mind that for two weeks I could hardly think of anything else."[19] A self-styled peasant of Chaillot recorded his anxiety in colloquial verses on the king's recovery:

> Las! quand notre pasteur au prône
> Recommandit votre parsonne,
> Tout aussitôt chacun de nous
> Se prosternait à deux genoux.
> Eh! jerni par la sainte ampoule,
> Jette-t'on les bons rois au moule?[20]
>
> [Alas! When our pastor in his sermon
> prayed for your person,
> every one of us immediately
> got down on his knees.
> Heh, zounds! By the Holy Ampulla,
> Do they make good kings with a mould?]

As the news of the restoration of the health of the body politic in the person of the sovereign spread across France, the devoted subjects of Louis "the Beloved" expressed their thanks with Te Deums and their joy with fireworks.

Given the unwritten character of the French constitution and the

19. Henri-François d'Aguesseau to his daughter, September 1, 1744, in his *Lettres inédites,* ed. D. B. Rives (2 vols.; Paris, 1823), II, 335.

20. "Discours prononcé au roi par un paysan de Chaillot," in *Recueil de pièces choisies sur les conquêtes et la convalescence du roi* (Paris, 1745).

illiteracy of a large proportion of the French people, spontaneous ju-
bilations and staged ceremonies that gave visible expression to the
principles of the traditional order played a didactic role in the public life
of the ancien régime. Official spectacles deployed an extensive yet
conventionalized repertoire of classical, biblical, and historical imagery
in the service of the crown. Stock symbolism and stylized panegyrics
extolled the might, justice, clemency, and piety of the ruler and reminded his subjects of the benefits of his reign, most notably peace
and plenty. In the eighteenth century these paternalistic motifs figured
more prominently than mythological and militaristic representations of
monarchy in royal imagery. Parisians, who cheered their king when
he appeared in public like "children who burst with joy" upon beholding
their father, had more opportunities than most French subjects to participate in the cult of kingship.[21] In 1763 and 1764, for example, they
celebrated the inauguration of the equestrian statue executed by
Bouchardon in the Place Louis XV and the laying of the cornerstone
of the Church of Saint Genevieve designed by Soufflot, built belatedly
by Louis XV out of gratitude for his recovery in 1744. Eighteenth-
century Parisians did not have the chance to witness the elaborate
entries and funerary rituals of the Renaissance, which stressed the
suzerainty and continuity of the monarchy. They did, however, see
the royal coach traverse the city on more than one occasion when
Louis XV left Versailles to exercise his absolute authority in the ceremony of the *lit de justice* behind the closed doors of the Parlement.

   The most theatrical manifestation of the traditions of Christian
kingship, of course, unfolded around the anointing and crowning of the
monarch in the cathedral of Reims, according to biblical precedent and
French custom. This magnificent spectacle, which dramatized the formula "King by the grace of God," emphasized the unaccountability of
the ruler and the submission of his people, who, "receiving their king
in some sense from the hands of God Himself," prayed that God would
bless their royal father with "the faith of Clovis, the zeal of Charlemagne, and the piety of Saint Louis." The coronation, at the same
time, underscored the obligations of the Most Christian King toward

   21. Nicolas-Toussaint-Lemoyne Desessarts, *Dictionnaire universel de police* . . .
(7 vols.; Paris, 1786–89), I, 38.

his subjects. Every sovereign ratified what the bishop of Langres referred to disingenuously as "the French social contract" in pronouncing the customary oaths at Reims.[22] Louis XV and Louis XVI, like their predecessors, promised before God to defend the Church and conserve the privileges of the clergy, to prevent iniquity and preserve justice, and to expel heretics from the realm.

The monarch, having recited these timeworn vows, was anointed with chrism mixed with oil from the Holy Ampulla of Clovis in nine locations, from the head to the hands. Following this consecration of wisdom and strength, he was invested with the emblems of royalty, including the sword and crown of Charlemagne, the spurs of chivalry, the scepter of justice, and the ring that symbolized indissoluble marriage with the kingdom. At the conclusion of the service, the dignitaries within the cathedral and the populace outside acclaimed their sovereign, enthroned in majesty as the resplendent image of the Divinity. The customs of releasing prisoners and distributing alms after the ceremony displayed the mercy and charity of the Most Christian King. The ritual of touching for scrofula, finally, exhibited his sacred character in the most graphic manner. As one staunchly orthodox account of the coronation of Louis XV declared, "this miraculous power is a gift of Heaven which has no other cause than the will of the Almighty, who, manifesting his favor for the Eldest Sons of His Church by visible means, makes them admired and respected by all peoples above all kings of the world."[23] Having acquired this thaumaturgic power through the reenactment of divine intervention at Reims, the French monarchs customarily exercised it on the most important religious holidays in the liturgical calendar.

The coronation service, which attached "the subjects to the sovereign and the sovereign to the subjects," also bound the French people as a whole to the God of their ancestors and illustrated their veneration for their collective past. It contained many archaisms like

22. D'Aguesseau, *Essai d'une institution au droit public*, ed. Louis Rigaud (Paris, 1955), 123; Nicolas Cabrisseau, *Sermon pour le sacre de Louis XV . . .* (Paris, 1724), 29; La Luzerne, "Sur l'harmonie entre les deux puissances," in *Collection intégrale*, LXXIII, 906.

23. Nicolas Menin, *Traité historique et chronologique du sacre et couronnement des rois et des reines de France . . .* (Paris, 1723), 308.

the prayer, spoken just before the enthronement, that God might endow the ruler with the strength of the rhinoceros. The ceremony of anointing and crowning, however, like the doctrine of divine right it embodied, did change in form and function between the eighth and the eighteenth centuries. Although the monarch still wore the customary clerical garments and received both bread and wine when he took communion at Reims, royal consecration no longer made him a quasi-sacerdotal personage. Formerly described as "the eighth sacrament," consecration sanctified him in the figurative sense of "calling down upon his person and his reign the abundance of celestial blessings." It attested "that his person is sacred and that it is forbidden to make any attempt upon his life, because, as the Scripture says of Saul, he is the Anointed of the Lord."[24] The holy oil of Clovis did not divest him of his mortality, but the royal mystique it symbolized did ensure his personal inviolability.

The constitutional as well as the ecclesiological significance of the coronation had changed by the time of the Bourbons. The ceremony no longer fulfilled the function of confirming the royal succession, because the rightful heir automatically acceded to the throne upon the death of his predecessor. Juridically speaking, it was "birth and not anointing which makes kings." The coronation had also lost any elective or contractual implications. The officiating bishops had traditionally asked the people assembled in the cathedral if they accepted the monarch as their ruler before he pronounced his oaths. The spectators in turn indicated their assent with a thunderous ovation, at least until 1654, when Mazarin prescribed "respectful silence" at this point in the proceedings. The cardinal presumably intended, in the wake of the Fronde, to emphasize the unmediated derivation of sovereignty from God. As an eighteenth-century priest reminded his congregation, "It is from Him alone that the king possesses his capacity and his power; it is consequently to Him alone that he is accountable for the use he

24. Nicolas Bergeat, *Explication des emblèmes inventés et mis en vers . . . pour la décoration des édifices, arc de triomphe, et autres monuments . . .* (Reims, 1775), 6; Jean-Georges Le Franc de Pompignan, "Défense des actes du clergé concernant la religion," in his *Oeuvres complètes,* ed. Jacques-Paul Migne (2 vols.; Paris, 1855), I, 1169; Pierre-Jean-Jacques Guyot *et al., Traité des droits, fonctions, franchises, exemptions, prérogatives, et privilèges . . .* (4 vols.; Paris, 1786–87), I, 45.

makes of his royal authority, because it is to God alone that he took the oath at his coronation."[25] The monarch vowed to rule his subjects according to the dictates of religion and justice, but they were neither party to the promise nor judges of his performance.

The transformation of the coronation, from necessary consecration to superfluous confirmation of sovereignty, reflected the consolidation of absolutism and the deformation of divine right by its apologists. Saint Paul, after all, suggested that God ordained whatever authorities existed, not just monarchies, and influential medieval theorists, cited by Monarchomachs, Ligueurs, and Frondeurs, assumed that the people cooperated with God in the making of kings. Apologists of absolutism, however, regarded monarchy as the only properly scriptural form of government and insisted that sovereignty derived immediately from God without consent or conditions on the part of the people. This version of divine right resulted from centuries of efforts to secure the independence of the French crown from the challenges of elective contractualism, papal ultramontanism, religious pluralism, and corporate constitutionalism. Because of the persistence of some of these challenges to royal authority and the inherent ambiguity of divine right, which the monarchy appropriated in order to deflect them, absolutism never added up to the impregnable ideology described by Bossuet and his eighteenth-century disciples.

In theory kingship "by the grace of God" exempted the French kings from accountability to their subjects. In reality, however, it failed to shelter them from criticism, opposition, and even assault in the last

25. Guyot *et al.*, *Traité des droits*, I, 44; François-Léon Réguis, *La Voix du pasteur* . . . (2 vols.; Paris, 1772), II, 477. On the changing political significance of the coronation, funeral, and entry ceremonies, see Ralph Giesey, "Models of Rulership in French Royal Ceremonial," in Sean Wilentz, (ed.), *Rites of Power: Symbolism, Ritual, and Power Since the Middle Ages* (Philadelphia, 1985), 41–64, and Giesey, *Cérémonial et puissance souveraine: France, XVe–XVIIe siècles* (Paris, 1987). On the coronation in particular see Richard A. Jackson, *Vive le roi! A History of the French Coronation from Charles V to Charles X* (Chapel Hill, 1984); Jacques Legoff, "Reims, ville du sacre," in Pierre Nora (ed.), *Les Lieux de mémoire* (4 vols.; Paris, 1984–86), III, 145–92; Marina Valensise, "Le Sacre du roi: Stratégie symbolique et doctrine politique de la monarchie française," *Annales*, XLI (1986), 543–78; Jean de Viguerie, "Les Serments du sacre des rois de France," in Yves Durand (ed.), *Hommage à Roland Mousnier: Clientèles et fidélités en Europe à l'époque moderne* (Paris, 1981), 57–70.

century of the ancien régime. Bishop Massillon acknowledged the dismaying discrepancy between the ideal of Christian kingship and the actual conduct of fallible monarchs in his eulogy of Louis XIV. "The holy anointment bestowed upon kings," he lamented, "consecrates their personage but does not always sanctify their character."[26] These words proved prophetic of Louis XV, only five years old when his great-grandfather was entombed in the royal necropolis at Saint-Denis. Miraculously preserved among the progeny of the Sun King, providentially restored to health in 1744, and saved by the hand of God from the blade of the regicide Damiens, Louis "the Beloved" apologized on his deathbed for offending God and scandalizing his subjects by his profligacy.

Louis XV's misconduct, whether or not it really scandalized his subjects, contributed to the discrediting of the sacred monarchy inasmuch as his inability to receive communion barred him from touching for "the king's evil." As he himself explained in 1769, the year before his daughter Louise joined the Carmelite convent at Saint-Denis in hopes of expiating her father's sins, "At my coronation I acquired the gift of being able to be the instrument of the grace of God for the curing of scrofula, but for this I must be in a state of grace myself, and it has been some time since this has happened."[27] At the time of Louis XV's coronation (1722), the words pronounced by the thaumaturgic monarch had already been altered from the confident formula "The king touches you; God heals you" to the more tentative "May God heal you." Louis XVI, like his grandfather, laid his hands upon more than two thousand scrofulous persons at Reims, but contemporaries expressed doubts, if not misgivings, about the rituals and mythology of Christian kingship at the time of his coronation (1775). Some not only voiced skepticism about the miraculous power attributed to the king

26. Jean-Baptiste Massillon, "Oraison funèbre de Louis le grand," in his *Oeuvres complètes*, ed. E.-A. Blampignon (4 vols.; Paris, 1886), III, 244–45.

27. Louis XV to Ferdinand of Parma, July 29, 1769, in the king's *Lettres à l'infant Ferdinand de Parme*, ed. Philippe Amiguet (Paris, 1938), 135. On Louis XV's first abstention from touching in 1739, see René-Louis de Voyer d'Argenson, *Journal et mémoires*, ed. E.-J.-B. Rathéry (9 vols.; Paris, 1859–67), II, 126–27; Edmond-Jean-François Barbier, *Chronique de la régence et du règne de Louis XV, 1718–1763* (8 vols.; Paris, 1866), III, 167; *Mémoires sur la cour*, II, 392.

but also dismissed the legend of the Holy Ampulla as a fraud, characterized the twice-anointed Pepin as a usurper, and even condemned the fanatical crusades of Saint Louis.[28]

Louis XIV's successors followed his example by commissioning portraits of themselves in their coronation robes, cluttered with all the emblems of sovereignty, but the royal icons in the style of Rigaud bore little resemblance to the scurrilous images of these monarchs in the Grub Street publications that circulated widely in the second half of the century.[29] This clandestine literature, which publicized the turpitude of Louis XV and his mistresses, also libeled his virtuous grandson, hailed as the reincarnation of the beloved Henry IV upon his accession to the throne. The political pornographers lampooned the alleged impotence of Louis XVI and credited his Austrian wife with voracious sexual appetites that she satisfied with lackeys, ladies-in-waiting, and the king's brothers. The eighteenth-century Bourbons were subjected to more of this personal defamation than their blameworthy predecessors, because of the breakdown of censorship, the expansion of literacy, the ineffectiveness of royal propaganda, and the vocal opposition to absolutism in their time. Whether or not such mud-

28. For traditional and skeptical comments on the royal touch, the Holy Ampulla, and Pepin, see, for example, Drouin Regnault, "Dissertation historique touchant le pouvoir accordé aux rois de France de guérir les écrouelles," appended to his *Histoire des sacres et couronnements de nos rois* . . . (Reims, 1722); Oroux, *Histoire ecclésiastique,* I, 179; Noël-Antoine Pluche, *Lettre sur la sainte ampoule et sur le sacre de nos rois* . . . (Paris, 1775); Louis-Vincent Goezmann de Thurn, *Essais historiques sur le sacre et couronnement des rois de France* . . . (Paris, 1775), 51; Menin, *Traité historique,* 75; and Etienne-Joseph Poullin de Lumina, *Moeurs et usages des Français* . . . (2 vols.; Lyon, 1769), II, 11. On Saint Louis see, for example, Nicolas-Jérôme Le Couturier, "Panégyrique de Saint Louis," in *Collection intégrale,* LXVI, 373.

29. On royal iconography see the catalogue of royal portraits by Gustave-Vincent Maumené and Louis d'Harcourt, *Iconographie des rois de France,* published as two volumes of the series Archives de l'art de France, n.s., XV–XVI (1929–32), and the analysis of the evolution of royal symbolism by Anne-Marie Lecoq, "La Symbolique de l'état: Les images de la monarchie," in Pierre Nora (ed.), *Les Lieux de mémoire* (Paris, 1984–86), II, 89–188. Antoine Danchet *et al., Le Sacre et couronnement de Louis XV* . . . (Paris, n.d.), contains splendid illustrations of the coronation ceremony, subsequently copied in Thomas-Jean Pichon *et al., Le Sacre et couronnement de Louis XVI* . . . (Paris, 1775). On the political pornography see Robert Darnton, *The Literary Underground of the Old Regime* (Cambridge, Mass., 1982).

slinging reached ordinary subjects and convinced them of the moral bankruptcy of their rulers, they had other grounds for disillusionment with the monarchy. Influenced by parlementary criticism of royal religious and fiscal policies, they greeted the sovereign with disapproving silence rather than the customary acclamations after *lits de justice.* They rioted in the countryside around Paris as well as in the streets of the capital after the crown abrogated the paternalistic regulations controlling the grain trade. Inflated prices suggested that the king had abandoned his fatherly interest in the affordability of their daily bread.

Depravity, "despotism," and deregulation undoubtedly tarnished the mystique of sacral kingship, yet it cannot be assumed that such failings—real, exaggerated, or imaginary—automatically dispelled long-standing respect for the institution of monarchy. Fallible monarchs, after all, and not the crown itself committed sins of the flesh, although the distinction between the king's "two bodies" surely eluded many of his subjects. Critics, furthermore, commonly blamed misgovernment on wicked councillors and tyrannical functionaries rather than the sovereign himself, if they really meant what they said. The myth of the omniscient and omnipotent royal father coexisted with the inconsonant faith that the benevolent monarch would rectify every wrong, if only he knew, if only he could. It is obviously difficult to assess the extent of popular disaffection, given the secondhand character of most of the sources. It is less difficult to trace the waning of the politico-religious traditions of the ancien régime in the minds of the literate parties to the prolonged ecclesiastical and constitutional conflicts that spanned the years between the coronations of Louis XV and Louis XVI. The protracted disputes involving the monarchy, the parlements, and the clergy, not the debauchery of the Parc aux cerfs, undermined the juridical principles of kingship "by the grace of God."

These politico-religious conflicts, of course, involved not only the sovereign himself but also a multitude of agents invested with royal authority who participated in the government of the kingdom. The monarch consulted informally with relatives, peers, and prelates at court, but he formalized decisions in his council, which always acted in his name, even in his absence. Its members included the prime minister, when the king appointed one; the chancellor (or the Keeper of the Seals, when the chancellor, who could not be removed from office, lost royal favor), the highest ranking officer of justice; the controller general of finances; the four secretaries of state, for war, the navy, foreign affairs, and the royal household; councillors of state named by the crown; and the *maîtres des requêtes* who reported on matters under consideration by the council. A changing cast of ministers, many though not all of them committed to financial and legal reforms, shaped the policies of the crown in the course of the eighteenth century. The administration dispatched royal declarations and ministerial directives to the provincial intendants (recruited mostly from the ranks of the *maîtres des requêtes*), who represented the crown throughout the realm. Having expropriated the functions of older judicial, financial, and military officers, the intendants played a leading role in the expansion of Bourbon absolutism, sometimes in collaboration with, but often at the expense of, corporate bodies and representative assemblies of various sorts.

The dozen parlements of France furthered the consolidation of royal authority inasmuch as they circumscribed the jurisdiction of ecclesiastical as well as seigneurial courts, but they also resisted it by defending corporate privileges in general and pressing their own representative pretensions in particular. The venal parlementaires, massively noble by the time of Louis XV, owned their public offices as private property, with the exception of the first presidents, named by the crown, who presided over the courts. The so-called *gens du roi* (the attorney general and his assistants, the solicitors general) sometimes found themselves caught in the middle of confrontations between the magistrates and the king, whom they represented in the deliberations of the courts. The *gens du roi* of the Parlement of Paris, which exercised jurisdiction over a third of the kingdom and led the parlementary opposition to absolutism in the eighteenth century, often played an influential role behind the scenes in the drafting of royal declarations, which the crown submitted to the magistrates for registration, and the decrees of the royal council, which it did not. The parlementaires, who issued decrees of their own in matters of *police*, recovered the right to make remonstrances against legislation referred to them, forty years after Louis XIV had suspended it, in 1715. When the monarch forced them to register his laws in the ceremony of the *lit de justice* by making a personal appearance in the Palais de

Justice and effectively retracting the authority delegated to the judges, they sometimes responded (typically led by the younger parlementaires in the *chambres des enquêtes* and *chambres des requêtes* rather than their senior colleagues in the *grande chambre*) by going on strike or even resigning their offices. Such recalcitrance provoked Louis XV to exile them from the capital more than once and to suppress the parlements altogether in 1771.

The magistrates wrangled not only with the king, whose religious and fiscal policies they frequently opposed, but also with the clergy, whose interpretations of the relationship between spritual and temporal authority they routinely contested. The quinquennial assemblies of the clergy, institutionalized by the monarchy for the purpose of collecting the "voluntary" *don gratuit* in lieu of taxes, regularly protested against parlementary as well as royal infringements of ecclesiastical jurisdiction over doctrine and discipline. The agents-general of the clergy, who enjoyed access to the king's council, looked after the corporate interests of the order in the years between these meetings. Convened in Paris, the assemblies were dominated by bishops, who typically exhibited less unanimity and less circumspection in episcopal mandements promulgated in their own dioceses than in the collective remonstrances drafted in the capital. In wealth and influence, the bishops outweighed the much more numerous parish clergy, overburdened by taxation and underrepresented in administration within the First Estate. The parish clergy provided a receptive audience for Richerism, which assigned them a more substantial role in the affairs of the Church, and Jansenism, which the prelates assembled in Paris repeatedly condemned.

The royal, parlementary, and ecclesiastical authorities of the ancien régime, who disagreed in some ways within their own ranks as well as with each other, agreed with the abbé Duguet that "in order to preserve the state it is necessary to maintain the ancient principles upon which it depends."[30] They all claimed to uphold the traditions of the realm, yet they all contributed to the undermining of these traditions before the Revolution. All parties to the politico-religious con-

30. [Jacques-Joseph Duguet], *Institution d'un prince* . . . (London, 1737), 171 (written in 1669).

flicts of the eighteenth century appealed to history and invoked divine right in order to defend their prerogatives in the corporate kingdom. Their disputes, commonly displaced into the times of the Fathers and the Franks, renewed the historical polemics of the civil wars and the Fronde and reopened the debate about the conventionalized version of the French past that bolstered the sovereignty of the crown. The monarchy attempted to reclaim the past for its own purposes, for example, by establishing the chair of public law at the Collège de France in 1773, but it showed considerably less respect for the customary order of things in other ways. The crown not only perpetuated but also challenged corporate privileges. Louis XV and Louis XVI continued the work of royal centralization and sponsored a variety of reforms, including the redistribution of taxes, codification of laws, abolition of judicial venality, restructuring of municipal government, deregulation of the grain trade, disbanding of the guilds, reorganization of religious orders, and civil toleration of Protestants. They did not succeed, of course, in implementing all of these changes, many of which provoked stubborn opposition.

Magistrates and bishops acknowledged that the king derived his authority from God and was accountable only to God, but many of them resisted the reforms undertaken by the administrative monarchy as innovations that endangered the customary order of the country. Elaborating upon the arguments of sixteenth- and seventeenth-century opponents of absolutism, they reminded their sovereign in remonstrances and mandements that God expected him to rule justly and defend the ancestral faith of the kingdom. The magistrates, who denounced despotism almost as eagerly as ultramontanism, refused to register legislation that violated the privileges of his subjects (and repudiated their own constitutional claims). The bishops, who insisted that conscience required them to obey God rather than humans (Acts 5:29), criticized royal policies that jeopardized the salvation of his people (and threatened their own worldly privileges). Both parties contributed to the desacralization of the monarchy by exploiting divine right to serve their corporate interests and by denying in practice the unaccountability of the crown that they recognized in principle. This assault on absolutism within the context of traditional principles, combined with the crown's inability to fulfill the role staked out for it in absolutist ideology by stifling the disruptive disputes, made divine right politically dysfunctional well before the Revolution.

The constitutional and ecclesiastical controversies that spanned the reign of Louis XV revolved around the interpretation of the ill-defined fundamental laws of the realm and the problematic relationship between spiritual and temporal authority. The monarchy, the magistrates, and the clergy argued for decades about such issues as whether royal pronouncements had the force of law without parlementary registration and which of the two powers had jurisdiction over the administration of the sacraments. The prolonged disputes about the meaning of the constitutive principles of the politico-religious order raised questions about the juridical fictions that bound it together: the identification of kingdom with kingship and the conjunction of citizenship and Catholicity. They discredited the divine ordination of the crown and subverted the confessional uniformity of the country. They nurtured the concepts of sovereign community disengaged from the person of the monarch and civil identity divorced from the faith of his ancestors. These conflicts, which made politics a more public concern and religion a more private matter in France, played a determinative role in the transformation of the Catholic kingdom of subjects divided by privileges into the pluralistic nation of citizens united in rights.

2

The Religious Obligations of the Monarchy and the Police *of the Christian Kingdom*

In the vocabulary of the ancien régime the word *police* referred not to the personnel responsible for the maintenance of law and order but to the broad range of administrative functions they fulfilled. Given the paternalistic character of the monarchy, *police* entailed royal regulation of and intervention in many aspects of public and private life with the objective of preserving "peace and concord among citizens" and "order and harmony in society."[1] Eighteenth-century treatises on *police* accordingly dealt with an extraordinary variety of subjects: assault, theft, fire hazards, food supply, epidemics, hospitals, guilds, taverns, mendicity, counterfeiting, clandestine gatherings, seditious pamphlets, irreligious books, Sabbath-breaking, cemeteries, gambling, domestic conflicts, sexual misconduct. As this selective catalogue suggests, the *police* of the kingdom involved not only concern for the safety, health, and industry of subjects but also surveillance of their obedience, orthodoxy, and morality.

Religion, described by the abbé Fauchet as "the first of the fundamental laws of the realm," figured prominently in discussions of *police*. The royal councillor Réal de Curban declared categorically that "people who have no religion are at the same time without *police*, without genuine subordination, and completely uncivilized." Nicolas Delamare,

1. Duchesne, *Code de police ou analyse des règlements de police* (Paris, 1757), 1.

one of the district commissioners responsible for the *police* of Paris, claimed that "if religion alone were well observed, all the other parts of the *police* would be fulfilled." Since religion not only marked the way to salvation but also preserved social order, the crown made Catholicism a collective obligation rather than a private option in France. The divinely ordained monarch and his magistrates accordingly collaborated with the clergy and defended the national faith through enforcement of sacramental conformity, censorship of unorthodox opinions, and punishment of irreligious and immoral conduct. The actual administration of the Christian kingdom, however, fell short of statutory ideals and clerical expectations in the eighteenth century. Jurisdictional conflicts disrupted collaboration between the two powers, and the secular authorities effectively renounced any visionary attempt, as one functionary put it, "to make society into a monastery."[2]

In theory, at least, there was nothing problematic about the relationship between the spiritual and temporal powers, commonly summarized in the form of a few incontestable principles: "Priesthood and sovereignty are two mutually independent but conjoined powers. Both depend only upon God. Sacred things are allotted to priests; civil things are reserved to sovereigns. Priests submit to the sovereign in temporal matters; sovereignty is subject to priesthood in spiritual matters."[3] The Church concerned itself with the Christian, the soul, the internal, salvation, eternal life. The monarchy assumed responsibility for the citizen, the body, the external, this world, public order. Conventional verbal dichotomies emphasized the differences between the two powers but did not imply their incompatibility. They not only enjoyed autonomy within their own jurisdictions but also supported each other in the execution of their respective functions. The clergy, who obeyed the king as his subjects, scrutinized the worldly conduct of Christians, and the king, who accepted the direction of the clergy as a Christian, policed the religious life of citizens. The missions of the

2. Claude Fauchet, "De la religion nationale," in *Collection intégrale*, LXVI, 31; Gaspard de Réal de Curban, *La Science du gouvernement*. . . (8 vols.; Paris, 1761–65), I, 390; Nicolas Delamare, *Traité de police* . . . (4 vols.; Amsterdam, 1729), I, 249; Jean Seznec (ed.), *Mémoire sur la réformation de la police de France soumis au roi en 1749 par M. Guillaute, officier de la maréchaussée de l'Ile-de-France* (Paris, 1974), 19.
    3. [Louis-Etienne de Foy], *Traité des deux puisssances* . . . (Paris, 1752), i–ii.

two powers, separable on paper, remained inseparable in practice, for God established them to work together for the spiritual and temporal welfare of His creatures.

The Church fixed the conditions of membership in the Catholic community transcending the borders of the kingdom and guided Christians from baptism to burial in every parish of the realm. The clergy alone formulated and interpreted the doctrines that embodied the word of God and administered the sacraments that dispensed His grace. Royal legislation of 1695 accordingly specified that "cognizance of cases involving the sacraments, monastic vows, divine worship, ecclesiastical discipline, and other purely spiritual matters" belonged to the ecclesiastical courts. Since God assigned the clergy jurisdiction over the soul and invested them with the spiritual sword of persuasion, they could not subject their parishioners to bodily punishments. The clergy could excommunicate sinners from the community of the faithful, but this penalty theoretically deprived them "only of the status of Christian and of the rights which belong to the Christian as a Christian."[4]

The French king served Catholicism not only through the example of his own piety but also by unsheathing the temporal sword of coercion to enforce the doctrinal decisions and disciplinary judgments of the clergy. Without meddling in spiritual matters as such, he incorporated the dogmas and canons of the Church into the laws of the realm and inflicted corporeal penalties upon subjects who violated its norms. Because, as Massillon pointed out, "the duties of religion enter into the public order," the monarchy punished offenses against the Divinity like heresy and blasphemy as crimes against society as well. Since the sovereign had jurisdiction over the body, he could not compel his subjects to embrace Catholicism in conscience, but he could and did maintain "the outward *police* of the Church" by repressing externalized deviations from its standards of belief and behavior.[5]

4. *Déclaration du roi*, April, 1695, in *Recueil général*, XX, 253; [René-Louis de Voyer d'Argenson *et al.*], *Histoire du droit public ecclésiastique français* . . . (2 vols.; London, 1750), II, 85.

5. Jean-Baptiste Massillon, "Petit carême," in his *Oeuvres complètes*, ed. E.-A. Blampignon (4 vols.; Paris, 1886), I, 17; *Recueil des consultations de Messieurs les avocats du parlement de Paris* . . . (Paris, 1740), 15.

Such collaboration between the spiritual and temporal powers sup-posedly ensured the order and orthodoxy of the realm. As one com-mentator on the edict of 1695 observed, however, "there is nothing so easy to reconcile in general and in theory as the competence of the jurisdictions" of the clergy and the crown, yet "nothing so difficult as to do so in particular cases and in reality."[6] The relationship between the two powers was considerably more complicated than conventional summaries suggested, because of the artificial character of the di-chotomies that distinguished their jurisdictions and because of the ongoing erosion of ecclesiastical jurisdiction by monarchs and magis-trates. Given these sources of dissension, clergy, crown, parlements, Jansenists, and Protestants argued endlessly about the differentiation of internal and external concerns and the limits of secular involvement in religious matters.

Because faith resided within the conscience of the individual, soci-ety had no assurance "that the religion of one person was the same as that of the next" without "an external, public, and uniform cult." Christ taught that His kingdom was not of this world, but the perpetu-ation of Christianity required its tangible presence in this world: clergy, churches, property, revenues, creeds, services. The exer-cises of the Church necessarily took external forms, because faith expressed itself only through visible and physical means such as professions of belief and participation in ritualized behavior that pre-sumably signified religious conformity. The clergy naturally main-tained that definitions of doctrine and administration of the sacraments, despite their externalized form, fell wholly within ecclesiastical juris-diction because of their spiritual content. The magistrates, on the other hand, often equated "spiritual" narrowly with "internal" and therefore denied the "purely spiritual" character of ecclesiastical dis-cipline, divine worship, monastic vows, and the sacraments them-selves. Invoking the standard of externality, they meddled in these matters and took cognizance even of excommunication, on the grounds that subjects could not be "excluded from the community of the faithful without being excluded from civil society" as well.[7]

---

6. Michel Duperray, *Notes et observations sur les cinquante articles de l'édit de 1695 concernant la jurisdiction ecclésiastique . . .* (Paris, 1718), 428.

7. Louis-Gabriel de Dubuat-Nançay, *Maximes du gouvernement monarchique . . .* (4 vols.; London, 1778), I, 99; Nicolas-Sylvestre Bergier, *Le Déisme réfuté par lui-*

Men and women, according to the maxim cited countless times by the parlementaires, were "born citizens before becoming Christians." Although citizens and Christians obviously did not constitute distinct persons, their membership in the state, juridically speaking, antedated their membership in the Church. Although Church and state, by the same token, obviously did not include distinct populations, "since the members of the Church are also the members of the state, it is nonetheless obvious, considering things in their natural progression, that the state must have antedated the Church."[8] Obvious, at least, to jurists who concluded from this version of human history that "the Church is in the state, but the state is not in the Church." This axiom allowed them to argue that the worldly privileges and external prerogatives of the Church derived conditionally from the concession of the state, which retained jurisdiction over all aspects of religion not "purely spiritual" in nature. Such Gallican readings of the relationship between the two powers provoked predictable counterarguments from the clergy, who denied that the inevitable externality of religious exercises or the hypothetical precedence of the state over the Church justified secular encroachments upon the jurisdiction assigned to them by God.

Gallicanism, of course, meant different things to the various parties involved in the jurisdictional conflicts of the eighteenth century. To the bishops, it meant the ultimate supremacy of councils over popes and considerable independence from Rome in their dioceses. To the king, it meant the right of royal nomination of bishops, the necessity of royal authorization of papal bulls and conciliar decrees, the immunity of royal authority from the threat of ultramontanism, and the legitimacy of royal intervention in the temporal affairs of the Church. To the parlementaires, it meant not only these royal prerogatives but also the more wholesale accountability of the clergy to the monarch and his magistrates in "the external exercise of the sacerdotal ministry which they derive from God alone." The judges circumscribed ecclesiastical jurisdiction in matters of doctrine and discipline by means of the *appel*

---

même . . . (Paris, 1765), 55; [D'Argenson *et al.*], *Histoire du droit public ecclésiastique,* II, 42.

8. [Jean Brunet], *Abrégé des libertés de l'église gallicane . . .* (N.p., n.d.), 8; [Thomas Pichon], *Les Droits respectifs de l'état et de l'église rappellés à leurs principes* (Avignon, 1766), 36–37.

comme d'abus (acknowledged but also restricted by the edict of 1695), which allowed for appeals to the royal courts in religious cases. Without this means of appealing clerical abuses, they warned, "the subjects of the king would find themselves in the very midst of the state totally deprived of his royal protection and at least in some regards under the rule of another power."[9] When Louis XV curbed their meddling in spiritual matters by supporting papal and ecclesiastical condemnations of Jansenism, the parlementaires linked their defenses of the prerogatives of the crown, the liberties of the Church, the privileges of French subjects, and their own constitutional pretensions in the name of Gallicanism.

The traditions of the ancien régime left no doubt about the importance of religion in the social and political order, but they left ample room for disputes about many of the details. The clergy emphasized the theoretical separability of spiritual and temporal concerns so as to defend the integrity of ecclesiastical jurisdiction, but also insisted upon the practical inseparability of spiritual and temporal concerns so as to demonstrate the necessity of secular intervention in support of Catholicism. They obviously did not advocate the neutrality of the crown in doctrinal or disciplinary affairs, but they did expect the crown to endorse their decisions and respect their prerogatives when it intervened in such matters. The monarch and his magistrates, guided by their own political agendas and their own interpretations of the relationship between the two powers, never failed to declare their support for the national faith but frequently challenged the privileges of the First Estate. The secular authorities did not question the concept of the Christian kingdom in principle. In practice, however, their extension of temporal at the expense of spiritual jurisdiction and their sporadic enforcement of the laws concerning religion effectively redefined its place in the public order.

"In a Catholic kingdom," declared the abbé Pey, "the citizen is also a Christian." This dictum embodied something more than wishful thinking on the part of the clergy, because royal legislation made civil status dependent upon sacramental conformity in France. The crown did not take much statutory interest in penance, communion, confir-

9. [Brunet], *Abrégé des libertés*, 21; [Vivien de La Borde], *Principes sur l'essence, la distinction, et les limites des deux puissances* (N.p., 1753), 87.

mation, and ordination, although it did require parents to send their children to catechism in preparation for confirmation and restricted monastic vocations in the 1760s. At the same time, it compelled subjects to attest births, marriages, and deaths through participation in the baptismal, matrimonial, and mortuary rites of the national faith. The facts of life and death, which verified subjects' identity in the eyes of the law, were recorded only in the parish registers. This dependence of civil status on religious acts provided a means of preserving confessional uniformity by forcing French men and women to have recourse to the sacraments of the Church in order to enjoy what Fauchet called "the prerogatives of French citizens in their full measure."[10]

Baptisms recorded in the parish registers not only cleansed newborn infants of Original Sin and inscribed them in the Christian community but also established their legitimacy (unless otherwise noted) and enrolled them among the subjects of the king. The divinely ordained monarch, "to whom the salvation of the citizen should not be less important than his worldly interests," punished the crimes of abortion and infanticide by death, directed midwives to report births to the parish priest, and required administration of the sacrament of baptism in the parish church within twenty-four hours of birth.[11] The spiritual and temporal authorities did not make marriage, like baptism, mandatory in the Christian kingdom, but they did make it impossible for non-Catholics to contract legitimate unions in France. The crown made the benediction of the parish priest a legal necessity, and the priest, for his part, commonly required prospective brides and grooms to attend confession, take communion, and/or make profession of their faith before uniting them in matrimony. Royal legislation also directed subjects to send for the parish priest when death knocked at the door. After confessing the moribund individual and questioning him or her concerning matters of faith, the priest granted absolution and administered the last rites. Death within the Catholic community guaranteed interment in consecrated ground adjoining the parish church or sometimes inside the sanctuary, depending on the social status of the de-

10. Jean Pey, *De l'autorité des deux puissances* (3 vols.; Strasbourg, 1781), II, 388; Fauchet, "De la religion nationale," in *Collection intégrale*, LXVI, 103.

11. Edme de La Poix de Fréminville, *Dictionnaire ou traité de police . . .* (Paris, 1758), 43.

ceased. Subjecting the dead to the same standards of belief and conduct as the living, canon law denied Christian burial to unbaptized infants, persons who had failed to fulfill their paschal obligations, usurers, duelists, actors, notorious sinners, excommunicates, schismatics, heretics, unbelievers, and suicides.

The jurisprudence of the Christian kingdom stigmatized infants not baptized by the Church as bastards, punished couples not married by the Church for living in concubinage, and consigned corpses not buried by the Church to the refuse dump. Exclusion from the sacraments meant disgrace in life and in death. It also meant exclusion from the parish registers, which entailed loss of legal identity. The crown had linked civil status and religious conformity in this way in the sixteenth century. The monarch and his magistrates unlinked them in the course of the eighteenth century. The royal declaration of April 9, 1736, circumvented the necessity of ecclesiastical certification of death by instructing the police to record the relevant facts and provide for burial in the cases of persons excluded from interment in the parish cemetery. The magistrates sometimes forced the clergy to bury allegedly unworthy parishioners in consecrated ground and routinely ordered them to administer the last rites to Jansenists in the 1750s. Having already arrogated cognizance of most matrimonial cases from the ecclesiastical courts, they tacitly recognized the legitimacy of Protestant unions in the second half of the century. Louis XVI completed the disjunction of Catholicity and citizenship in 1787 by providing for secular registration of births, marriages, and deaths.

The clergy expected their sovereign to defend the national faith through censorship of unorthodox opinions as well as enforcement of sacramental conformity. They warned him repeatedly against dangerous schismatics, heretics, and unbelievers, who intended, according to the bishop of Lodève, "to allow everyone the liberty to think, to speak, to live, and to act as he pleases, thus abolishing the most elementary principles of dependence and subordination." Such license contravened the will of God, because it deprived His Church of its statutory monopoly on the consciences of His creatures. It also threatened the peace of the realm, because it encouraged independence and insubordination. Kingship "by the grace of God" invested the king with the power to control the verbal space of the kingdom and charged him with the responsibility to use this power to proscribe unorthodoxy in its Jansenist, Protestant, and philosophic forms. Because "religion is part of our constitution," as the solicitor general Séguier put it, "one cannot attack religion without disturbing the public order."[12] The crown, the clergy, and Séguier's parlementary colleagues therefore resorted to censorship in order to protect Catholic subjects from errors that might jeopardize their salvation or mislead them into unsubmissive conduct.

Since religious beliefs influenced worldly behavior, according to the abbé Bergier, "there are no private opinions in matters of religion that are of no consequence to the community." Private opinions, however, eluded the scrutiny of the authorities as long as they remained private. As long as a French subject "conducts himself outwardly as a good citizen," Bergier admitted, "neither the law nor the *police* has anything to do with his beliefs." Since the Most Christian King had no jurisdiction over unverbalized private opinions, he discharged his obligation to promote orthodoxy by other means. He supported the inculcation of proper beliefs through catechismal instruction, attached temporal disabilities to the spiritual penalties by which the clergy stigmatized nonconformity, required professions of Catholicity from functionaries as diverse as midwives and executioners, and punished what the clergy condemned as "the public, flagrant, and voluntary expression" of unorthodox opinions in print or in the streets.[13]

According to the laws of the ancien régime nothing could be published in France (with some exceptions, notably episcopal instructions and parlementary decrees) without the permission of the king. The monarchy required preliminary submission of manuscripts to royal censors, who marked passages for revision or deletion before publication. The standard authorization on the title page certified that authors had not abused the medium of the printed word by expressing

12. Jean-Félix-Henri de Fumel, *Instruction pastorale de Monseigneur l'évêque de Lodève sur les sources de l'incrédulité du siècle* (Paris, 1765), 182; Antoine-Louis Séguier, *Réquisitoire sur lequel est intervenu l'arrêt du parlement du 18 août 1770 . . .* (Paris, 1770), 57.

13. Bergier, *Déisme réfuté*, 223, 133; *Procès-verbal de l'assemblée générale extraordinaire du clergé de France tenue à Paris au couvent des Grands Augustins en l'année 1780* (Paris, 1782), 337.

unorthodox opinions. The crown, the clergy, and the parlements shared the prerogative of condemning published works (commonly but not always unauthorized) that contradicted the political principles, religious beliefs, or moral standards of the Christian kingdom. The royal council suppressed the first two volumes of the *Encyclopédie*, for example, on the grounds that they contained "maxims tending to subvert royal authority, to promote the spirit of independence and revolt, and, by means of obscure and ambiguous terms, to raise the foundations of error, moral corruption, and incredulity."[14] The magistrates frequently ordered the ritualistic tearing and burning of condemned books in order to avenge their violation of conventional norms and purge their errors from public consciousness.

Despite the promulgation of the draconian edict of April 4, 1757, which sentenced authors, publishers, and distributors of irreligious and seditious books to death, the severity of censorship diminished in the eighteenth century. Royal control over the medium of print broke down because of laxity in the enforcement of the laws and the impossibility of enforcing them. During his administration as director of the book trade, Malesherbes standardized the use of *permissions tacites*, which permitted the publication of books that could not appear with the formal authorization on the title page. Royal officials responsible for the censorship of the printed word did not enforce the regulations strictly, both because they obviously did not want to do so in the cases of books they had decided to tolerate and because they simply could not do so in the cases of other titles they would have liked to suppress. Given the proliferation of clandestine presses and the resourcefulness of smugglers, they could not arrest the flood of unauthorized pamphlets engendered by the politico-religious disputes that spanned the reign of Louis XV or the influx of so-called "philosophic" books from Switzerland and Holland in the second half of the century. The authorities could not stop the dissemination of these subversive and ungodly works, as one bookseller incarcerated in the Bastille explained, "because people are set on obtaining them at any price. And who? The very people who, given their birth, their status in society, their faith, their learning, and their zeal for religion, ought to be the first to con-

14. *Arrêt du conseil*, February 7, 1752, in *Recueil général*, XXII, 250.

demn them."[15] "The public," excluded from participation in politics, expressed itself not only by means of occasional demonstrations and riots but also through steady consumption of controversial literature and illicit publications.

The crown, the clergy, and the magistrates invariably reaffirmed their zeal for religion when they condemned unorthodox works, but their prolonged jurisdictional conflicts undermined the efficacy of censorship in France. Bishops condemned parlementary decrees, judges condemned episcopal instructions, and the sovereign condemned both from time to time, in order to silence wrangling over the interpretation of contested traditions. Even when the authorities made common cause against "philosophic" errors, they often did so—as in the celebrated affairs of the thesis of the abbé de Prades and Helvétius' *De l'Esprit*, set against the background of the ecclesiastical and constitutional strife of the 1750s—with purposes of their own in mind. By accentuating the partisan character of censorship and awakening the political consciousness of the literate public, the controversies concerning Jansenism and taxation, as much as the Enlightenment, thwarted royal efforts to police the verbal space of the Christian kingdom.

The divinely ordained king served God, the Church, and the people entrusted to his care by criminalizing various sorts of irreligious and immoral behavior as well as the expression of unorthodox opinions. Such misconduct, like unorthodoxy, showed contempt for the Almighty, challenged clerical authority, and threatened to lead French subjects astray. The monarch regarded offenses against God prohibited by the Decalogue (namely Sabbath-breaking, blasphemy, and suicide) and violations of the standards of morality defined by the clergy as transgressions against the public order. Religion played a visible role not only in the demarcation of right and wrong but also in the rituals of criminal procedure. Judges sometimes ordered the publication of ecclesiastical monitions, which required parishioners to disclose information concerning cases under investigation on penalty of excommunication. They routinely included the *amende honorable* out-

15. Quoted in Nicole Hermann-Mascard, *La Censure des livres à Paris à la fin de l'ancien régime* (Paris, 1968), 97.

side the church doors in the sentences of malefactors whom they condemned to death. This penalty required criminals, barred from sanctuary, to acknowledge their guilt and apologize for offending God, the king, and justice before the mutilation and immolation of their bodies, which could not rest in consecrated ground.

The king did not compel his subjects to attend mass in the parish church on the Sabbath and the numerous holy days that punctuated the calendar, but he did encourage observation of the Third Commandment by prohibiting other activities that might distract them from their Christian duties. The crown banned manual labor and merchandizing on days consecrated to God and ordered the closing of taverns and theaters during the hours of divine services. Royal judges as well as parish priests, however, could grant dispensations for urgent labors, such as harvesting and building repairs. The temporal authorities also incorporated Catholic dietary restrictions into the *police* of the realm by restricting the sale of meat during Lent to sick and elderly persons. The Hôtel Dieu of Paris enjoyed a monopoly on the sale of meat during the quadragesimal season until Turgot abolished the privilege in 1774. By that time the clergy complained regularly about the increase of Sabbath-breaking and the nonenforcement of the laws against this species of irreverence.[16]

French jurisprudence protected the sacred character of persons, places, objects, and ceremonies as well as times consecrated to God. The monarchy punished sacrilegious attacks on members of the First Estate, profanation of cemeteries, desecration of the Host, and failure to cover the street in front of the house with rugs for processions on holy days. It also disciplined blasphemers, who abused the gift of speech and scandalized their neighbors by verbally abusing the Creator, the Virgin Mary, or the saints. Louis XIV, who attempted to extirpate what Delamare called the three monsters of heresy, dueling, and blasphemy, established a graduated scale of penalties for repeated infractions of the Second Commandment. His declaration of 1666 punished the first four offenses by progressively more sizable fines (or periods of imprisonment on bread and water if the culprit could not

16. See for example PV, VIII/1, *Pièces justificatives*, 205–206 (1755), 307 (1760); VIII/2, *Pièces justificatives*, 489–90 (1765), 621 (1770); IX, *Pièces justificatives*, 1307 (1775).

pay), the fifth by exposure in an iron collar attached to a stake on a Sunday or holy day, the sixth by exposure in the pillory and splitting of the upper lip, the seventh by splitting of the lower lip as well, and the eighth by amputation of the incorrigible tongue. It left the more thorough punishment of "enormous blasphemies" to the discretion of the magistrates.[17]

The most celebrated incident of sacrilege and blasphemy in the ancien régime occurred a century after the promulgation of this legislation. On the morning of August 9, 1766, the residents of Abbeville realized that someone had mutilated the venerated wooden cross on the main bridge of the town during the night. They blamed the crime on several rowdy youngsters, including the chevalier Jean-François de La Barre, an orphaned adolescent from Paris who lived with his cousin in Abbeville. Fueled by personal conflicts within the community, the case against La Barre manifested hostility to the fashionable outsider whose irreverent behavior reflected a deplorable lack of paternal correction and threatened to corrupt the local youth. The judicial investigation, expedited by the publication of ecclesiastical monitions, revealed that the chevalier collected pornographic books and made a habit of singing irreligious songs. Townspeople remembered that he had failed to remove his hat and kneel upon encountering the Corpus Christi procession in the street and suspected him of desecrating the Host as well as crosses in the cemetery. After the Parlement of Paris confirmed the death sentence and Louis XV declined to suspend it, La Barre was decapitated and burned at the stake, along with a volume of Voltaire's *Dictionnaire philosophique* discovered in his room.

The monarch and his magistrates, anxious to demonstrate their devotion to Catholicism at a time when they were embroiled in jurisdictional conflicts with the clergy, rejected the argument that La Barre's sins did not constitute crimes against the public order. The most noteworthy fact about the death sentence they sanctioned in this case, however, was its exceptional character. Treatises on *police* in the second half of the eighteenth century acknowledged that blasphemy, if not sacrilege, had become "very common among ordinary people" and admitted that the magistrates, who considered the laws too harsh, rarely punished it. La Barre himself suffered only figurative

17. *Déclaration du roi*, July 30, 1666, in *Recueil général*, XVIII, 87.

amputation of the tongue: the executioner passed his hand symbolically in front of the chevalier's face. According to the jurist Guyot, the
judges recognized "that it is not for humans to avenge the Deity" and
therefore confined themselves to considering "the harm that might
result to society from impious and scandalous acts and punishing these
sorts of offenses according to the injury that public morals suffer from
them."[18] By the last decades of the ancien régime they no longer
shared Louis XIV's assumption that such offenses against God automatically threatened society and required exemplary retribution in this
world.

The stern laws of Louis XIV, inspired by his awareness of his obligations as Most Christian King, fined persons who overheard blasphemous remarks and failed to report them within twenty-four hours.
They also ordered the police to investigate the deaths of individuals
who did not die of natural causes, so as to identify and punish cases of
suicide. Self-destruction constituted a crime not only against God,
who endowed humans with life and commanded them not to kill, but
also against the ruler, the country, and the family, to whom "every
citizen is accountable for his days."[19] After posthumous trial and conviction, the corpses of suicides were dragged through the streets face
down on a hurdle, hung by the feet, and thrown in the refuse dump.
The monarchy punished the survivors as well as the deceased by condemning the memories and confiscating the property of persons who
killed themselves. In spite of these draconian penalties, contemporary
witnesses like the Parisian printer and bookseller Siméon-Prosper
Hardy reported large numbers of suicides in the second half of the
eighteenth century.

Hardy attributed the alleged epidemic of self-destruction to "the
decay of religion and morality" in his time, which he blamed on
"the lack of education and the reading of pernicious books." Few of the
tragic stories he recorded, however, betrayed any evidence of "philosophic" sentiments, with the notable exception of the notorious case

18. Nicolas-Toussaint-Lemoyne Desessarts, *Dictionnaire universel de police* . . .
(7 vols.; Paris, 1786–89), I, 616; Pierre-Jean-Jacques-Guillaume Guyot *et al.*, *Repertoire universel et raisonné de jurisprudence* . . . (17 vols.; Paris, 1784–85), II, 403.

19. Pierre-François Muyart de Vouglans, *Instituts au droit criminel* . . . (Paris,
1762), 537.

of Bourdeaux and Humain, the young dragoons who shot themselves in a tavern at Saint-Denis on Christmas Day, 1773. They penned a testament in which they claimed that "distaste for life is the only motive which makes us leave it" and contemptuously consigned their corpses to the king's justice.[20] Louis XV reportedly blamed their suicide on the Encyclopedists, but other contemporaries suggested that dishonesty and dissolution had driven the dragoons to take their own lives. Their bodies, in any case, were buried in the Parisian cemetery of the Holy Innocents, but the criminal chamber of the Parlement condemned them four months later to be hanged in effigy in the Place de Grève.

The alleged motivation and the belated punishment of Bourdeaux and Humain made their case the exception rather than the rule. Families sometimes tried to cover up the real cause of death, in order to avoid the penalties prescribed by the laws, but such deceptions were no longer necessary in Hardy's time. Despite the perceived increase in the incidence of suicide, the magistrates almost never enforced the letter of the law in the last decades of the ancien régime. Concerned about the health hazards posed by unburied bodies, they routinely ordered interment, ordinarily without ceremony and occasionally over the objections of the clergy, in what Hardy called "the usual and customary manner, without putting the corpse on trial, as is sometimes done, a means little capable, as proved by experience, of preventing a person from killing himself when given up to despair."[21] The judges clearly recognized the futility of the statutory punishments and probably intended to defend the property rights of the relatives of the deceased. They generally attributed suicide to madness, which legally exempted its victims from posthumous prosecution. Inclined to regard Sabbath-breaking and blasphemy as evidence of crudeness rather than criminality, they effectively decriminalized suicide by making a standard assumption out of extenuating circumstances in the cases of persons who killed themselves.

20. Siméon-Prosper Hardy, "Mes loisirs ou journal des événements tels qu'ils parviennent à ma connaissance" (1764–89), in FF, Vol. 6681, fols. 41, 379; Maurice Tourneux (ed.), *Correspondance littéraire et critique par Grimm, Diderot, Raynal, Meister, etc.* (15 vols.; Paris, 1877), X, 344.

21. Hardy, "Mes loisirs," in FF, Vol. 6681, fol. 35.

The king, the magistrates, and the police concerned themselves with immorality as well as irreligion, since many vices not only violated conventional standards of godly conduct but also threatened the familial order of French society. The authorities outlawed games of chance and restricted the operating hours of taverns, for example, so as to prevent the disruptive consequences of gambling and drunkenness: blasphemy, confusion of ranks, brawling, impoverishment, domestic discord. The fatherly sovereign, who imprisoned rebellious children and wayward wives, endeavored to restrain the passions that led his subjects into dissipation and delinquency. Collaborating with the clergy in the regulation of the most unruly of these passions, the monarchy tacitly endorsed the ecclesiastical assumption that vaginal intercourse within marriage for the purpose of procreation constituted the only legitimate form of sexual activity. The laws of the Christian kingdom, according to several eighteenth-century jurists, authorized the punishment of masturbation by banishment, but the police simply reprimanded boys for this offense. The shoemaker Lenoir and the domestic Diot, apprehended *flagrante delicto* in a Parisian street and charged with the crime of sodomy, did not get off so lightly. The magistrates made an example of these young men, burned at the stake in 1750, as they did of La Barre, Bourdeaux, and Humain, but they usually punished sodomy by imprisonment and enforced the death penalty only in cases involving violence. They commonly mitigated the severe penalties for extramarital as well as nonprocreative sex: adultery, bigamy, prostitution. The police routinely imprisoned prostitutes who scandalized their neighbors, endangered family interests, or corrupted other women. At the same time, they openly tolerated venal traffic in sex, since they not only accepted the conventional rationalization that the availability of prostitutes protected the virtue of respectable women but also made use of prostitutes in the investigation of other crimes.

The punishment of irreligion and immorality, like the enforcement of sacramental conformity and the censorship of unorthodox opinions, declined in the eighteenth century. Many magistrates apparently agreed with the lawyers from Bordeaux who denied that the *police* of the kingdom required them "to bring about rectitude in the conduct of individuals, for which the responsibility is left to the preachers and ministers of the Church." Without abandoning traditional norms in principle, they confined themselves in practice to punishing flagrant cases of private misconduct that disturbed public order. Their laxity compounded the disparity between social reality and the ideal of the "wholly Christian *police*" constructed by Charlemagne, Saint Louis, and Louis XIV. Monarchs and magistrates, to be sure, had never managed to make the French people abide by the standards enshrined in legislation, but critics complained more loudly than before that the laws regarding religion and morality had "fallen into disuse" in the eighteenth century.[22] Historical research has produced abundant evidence of dechristianization of various sorts among various segments of the population in various parts of the country: More delayed baptisms, indifference concerning burial, omissions of religious invocations and intercessory clauses from wills, bequests to subsidize charity for the living rather than masses for the dead. More novels, newspapers, historical and scientific works, and unorthodox books, but fewer theological titles in print. More Sabbath-breaking, blasphemy, suicide, premarital sex, illegitimate births, abandoned children, contraception, adultery, prostitution. Less regularity in attendance at Sunday mass and fulfillment of paschal obligations, fewer confraternities and ordinations, more friction between clergy and laity over tithes, ecclesiastical fees, parish expenditures, administration of the sacraments, observance of holy days, and standards of moral conduct.

Historians, of course, have raised questions about the interpretation of the evidence and about the concept of dechristianization itself.[23] It seems to assume the existence of homogeneous Christianity before

22. Memorandum from the lawyers de Lamothe and de Lisleferme to the police of Bordeaux, December 1, 1775, quoted in Josette Pontet, "Morale et ordre publique à Bayonne au XVIIIe siècle," *Bulletin de la société des sciences, lettres, et arts de Bayonne,* CXXXIII (1974), 132–33; Paul-César de Cicéri, "Panégyrique de Saint Louis," in *Recueil de plusieurs pièces de poésie présentées à l'Académie française* (Paris, 1721), 243; Meusy, *Code de la religion et des moeurs* . . . (2 vols.; Paris, 1770), I, viii.

23. Indispensable works on the Counter-Reformation and dechristianization include Jean Delumeau, *Le Catholicisme entre Luther et Voltaire* (Paris, 1971); Michel Vovelle, *Piété baroque et déchristianisation en Provence au XVIIIe siècle* (Paris, 1973); and John Bossy, *Christianity in the West, 1400–1700* (Oxford, 1985). See the bibliography of the present work for numerous references concerning the various matters discussed in these paragraphs.

the eighteenth century and to equate changes in collective behavior with changes in collective mentalities. Ordinary subjects in the sixteenth and seventeenth centuries surely thought of themselves as Christians, but their version of Christianity did not satisfy the post-Tridentine Church. The Counter-Reformation, which lasted into the eighteenth century in many ways, involved a massive campaign both to reform the clergy and to Christianize the laity by reordering their lives according to ecclesiastical standards of belief and behavior. Intent upon disengaging the sacred from the profane and consolidating their monopoly over the sacred, the reformed clergy attempted to purge popular religion of paganism, to reindoctrinate the population through catechism, and to centralize religious devotions in the parish church under the authority of the parish priest. They condemned what they regarded as superstitious customs surrounding birth, marriage, and death and emphasized sacramental intervention in the life of the individual at the expense of the family and community celebrations that marked the rites of passage. They attacked confraternities, pilgrimages, and unauthorized cults of local saints, which diffused religious energies and eluded clerical control. They condemned popular festivities and even abolished some holy days—Archbishop Christophe de Beaumont of Paris, for example, abolished thirteen in 1778—in order to stop the profanation of sacred times and places by drinking, dancing, and debauchery.

The reforms effected by the clergy contributed in obvious ways to the belated Christianization of the realm under the Bourbon monarchs. It seems likely that they also contributed in the long run and in less obvious ways to the so-called dechristianization before the Revolution. The Counter-Reformation, aided and abetted by the Most Christian Kings, underscored the official character of Catholicism in France and staked out a more obtrusive role for the Church in the lives of the French people. Inasmuch as it made the clergy (tonsured, celibate, educated, and more commonly from outside the parish) more alien, and Christianity more repressive, than before, the Counter-Reformation probably aggravated anticlericalism and caused disaffection from the rites of the national religion. If so, eighteenth-century changes in religious behavior reflect not only "philosophic" changes in mentalities but also hostility to the imposition of a redefined and reorganized version of Catholicism. It is not altogether obvious, in any case, that the behavioral nonconformity documented by historians demonstrates the dechristianization of the minds and hearts of French Catholics, any more than the behavioral conformity demanded by the post-Tridentine Church demonstrates their genuine Christianity.

The monarchy and the magistrates collaborated with the clergy in the implementation of the reforms that transformed the religious life of the French people. The Most Christian Kings promoted the differentiation of the sacred and the profane by ordering the enclosure of cemeteries, traditionally used for such worldly purposes as grazing, marketing, dancing, elections, and assignations. They forbade their subjects to undertake unauthorized pilgrimages in order to prevent them from using this form of devotion as a pretext for escaping burdensome family obligations. The crown ratified suppressions of holy days by the prelates, and the parlementaires joined them in condemning the vulgar revelries of the peasantry. The campaign to civilize the populace, endorsed by bishops and judges well before philosophes took up the cause, found quintessential expression in the parlementary decree of May 24, 1784, which prohibited the dangerous custom of ringing church bells to dispel storms. The clergy disavowed the magic that unlettered Catholics confused with religion, and the magistrates applied the principles of the new science of electricity to the public welfare.

As the state assumed more active responsibility for the public welfare in the eighteenth century, several controversies demonstrated that the claims of religion and science did not always harmonize as they did in the case of the church bells. Obsessed by the fear of depopulation, the authorities concerned themselves with the health of French subjects in many ways. The police of Paris, for example, published regulations concerning the inspection of foodstuffs, the collection of refuse, the surveillance of quacks, and the resuscitation of Parisians who fell into the Seine. The monarchy promoted the certification of doctors and the registration of medical remedies, subsidized courses for the training of midwives, and established facilities for the care of abandoned children and the treatment of venereal disease. The king and the archbishop of Paris as well backed the efforts of the doctors to reform the medical regimen of the Parisian Hôtel Dieu in the

1780s, but they encountered stubborn resistance from the nuns who staffed the hospital. The nuns, who regarded healing as a religious calling rather than a clinical business, managed to delay their subordination to the doctors because they found supporters among the parlementaires who respected their piety and defended their privileges.

Reformers did not complete the "medicalization" of the hospital, but they did win the disputes about inoculation for smallpox and relocation of urban cemeteries before 1789. Many doctors and clergy opposed inoculation because of its novelty and because it seemed to involve meddling in the designs of Providence. After a decade of public debate about its reliability and permissibility, the Parlement of Paris prohibited the practice in cities in 1763, pending full investigation by the Faculties of Medicine and Theology. It took the physicians four years to approve the treatment, and the theologians never ruled on the subject. The lieutenant of police Sartine, meanwhile, permitted the practice in the capital in spite of the parlementary ban, and Choiseul had the cadets of the Ecole Militaire inoculated in 1769. Although "the fanatical priests raised a ruckus," according to one anti-clerical *nouvelliste,* Louis XVI symbolically settled the matter by having himself and his brothers inoculated in 1774 after their grandfather's death from smallpox.[24]

Just months before they referred the question of inoculation to the experts in 1763, the parlementaires consulted the Faculty of Medicine and the Academy of Sciences about the health threat posed by noxious vapors emanating from parish cemeteries. After thorough investigation of conditions in Paris, they prohibited further interments inside churches and prescribed the relocation of cemeteries outside the city walls. These regulations, which effectively abolished many of the traditional rituals of death in the name of hygiene, did not take effect for more than a decade. After Loménie de Brienne, the archbishop of Toulouse, raised the issue again and the assembly of the clergy of 1775 seconded his recommendations, the crown promulgated the declaration of March 10, 1776, ordering the relocation of insalubrious cemeteries. This declaration provoked riots in several provincial cities and opposition from the parish clergy of Paris, who realized that it

24. Nicolas Baudeau, "Chronique secrète de Paris sous le règne de Louis XVI en 1774," *Revue retrospective,* III (1834), 87.

would decrease their income from burial fees and claimed that it would undermine the faith of their parishioners. The Parlement subsequently closed the cemetery of the Holy Innocents, the largest graveyard in the city, in 1780. The remains of countless generations of Parisians buried there were eventually removed, with the approval of the archbishop and under the supervision of the lieutenant of police, during the years 1786 to 1788.

Changes in the administration of mendicity and education, as well as health, manifested the growth of royal and parlementary involvement in the management of the public welfare. Charitable orders, foundations, and confraternities spawned by the Counter-Reformation embraced the traditional view of the poor as representatives of Christ, but royal and local officials regarded them more often as criminals. During the reign of Louis XIV the monarchy confined beggars in the general hospitals in order to Christianize them and put them to work. Eighteenth-century intendants consigned them to workhouses or employed them in public works designed to promote productivity more than piety. Clergy and religion alike retained a more visible role in the staffing and curriculum of schools than in the repression of poverty. Louis XIV required all parishes to establish primary schools to teach the catechism, first and foremost, along with the rudiments of reading and writing. Louis XV assigned responsibility for the supervision of secondary schools to local boards composed largely of lay notables, but he also entrusted instruction in most of the former Jesuit schools to other religious orders in the 1760s. This reorganization disappointed parlementary reformers like La Chalotais, convinced of the Jesuits' blind devotion to Rome, the classics, and the next world. He called for modernization and "secularization" of the "monkish" education offered by "men having interests different from those of the country."[25]

La Chalotais, who wanted to reduce the visibility of religion in the schools but hardly exclude it from the curriculum, advocated secularization in the literal sense of the word, involving some tangible change from ecclesiastical to secular status, use, and/or jurisdiction. Reforms in the administration of health, mendicity, and education that entailed

25. Louis-René de Caradeuc de La Chalotais, *Essai d'éducation nationale ou plan d'études pour la jeunesse* (N.p., 1763), 18, 15.

such alterations in the social functions of the Church may well reflect some measure of secularization in the more figurative sense of changes in assumptions about the role of religion in the world. Like the nonenforcement of the legislation concerning the sacraments, censorship, irreligion and immorality, and like the behavioral deviations from the standards of the post-Tridentine Church, however, these reforms do not constitute transparent evidence of dechristianization. The Enlightenment undoubtedly had something to do with some changes in the religious life of literate subjects and some changes in the traditional roles of religion in the Christian kingdom, but these changes do not mean that the French people in general or the secular authorities in particular abandoned the faith of their ancestors under the influence of the philosophes. Changes in the jurisprudence and administration of the realm reflected long-standing concern for the effective and productive management of the human resources of the country as well as the ongoing centralization of authority in the hands of the crown. The monarch and his magistrates reconsidered the extent of their obligation to serve the institutional Church during the politico-religious conflicts that spanned the reign of Louis XV. These conflicts accelerated the expansion of secular at the expense of ecclesiastical jurisdiction, the subordination of the ideals of orthodoxy to the demands of public order, and the withdrawal of the state from the business of compelling subjects to abide by the prescriptions of the Church.

3

Politico-Religious Strife from Unigenitus to the Vingtième, 1714–1751

When the Parisian lawyer Matthieu Marais complained in 1729 that he was "very tired of the Constitution," he referred not to the unwritten constitution of the country but to the papal Constitution *Unigenitus* (1713), which condemned 101 allegedly erroneous propositions extracted from Pasquier Quesnel's Jansenist commentary on the New Testament.[1] Designed by Rome and Versailles to end more than a half-century of controversy about the workings of divine grace, this notorious bull instead provoked decades of disruptive debate about the religious and political order of the kingdom. The tiresome disputes engendered by the Constitution may have exasperated Marais, but they had momentous constitutional consequences. These conflicts, more than the Enlightenment, undermined the juridical fictions that bound the ancien régime together: the identification of the corporate kingdom with the divinely ordained kingship and the conjunction of citizenship and Catholicity. Prolonged dissension involving the crown, the clergy, and the parlements shattered the deceptive consensus concerning the interpretation of the traditions that made the realm an extension of its ruler and civil identity dependent upon confessional conformity.

1. Matthieu Marais, *Journal et mémoires sur la régence et le règne de Louis XV, 1715–1737*, ed. Mathurin-François-Adolphe de Lescure (4 vols.; Paris, 1863–68), IV, 75. Where capitalized, the word *Constitution* refers to *Unigenitus*.

The interminable strife spawned by *Unigenitus* accentuated the subversive character of Jansenism. The Church and the crown had already condemned this protean heresy on doctrinal, ecclesiological, and political grounds during the reign of Louis XIV. Seventeenth-century Jansenists espoused Augustinian predestinarianism and advocated moral rigorism. They attacked the semi-Pelagianism and casuistry associated with the Jesuits, who quickly cast themselves in the role of their inveterate adversaries. Roman hostility encouraged Jansenists to embrace Gallicanism, which allowed them to appeal to councils over popes. Episcopal hostility encouraged them to embrace Richerism, which denied the subordination of the parish clergy to the bishops. Their schismatic theology and "republican" ecclesiology made the Jansenists politically suspect, in spite of their protestations of loyalty to the crown. Richelieu regarded them as unfaithful subjects because of their criticism of French foreign policy during the Thirty Years' War, Mazarin suspected them of complicity in the Fronde, and Louis XIV resented their criticism of his extension of regalian rights over vacant benefices. Royal hostility encouraged Jansenists to embrace the constitutionalism of the parlementaires, who attempted to protect them from persecution incited by the so-called "devout party"—the Jesuits, the majority of the bishops, members of the royal family, and various ministers—during the reign of Louis XV.

In the course of the conflicts provoked by *Unigenitus*, Jansenism became loosely synonymous with opposition to ecclesiastical and ministerial "despotism" because of its coalescence with the defense of Gallican liberties, the agitation of disgruntled parish priests, and the political pretensions of the magistrates. Elaborating upon arguments articulated during the civil wars and the Fronde, the parlements assigned themselves an essential role in the history and constitution of the French monarchy. They described themselves as the descendants of the general assemblies of the Frankish people and the guardians of the traditions that preserved the order of the kingdom. They claimed the responsibility of registering royal declarations and the right to remonstrate against legislation that violated the fundamental laws of the realm. Formulating their arguments within the framework of traditional principles, the judges insisted that the crown abused its absolute authority by resorting to arbitrary means to enforce the Constitution.

A vocal and influential minority of Jansenists in the Parlement of Paris, seconded by lawyers and pamphleteers who shared their religious convictions, led the crusade against the bull. Gallicanism and legalism prompted other magistrates to take up the cause of Jansenism, which sharpened their constitutional arguments and fueled their opposition to absolutism.

In the penultimate year of his long reign, Louis XIV made one last effort to ensure religious uniformity in his realm by securing the ratification of *Unigenitus* by an ad hoc assembly of French bishops and by the Parlement of Paris. In accepting the bull, the prelates and the magistrates both commented on the ninety-first of the 101 propositions it censured: "The fear of an unjust excommunication must never prevent us from doing our duty." The bishops explained that the condemnation of this seemingly unexceptionable maxim targeted insubordinate Jansenists who obstinately appealed to conscience in order to justify their resistance to the decisions of the Church. They carefully denied that the pope intended to suggest that he could legitimately excommunicate subjects who failed to obey papal injunctions that conflicted with their imprescriptible obligations toward their sovereign. The possibility of this ultramontane interpretation of the censure alarmed the magistrates, who read the condemnation of the ninety-first proposition as an attempt to resurrect the pernicious doctrine of Roman supremacy over temporal rulers. In registering the Constitution with qualifications to protect the Gallican liberties of the realm, they specifically noted that "the fear of an unjust excommunication" should never deter subjects from "the loyalty and obedience owing to the king."[2] Although *Unigenitus* dealt for the most part with abstruse theological questions, it provoked political dissension in France, largely

---

2. Léon Mention (ed.), *Documents relatifs aux rapports du clergé avec la royauté de 1705 à 1789* (Paris, 1903), 50. Nine of the forty-nine bishops who attended the ad hoc assembly refused to subscribe to the bull. For the resistance of the *gens du roi*, see Augustin-Louis Gazier (ed.), "Fragment inédit des mémoires du chancelier d'Aguesseau," *Bulletin philologique et historique*, XXXVI (1918), 38; Guillaume-François Joly de Fleury, "Mémoires historiques," in JF, Vol. 2476, fols. 144–45 v; Henri Courteault (ed.), "Journal historique de Guillaume de Lamoignon, avocat-général au parlement de Paris, 1713–1718," *Annuaire-bulletin de la société de l'histoire de France*, XLVII (1910), 246.

because the parlements never ceased to regard it as a threat to the independence of the monarchy, in spite of repeated ecclesiastical explanations and royal assurances to the contrary. As the magistrates exploited the menace of ultramontanism in order to advance their own constitutional claims, conflicts over the Constitution escalated into conflicts over the disposition of authority in the realm.

Opposition to *Unigenitus* mushroomed during the Regency as Jansenists polemicized against the bull and dissident ecclesiastics appealed to a future council for review of the papal condemnation. To defend the authority of the Church and restore tranquillity in the kingdom, the Regent prohibited further controversy, pending doctrinal clarifications from Rome, in the declaration of October 7, 1717. While acknowledging that the Most Christian King was obliged to protect the Catholic faith, the crown thereby refrained from meddling in dogmatic questions which the Church alone could resolve: "More submissive to its decisions than the least of our subjects, we believe that it is from the Church that kings and peoples alike must learn the truths necessary to salvation, and we have no intention of extending our power over that which concerns doctrine, of which the sacred trust has been committed to another power."[3] Clement XI responded in 1718 with the encyclical *Pastoralis officii*, excommunicating ecclesiastics who refused to accept the bull without reservations. Less deferential than the crown, the Parlement promptly suppressed the inflammatory papal letter, which disregarded the Gallican modifications it had appended to *Unigenitus*.

The magistrates portrayed themselves as defenders not only of the Gallican liberties of the realm but also of the "fixed and inviolable laws as ancient as the monarchy," which they expected the crown to respect. They invoked these laws during the minority of Louis XV to justify their opposition to the fiscal policies of the Regent, who eventually exiled them to Pontoise. During this exile he announced the bishops' acceptance of doctrinal clarifications about issues addressed by the Constitution. In the declaration of August 4, 1720, as in 1717, he cited the edict of 1695 on ecclesiastical jurisdiction and studiously

---

3. *Déclaration du roi*, October 7, 1717, in *Suite du supplément à la nécrologie des défenseurs de la vérité* (N.p., 1764), 219.

avoided trespassing upon clerical prerogatives. The Regent's acceptance of the doctrinal compromise as representing the genuine sense
of *Unigenitus* depended, in the first place, upon its ratification by the
clergy. The crown, furthermore, set aside the conciliar appeals of the
preceding years in noncommittal terms "*as* of no effect," without presuming to rule that they were canonically "of no effect." Having endorsed the "true" interpretation of the bull and thereby reaffirmed the
young king's claim to "the glorious title of Eldest Son of the Church,"
the Regent endeavored to restore public order by reiterating his injunction of silence. The Parlement registered the accommodation after
several months of negotiation in order to expedite its return from exile, but not without reaffirming the qualifications of 1714.[4]

Royal prohibitions notwithstanding, disgruntled clergy renewed their
appeals, and pamphleteers of all stripes continued their polemics
after 1720. The Jansenist weekly, *Nouvelles ecclésiastiques*, appeared
in the wake of the controversial council of Embrun, which characterized the Constitution as a "dogmatic judgment of the Church" and
deposed the Jansenist bishop of Senez in 1727. The police never succeeded in arresting the circulation of this unauthorized periodical,
which provided the literate public with news about ecclesiastical and
parlementary opposition until the Revolution. "Miracles" at the tomb
of the Jansenist deacon François de Pâris following his death in the
same year gave birth to the cult of the convulsionaries. Their entan-
glement in the ongoing dissension about the bull led the king to close
the cemetery of Saint-Médard where they congregated, but mil-
lenarian conventicles survived underground for many years.[5] The
closing of the cemetery had the enthusiastic support of Vintimille,
the new archbishop of Paris, who collaborated with cardinal Fleury in
his efforts to impose orthodoxy upon the religious orders, the parish
clergy, and the faculty of theology of the Sorbonne. In 1729, the year
of Vintimille's appointment, the Holy See inadvertently played into

4. *Les Remontrances*, I, 95; *Déclaration du roi*, August 4, 1720, in Mention (ed.),
Documents, 52. Marais commented in his *Journal*, II, 5, that the declaration had been
registered as if it had not been registered.

5. On the vaguely subversive character of the convulsionaries, see B. Robert
Kreiser, *Miracles, Convulsions, and Ecclesiastical Politics in Early Eighteenth-Century
Paris* (Princeton, 1978), 304, 317, 335.

the hands of critics of the Constitution by issuing an office for the festival of Saint Gregory VII, the eleventh-century pope who deposed the Emperor Henry IV during the Investiture Conflict. Defending "the inviolable and sacred principles of the attachment of subjects to their sovereign," the parlementaires banned the ultramontane text, which seemed to belie the explanations of the French bishops and confirm the worst apprehensions of Gallican opponents of *Unigenitus*.[6]

Exercising the royal prerogative of "fixing the true sense of previous laws often obscured by the diversity of interpretations," Louis XV made another effort to clarify his intentions and resolve disputes over the Constitution in the declaration of March 24, 1730.[7] He recognized the bull as a "judgment of the universal Church in matter of doctrine," as a "law of the Church and of the state," and required all candidates for orders and benefices to subscribe to the papal formulary condemning Jansenism. Denouncing opposition to *Unigenitus* founded upon the pretext of Gallicanism as rebellion against the throne, he forbade the Parlement to take cognizance of appeals from recalcitrant ecclesiastics. He again prohibited further controversy but specifically authorized the clergy to fulfill their pastoral function of instructing the faithful with regard to the dogmatic issues addressed by the Constitution.

Consulted during the drafting of these articles, cardinal de Bissy, who had attended the assembly of prelates which ratified *Unigenitus* in 1714, warned against compromises to mollify the magistrates.[8] Joly de Fleury, the attorney general of the Parlement of Paris, warned, on the other hand, that the magistrates would bridle at the words "judgment of the universal Church in matter of doctrine." This formula, more or less equivalent to the denomination "rule of faith," implied that the Constitution was not susceptible to amendments like the qualifications of 1714. Many of the judges, as Joly de Fleury anticipated, protested "vigorously and vociferously" against the declaration in the *lit de justice* of April 3. The outspoken abbé Pucelle, who

6. *Arrêt du parlement*, July 20, 1729 (Paris, 1729), 5. Unless otherwise specified, the word *parlement* in texts entitled *Arrêt du parlement* refers to the Parlement of Paris.

7. Henri-François d'Aguesseau to Polinchove, first president of the Parlement of Flanders, April 14, 1730, in FF, Vol. 6822, fol. 122. For the text of the declaration, see Mention (ed.), *Documents*, 62–69.

8. Henri-Pons de Thiard de Bissy, "Remarques sur le projet de la déclaration à faire," in Vol. 448, no. 32, PR.

charged that it made the king the vassal of the pope, underscored the constitutional aspect of their resistance to *Unigenitus*. He reminded his colleagues that "there were occasions when the interest of the king and the state was involved when it was necessary to show resoluteness against the king himself, who did not know his rights."[9] According to this line of reasoning, which became standard fare in remonstrances increasingly designed for public consumption, disobedience to royal commands amounted to genuine obedience to the crown when the monarch disregarded the fundamental laws of the realm. Contemporaries interpreted the failure of the Parisian populace to acclaim Louis XV in the usual fashion on April 3 as a sign of their support for the magistrates and hostility to the bull. Placards appeared in the Palais de Justice after the king's appearance calling upon Saint Genevieve to deliver the capital from the Constitution as she had from Atilla.

The quinquennial assembly of the clergy, meeting during the summer months, complained about abusive interpretations of *Unigenitus* by its ecclesiastical and parlementary critics. Anxious to dissociate themselves from ultramontane readings of the bull and the office of Gregory VII, the prelates reassured the monarch of their unfailing reverence for his "sovereign, independent authority subject only to God." They reminded French subjects of the "sacred duty" of submission to the crown from which no power could release them. In the closing address of September 17, however, La Parisière, the bishop of Nîmes, admonished Louis XV that his reign was "based upon Catholicity and must always be supported by the same principle." The *Nouvelles ecclésiastiques* asked maliciously if the bishop meant that the king would lose his crown and that his subjects would no longer have to obey him if he was no longer Catholic.[10] Disclaiming any such subversive interpretation of his words in a letter to Fleury, La Parisière explained that the Most Christian King's manner of ruling, not his claim to the throne, was "based on Catholicity," and acknowledged that even defection from the true faith could not undermine his legiti-

---

9. Joly de Fleury to d'Aguesseau, May 22, 1730, in JF, Vol. 84, dossier 858, fol. 191; FF, Vol. 10908, fol. 74 v; Edmond-Jean-François Barbier, *Chronique de la régence et du règne de Louis XV* (8 vols.; Paris, 1866), II, 112.

10. PV, VII, 1075, 1220; *Nouvelles ecclésiastiques*, October 18, 1730, p. 11.

macy. With the unruly conduct of the magistrates in the *lit de justice* of April 3 in mind, he emphasized the axiom that the monarch was not accountable to anyone on earth, including those whom he entrusted with the authority he derived from God "for the maintenance of the laws."[11]

Before the end of September the lawyers in the Parlement of Paris—who had already distinguished themselves by their strident criticism of the council of Embrun and the office of Gregory VII— entered the fray once more with an inflammatory consultation in favor of a number of appellant priests against their bishops. Contending that the definition of the jurisdiction of the two powers was a temporal matter, the forty signatories defended the *appel comme d'abus*, recently denounced by the assembly of 1730 and routinely circumvented by the evocations of the royal council. They argued that the clergy derived whatever "external and coercive jurisdiction" they exercised from the king and that ecclesiastics, as his subjects, were therefore accountable to his magistrates for any misuse of this authority. In making their case, the lawyers referred to the Parlement as the senate of the nation and the repository of public authority and described laws as conventions between rulers and subjects. The royal council singled out these unorthodox expressions in its suppression of the consultation, which tended not only to slight the Church but also to "attack the fundamental principles of the government of France and diminish the respect of the people for that supreme authority which, residing entirely in the sole person of the sovereign, constitutes the essential character of the monarchy." Two hundred lawyers inscribed their names on a petition intended to reconcile the language of the consultation with the traditions of the kingdom and disavow "every other interpretation." As Barbier noted, this petition amounted to "saying in plain French that the royal council was wrong."[12] The crown rejected this justificatory text, crammed with verbal precedents, and, after weeks of negotia-

11. Jean-César Rousseau de La Parisière to André-Hercule de Fleury, November 18, 1730, in JF, Vol. 1476, fol. 222.

12. *Mémoire pour les sieurs Samson, curé d'Olivet . . .* (Paris, n.d.), 2–3; *Arrêt du conseil,* October 30, 1730 (Paris, 1730), 2; *Requête de messieurs les avocats du parlement au sujet de l'arrêt du conseil du roi du 30 octobre 1730* (N.p., n.d.), 10; Barbier, *Chronique,* II, 137.

tions, accepted instead a more submissive statement by the signatories of the consultation designed to erase any suspicions concerning their loyalty to the throne.

In this declaration the lawyers summarized the conventional principles of French absolutism. They acknowledged "that the kingdom of France is a purely monarchical state, that the supreme authority resides solely in the person of the sovereign, that Your Majesty occupies in the realm the place of God Himself, of whom he is the image." They accordingly recognized that the magistrates derived their authority from the divinely ordained king. Recapitulating familiar Gallican maxims, they maintained "that there is no power on earth which has the authority to release peoples from that inviolable loyalty which they owe their sovereign." Even excommunication "could never break the sacred bond which ties subjects to the king." Having expressed their opposition to *Unigenitus* in this roundabout manner, the lawyers concluded by reiterating their restrictive interpretation of ecclesiastical prerogatives. They granted that the clergy derived their authority over the salvation of souls directly from God but maintained that "it is to Your Majesty alone that they owe the external jurisdiction which they exercise in your realm, for the use of which they are necessarily accountable to Your Majesty and consequently to the Parlement, which renders justice in your name."[13] They incorporated their broad construction of secular prerogatives in religious matters into their reaffirmation of royal sovereignty, as chancellor Lamoignon observed some twenty years later, in order to subject the clergy to the jurisdiction of the magistrates.[14]

The crown announced its acceptance of this aggressive retraction in the decree of November 25, 1730. Since the lawyers did not explicitly acknowledge the errors imputed to them by the royal council in October, one contemporary commented that the crown's acceptance of their declaration, which only explained what they "really" meant in

13. The lawyers' declaration takes up most of the three pages of the *arrêt du conseil* of November 25, 1730 (Paris, 1730).

14. Guillaume de Lamoignon de Blancmesnil, "Observations sommaires sur la déclaration des avocats inserée dans l'arrêt du conseil d'état du 25 octobre 1730 en ce qui concerne la jurisdiction eccléstiastique," in Ser. 177 Mi, Vol. 75 [Ser. 154 AP, Vol. 10], no. 34, fol. 1 v., AN.

the first place, amounted to admission that the council "misunderstood the meaning" of the consultation. The clergy, meanwhile, continued to inveigh against the "republicanism" and "Anglicanism" of the lawyers. As the bishop of Embrun complained to Louis XV, "everything they say about the Church" in the declaration "leaves entirely untouched, even confirms what they had stated" in the consultation.[15] Cardinal Fleury, who congratulated the lawyers for underlining "the genuine and leading principles of the fundamental constitution of the monarchy" in their declaration, reassured the agents-general of the clergy that the decree of November 25 did not mean that the crown intended to abandon its defense of ecclesiastical jurisdiction.[16] Acting on the same assumption, cardinal de Bissy circulated a model condemnation of the lawyers as rebels against both God and king.[17] Some of his colleagues broadened the indictment to include the magistrates, who adopted the lawyers' language in censuring episcopal pronouncements and remonstrating against evocations of *appels comme d'abus.*

The prelates argued that their "external and coercive jurisdiction" in religious matters, like their authority over consciences, derived from divine institution, not royal concession. As defined by the archbishop of Paris in his pastoral instruction of January 10, 1731, this jurisdiction meant the right to pronounce judgments outside of the tribunal of penitence and to impose spiritual penalties that took effect on the souls of offenders regardless of their resistance. The Church, though spiritual in its ends, necessarily expressed itself through external acts such as the administration of the sacraments. Externality, as Vintimille explained, did not automatically entail subjection to secular authority. The differentiation of the two powers, ordained by God for distinct ends, guaranteed the independence of the clergy in the exercise of their spiritual functions, just as it protected monarchs from papal deposition. The prelates acknowledged their accountability to the king in temporal affairs. They insisted, at the same time, that the king and his magistrates must defer to them without presuming to

---

15. NAF, Vol. 3334, fol. 136 v; Pierre-Guérin de Tencin to Louis XV, December 18, 1730, in Vol. 449, unpaginated, PR.

16. NAF, Vol. 3334, fols. 141 v., 193.

17. Model condemnation in Vol. 449, PR.

meddle in matters of doctrine and discipline assigned by God to the spiritual power.

The polemics provoked by the declaration of 1730, the assembly of the clergy, and the consultation of the lawyers escalated in 1731. The bishops denounced temporal interference in spiritual affairs, as preached and practiced by the parlementaires. The magistrates, in turn, accused them of "distorting the proper sense of terms" by claiming "external and coercive jurisdiction." In his condemnations of Vintimille and other prelates—notably La Fare, bishop of Laon, and Tencin, bishop of Embrun—the solicitor general Gilbert de Voisins charged that these terms misrepresented the more restricted authority that the Church derived from God and threatened the sovereignty of the crown. In his repeated efforts to stop this brawling over terms, the monarch sought to fulfill his paternal obligation to mediate disputes involving the interpretation of the religious and political traditions of the realm. Dismissing attempts to equate resistance to the king with adherence to the genuine interests of the kingdom, Louis XV ignored the judges' exaggerated anxieties concerning the ninety-first proposition, the office of Gregory VII, and the address of the bishop of Nîmes. He tried to quiet the clergy, meanwhile, with assurances that the lawyers had adequately recanted their errors. On the one hand, he protected ecclesiastical jurisdiction by evoking religious matters from the Parlement to the royal council, insisting that the magistrates must, like the Most Christian King, "respect the limits which God Himself has laid down between two authorities whose rights are distinct without being contradictory." [18] On the other hand, he endeavored to restrain prelates whose intemperate language and imprudent conduct prolonged dissension. Through these complementary strategies, implemented as much by means of negotiations behind the scenes as through public pronouncements, the crown hoped to encourage moderation in both parties yet satisfied extremists in neither camp.

Disturbed by what he referred to disingenuously as "new disputes" occasioned by "some writings" widely distributed "in the public,"

---

18. *Arrêt du parlement,* March 5, 1731 (Paris, 1731), 2; Royal reply to remonstrances of January 9, 1731, in *Les Remontrances,* I, 241.

Louis XV attempted to clarify "the nature, scope, and limits of ecclesiastical authority and secular power" in the decree of March 10, 1731.[19] He granted, in the first place, that God had vested authority over doctrinal and disciplinary matters in the Church and specifically empowered the Church to impose irresistible spiritual penalties on sinners in accordance with its canons. He also reconfirmed his predecessors' concession of the forms of externality of ecclesiastical judgments. Concerned that the disputes involved disagreements not only about words but also about substance, the king imposed silence on his quarrelsome subjects and announced the appointment of a commission of prelates and royal councillors to advise him on the means of restoring concord between the two powers. In his cover letter to the bishops he called attention to his defense of their "jurisdiction," a verbal red flag he deliberately avoided in the decree itself, and exhorted them to second his irenic designs.[20] The bishops, of course, would have preferred that the king recognize their jurisdiction explicitly in the text of the decree and overrule the parlementary condemnation of Vintimille's pastoral instruction, which justified their usage of the controversial term.

The commission met during the summer months under the supervision of Fleury, the architect of royal religious policy. Fleury had lectured the belligerent bishop of Laon "that the subject of ecclesiastical jurisdiction is so sensitive and that it is so difficult to lay down its precise limits that the terms cannot be too carefully weighed and concerted." He urged the uncooperative La Fare to adopt the language of the archbishop of Paris, "who leaves nothing to be desired with regard to the power of the Church" in his pastoral instruction.[21] The prelates named to the commission—cardinal de Bissy, who had publicly denounced the forty lawyers; cardinal Rohan, who, like de Bissy, had attended the assembly which ratified *Unigenitus*; and the archbishop of Rouen, Fleury's agent in the stage-managing of the assembly of the clergy of 1730—reiterated the prime minister's advice in their own letters to La Fare.[22] The ecclesiastical commissioners, like La

19. *Arrêt du conseil*, March 10, 1731, in *Recueil général*, XXI, 354.

20. Royal letter to bishops, in FF, Vol. 23442, fol. 84.

21. Fleury to Etienne-Joseph de la Fare, January 16, 1731, in Ser. 257 AP, Vol. 14, dossier I, no. 77, and June 27, 1731, in Ser. 257 AP, Vol. 14, dossier III, no. 2, AN.

22. Henri-Pons de Thiard de Bissy to La Fare, March 11, 1731, in Ser. 257 AP,

Fare, supported the Constitution and opposed parlementary encroach-
ment upon ecclesiastical prerogatives. They were more disposed to
collaborate with the ministry in order to attain these objectives, however, than their intransigent colleague.

The lay commissioners included three royal councillors—d'Argenson, Fortia, and d'Ormesson—and Chancellor d'Aguesseau, who had
risked Louis XIV's wrath by balking at registration of the Constitution
but subsequently presented the declaration of 1730 to the Parlement
at the *lit de justice* of April 3. More faithful to his Gallican convictions
on paper than in public, d'Aguesseau believed that "the present disputes turn upon questions of words to which everyone attaches different meanings." He concluded off the record that proper definitions of
the terms *external, coercive,* and *jurisdiction,* employed loosely by
Vintimille, would vindicate the magistrates and infuriate the bishops.
Given the likely backlash from one party or the other against any pronouncement concerning the two powers, the chancellor realized that
the crown had to try to avoid compromising itself by "defining anything
in this matter by a law emanating from royal authority."[23]

Judging from the papers collected by the comte d'Argenson, the
commissioners reviewed the polemics on both sides of the question.
Several of the memoirs submitted for their consideration restated the
Gallican argument that "the Church derives from temporal rulers the
civil and purely external exercise of the powers which it received from
Jesus Christ." These memoirs contained ominous warnings about the
threat of ultramontanism, which other memoirs dismissed as provocative nonsense. Anxious to avoid further disputes regarding matters
"about which they would have wished no explanation had ever been
required," the commissioners reported that "the substance of the
power of the Church is not contested."[24] Having reiterated and elaborated upon the generalized catalogue of ecclesiastical prerogatives in

Vol. 15, dossier II, no. 17, AN; Armand-Gaston-Maximilien de Rohan to La Fare, June
27, 1731, in Ser. 257 AP, Vol. 15, dossier III, no. 2, AN; Louis de La Vergne de Tressan
to La Fare, in Ser. 257 AP, Vol. 16, dossier XI, nos. 2 and 5, AN.

23. D'Aguesseau, "Précis des réflexions à faire sur la querelle des limites des
deux puissances," in Vol. 449, PR. The other lay commissioners were Henri-François
de Paule Lefèvre d'Ormesson, Joseph-Charles de Fortia, and Marc-Pierre de Voyer de
Paulmy d'Argenson.

24. Vol. 3053, fols. 283 v., 345, 342 v., Arsénal.

the decree of March 10, they addressed themselves to the more specific issues of terminology raised by the archbishop of Paris. After explaining that words ought to convey the intended meaning literally and exactly in a manner consecrated by common usage, they concluded that Vintimille's exposition of "external and coercive jurisdiction" satisfied these requirements. They therefore assured the king that he could ignore parlementary protests and approve this language without detracting from the plenitude of his authority.

In the end the recommendations of the commissioners justified the hope expressed by the bishop of Chartres that they would "insist upon the prerogatives of the Church." They did so after having studied the memoir in which Vintimille responded to the magistrates' suppression of his pastoral instruction and reminded Louis XV of his coronation oath to defend the Church. The archbishop explained that he had spoken out against the consultation and the declaration of the forty lawyers in order to correct their heretical assertions concerning the Church, which the king, according to him, had not presumed to correct. Exercising the episcopal prerogative of instructing the faithful in such matters, he claimed to have defined terms "with exactitude which scrupulously preserves the characteristic distinctions between the two powers." He condemned those who challenged the formula "external and coercive jurisdiction," carefully defined and supported by innumerable verbal precedents, for "wanting to disturb the Church and the state by disputes over words." Informed of the commission's conclusions regarding these disputes, Louis XV overruled the parlementary condemnation by the decree of July 30. This decree summarized Vintimille's memoir without putting his words in the king's mouth and allowed the archbishop to publish his pastoral instruction. Resorting to sleight of hand to reconcile this implicit reprimand with its previous acceptance of the lawyers' declaration, the crown announced that Vintimille had censured only "false principles which are rejected by all Catholics," including, presumably, the signatories of the consultation.[25]

25. Charles-François de Montiers de Mérinville to La Fare, March 28, 1731, in Ser. 257 AP, Vol. 17, dossier X, no. 10, AN; Charles-Gaspard-Guillaume de Vintimille, *Mémoire présenté au roi* . . . (Paris, 1731), 11; Vintimille, "Projet du mémoire à présenter au roi," in Vol. 3053, fol. 333, Arsénal; *Arrêt du conseil*, July 30, 1731 (Paris, 1731), 12.

Just a week before he sanctioned the archbishop's justification of his words, Louis XV made a significant terminological gesture of his own concerning *Unigenitus*. Gilbert de Voisins had urged the crown in January to clarify the declaration of 1730 by stating that this legislation did not recognize the bull as a "rule of faith" or disallow the qualifications of 1714. Fleury had responded evasively at the time that "there are matters about which it is not appropriate for the king to express himself, because they are not within his competence." In a circular letter dated July 22, however, Louis XV asked the bishops not to describe the Constitution as a "rule of faith." Since he had already endorsed the denomination "judgment of the universal Church in matter of doctrine" and recognized *Unigenitus* as a "law of the Church and of the state," he urged the prelates "to avoid an expression which is not necessary and which has become an occasion for new disputes which are equally dangerous and pointless."[26] Stressing the need for uniformity in conduct as well as language, the king also asked the clergy, in guardedly vague terms, not to interrogate untroublesome Catholics about doctrinal matters beyond their capacity, by which he meant submission to the bull.

Although the Church had not officially approved the designation "rule of faith," some prelates regarded the royal proscription as a violation of ecclesiastical jurisdiction comparable to the transgressions of the magistrates.[27] The bishops of Evreux, Marseilles, and Verdun criticized Louis XV's letter by citing d'Aguesseau's published rebuke to the parlement of Bordeaux in 1730 for its meddling in spiritual matters.[28] Tencin, the bishop of Embrun, protested that "the king is made to speak as though he had the prerogative of fixing the language of the

26. Fleury to Pierre Gilbert de Voisins, January 14, 1731, in Ser. U., Vol. 877, no. 73, AN; Royal letter to bishops, July 22, 1731, in NAF, Vol. 3334, 230 v. Marais wondered in his *Journal*, IV, 268, if the French Academy could explain the difference between the expressions "rule of faith" and "dogmatic judgment of the universal Church."

27. The Parlement condemned various pronouncements in which La Fare mentioned the conclusions of a Roman council, not recognized in France, which had characterized *Unigenitus* as a "rule of faith." See Fleury's undated rebuke in Ser. 257 AP, Vol. 14, dossier III, no. 149, AN.

28. Jean Le Normand to Fleury, undated, in FF, Vol. 7027, fol. 542; Statements by Henri-Xavier de Belsunce de Castelmoron and Charles-François d'Allencourt, dated August 18 and 19, respectively, in Vol. 449, PR.

faith."[29] Tencin—who had characterized the Constitution as a "rule of faith" in his condemnation of the lawyers and scorned Vintimille's pastoral instruction as a sellout—complained to cardinal de Rohan, a member of the royal commission, that Louis XV had in effect reneged on the declaration of 1730 and endorsed the encroachments of the magistrates.

The magistrates, repeatedly thwarted in their attempts to undo the declaration of 1730, naturally referred to the circular letter in their remonstrances of July 24 against the evocation of cases involving the withholding of sacraments. Invoking the familiar Gallican maxim "The Church is in the state," they reasoned that the monarch was entitled, indeed obliged, to take cognizance of abuses committed by ecclesiastics so as to protect his subjects against arbitrary departures from the canons of the Church recognized in the realm. Because *Unigenitus* lacked the status of "rule of faith" in France, they denounced the refusal of sacraments—which they equated with excommunication—to persons who refused to accept the bull on their deathbeds as a dangerous and indefensible innovation that not only endangered the salvation of the subjects in question but also threatened the sovereignty of the crown. They claimed that they respected the legitimate rights of spiritual authority in this mixed matter inasmuch as they distinguished between "that which constitutes the matter and the substance of the sacraments and that which regards only the external and public exercise of administering them."[30] They distinguished, that is to say, the invisible grace dispensed exclusively by the clergy from the visible dispensation of that grace, in which the clergy had to abide by rules as well known to the parlementaires as the clergy themselves. The judges, who would have liked the king to ban the denomination "rule of faith" outright and forbid interrogations altogether, persevered in their argument that the clergy had no external jurisdiction of their own and that the discipline of the Church, insofar as it was external in character, fell under secular jurisdiction.

The circular letter of July 22 and the royal decree of July 30, designed to restrain the clergy and the Parlement, respectively, did not

29. Tencin to Nicolas-Prosper Bauyn d'Angervilliers, August 6, 1731, in NAF, Vol. 3334, fol. 244.

30. *Les Remontrances*, I, 252.

put a stop to disputes about the Constitution and the relationship between the two powers. Some bishops, notably La Fare and Tencin, defiantly insisted upon the denomination "rule of faith" and denied their accountability to the crown in what they regarded as spiritual affairs. The king himself suppressed some of their pastoral letters, at least partly in order to forestall intervention by the magistrates, who continued to complain about royal evocations in such matters. Louis XV made a concession to the parlementaires when he renewed the injunction of silence in the decree of September 5. He mentioned the qualifications of 1714 in prescribing submission to *Unigenitus,* qualifications they regarded as material evidence that the bull could not be described as a "rule of faith." Two days later, however, the king rebuffed their remonstrances against his decision in favor of the archbishop of Paris, just as he had rebuffed their remonstrances concerning the refusal of sacraments. Explaining once more that Vintimille had censured only "false principles which are rejected by all Catholics," he assured the judges that he would not tolerate the sort of violations of religious and political traditions that they had read into the archbishop's pronouncement.[31]

Urged on by Pucelle and several other ardent Gallicans, the magistrates took Louis XV's words as an invitation to defend royal authority and advance their own pretensions by defining these traditions. They criticized the clergy's attempts, "under the pretext of instruction" sanctioned by the king, to fix the relationship between the two powers and then proceeded to do so themselves. As if to suggest that the prelates still harbored ultramontane sentiments, they reaffirmed the independence of the crown in uncategorical terms. Unlike the commissioners of 1731, they attributed "jurisdiction" only to the temporal power. They consequently declared that the clergy were answerable to the monarch "and, in the case of abuse, to the court under his authority for the exercise of the jurisdiction which they derived from the king himself." Stretching their competence in religious matters to the maximum, the parlementaires contended that ecclesiastics were likewise accountable "for everything in the exercise of the power

31. Royal reply to remonstrances of September 3, 1731, in *Les Remontrances* I, 272.

which they derive from God which might disturb public tranquillity, the laws, and the maxims of the kingdom."[32] Their summary account of "the maxims of the kingdom" on the subject of the two powers, in other words, reiterated the claims expounded in their remonstrances against Vintimille and the refusal of sacraments recently rejected by the king.

Before the bishops had a chance to counterattack, the crown suppressed this decree as a violation of silence and usurpation of its legislative authority. When Louis XV reprimanded the magistrates on September 9 for publishing such a decree, he did not expressly condemn its contents, so as to avoid the awkward necessity of formulating and attempting to impose his own definitions of contested traditions. "The king," as Gilbert de Voisins observed, "cannot pronounce on these sorts of disputes without considerable drawbacks."[33] Given the difficulty of satisfying both parties involved in the conflicts, the monarch frequently exercised his least compromising—and often least effective—option by renewing the injunction of silence. During the fall of 1731, the crown considered further legislation, modeled on the decree of March 10, dealing with the thorny issues it had sidestepped in its pronouncements of July 30 and September 9. The legislation in question was designed in part to end the strike staged by the lawyers in the Parlement of Paris. They regarded the decree concerning Vintimille's pastoral instruction as an abrogation of the previous decree by which Louis XV had accepted their retraction.

Joly de Fleury, who drafted and redrafted the text, had already revealed his thinking on the subject of "external and coercive jurisdiction" when consulted by d'Aguesseau during the deliberations of the royal commission. Scorning "the language of theologians," the attorney general warned that the clergy used these terms incorrectly and in a manner prejudicial to the sovereignty of the crown. He sounded the same Gallican note in the opening lines of his first draft, dated November 17. In these lines the monarch recognized, in uncommonly restrictive language, "the *wholly* spiritual power established by God to guide souls in religious matters" but also declared that he would not countenance the slightest detraction from the plenitude of temporal

32. *Arrêt du parlement*, September 7, 1731, in Mention (ed.), *Documents*, 70.
33. Gilbert de Voisins to Fleury, July 24, 1731, in Ser. U, Vol. 877, no. 70, AN.

authority he derived from God.[34] The attorney general had the king attribute the disputes concerning the two powers to differences over words and then decline to settle these terminological questions outright. Instead, he had the sovereign explain what those who claimed "external and coercive jurisdiction" for the Church meant by that expression, in such a way as to exclude the sorts of connotations Joly de Fleury found objectionable. Since this artful declaration prohibited innovations in language, as its author pointed out in his cover letter to d'Aguesseau, it would have allowed the magistrates to take action against clerics who abused the terms by interpreting them in ways other than the king had specified.[35]

The lawyers in the Parlement resumed their duties after intensive negotiations that resulted in the decree of December 1. In this decree Louis XV explicitly acknowledged that they did not advocate the "false principles" condemned by the archbishop of Paris. Joly de Fleury advised d'Aguesseau two days later that a declaration in the style he had proposed was "the only way of settling everything." The chancellor remained skeptical about the possibility of placating the magistrates, many of them still nettled by the suppression of their decree of September 7, without offending the prelates, some of them still offended by the circular letter. He predicted that the declaration, if "drawn up with all the strength demanded by the most zealous defenders of royal authority," would "stir up the bishops." On the other hand, if the king "explains himself more tentatively, weighing and choosing his words circumspectly, leaving ambiguities inevitable in this matter," then "the Parlement will not be satisfied."[36]

The attorney general, who had suggested disingenuously that the crown could mollify the judges by adopting the principles they had expounded in September, composed a number of further drafts, more aggressively Gallican in spirit than the first, during the month of December. In these versions he baldly sanctioned appeals against "the

34. Joly de Fleury to d'Aguesseau, July 6, 1731, in JF, Vol. 101, dossier 960, fols. 27, 128.

35. Joly de Fleury to d'Aguesseau, November 17, 1731, in JF, Vol. 101, dossier 960, fol. 191.

36. *Arrêt du conseil,* December 1, 1731 (Paris, 1731), 2; Joly de Fleury to d'Aguesseau, December 3, 1731, in JF, Vol. 101, dossier 960, fol. 158; D'Aguesseau to Joly de Fleury, December 12, 1731, in JF, Vol. 101, dossier 960, fol. 175 v.

abuses which can be met with in acts emanating from the spiritual power." He effectively denied the clergy the use of the terms *external, coercive,* and *jurisdiction,* which they had appropriated from secular tribunals. By the end of the month, Joly de Fleury was thoroughly exasperated by the evasive tactic of prefacing any legislation with reassurances that the disputes concerned words more than substance. As he complained to d'Aguesseau, "This amounts to reproaching the bishops and the parlements for fighting over nothing but shadows."[37]

After cardinal Fleury pointedly reminded the attorney general at a conference on December 30 that "the king wishes to preserve the rights of *both* powers," discussions reverted to the model of March 10. Legislation concerning the demarcation of spiritual and temporal jurisdictions became irrelevant, however, as frictions between the crown and the Parlement escalated into a full-scale constitutional crisis in 1732. After Louis XV evoked all cases involving the "miracles" of Saint Médard to the royal council and overruled their suppression of Vintimille's pastoral instruction condemning the *Nouvelles ecclésiastiques,* the judges offered to resign their offices in protest. They recognized that "it is for the sovereign to make the laws" and that "it is for the magistrates to see that the laws are executed with all the authority which he has vested in them for this purpose."[38] At the same time, they implicitly criticized repeated royal interventions in their proceedings by insisting that they must be allowed to exercise this authority without such interference in order to uphold the laws of the realm and protect the interests of the crown. When the Parlement responded to the king's imposition of disciplinary restrictions on their deliberations by going on strike, he exiled many members of the company to the provinces for several months.

As voluble in professing submission to the monarch as they were in defending his crown against ultramontanism, the magistrates had condemned the *Judicium francorum* in August. This anonymous tract, adapted from a pamphlet published during the Fronde, described the Parlement as the guardian of the constitutive principles of the mon-

---

37. JF, Vol. 101, dossier 960, fol. 186 v.; Joly de Fleury to d'Aguesseau, December 23, 1731, in JF, Vol. 101, dossier 960, fol. 212.

38. JF, Vol. 101, dossier 960, fol. 188; *Les Remontrances,* I, 283.

archy. It argued that resistance to arbitrary measures such as evocations did not contradict the sovereignty of the king, since he remained absolute only as long as he respected the fundamental laws that distinguished monarchy from despotism. The judges denounced this seditious disclosure of the latent disjunction between kingship and kingdom, more explicitly formulated than the consultation of the forty lawyers or their own remonstrances.[39] They persisted nonetheless in their opposition to royal efforts to circumscribe their cognizance of religious matters and thereby curb their political pretensions.

Once the turmoil of 1732 had subsided, the chastened magistrates resumed their guerilla warfare against the bull *Unigenitus.* Louis XV promptly suppressed the decree of April 25, 1733, by which they banned the denomination "rule of faith," and likewise ignored the remonstrances of June 29, 1738, in which they condemned the refusal of sacraments. Describing "admittance to the Church, attendance at divine worship, participation in the sacraments, and access to ecclesiastical burial" as "external goods" to which all Catholics were entitled, the judges protested against arbitrary deprivation of these spiritual possessions, which they equated with excommunication. Arguing from the canons of the Church that the clergy could impose this penalty "only for a notorious, public, scandalous crime accompanied by contumacy and rebellion," they maintained that exclusion from the sacraments under other circumstances involved defamation of character, because it implied the commission of some serious offense. They charged that ecclesiastics abused their authority by inflicting such defamatory sentences on the basis of interrogations concerning *Unigenitus* "which the Church does not authorize by its ritual and which," they added, "the state forbids." The parlementaires, in short, claimed jurisdiction over religious status insofar as it affected civil status in the Christian kingdom, insisting that the clergy were accountable to them "even in that which regards the dispensation of sacred things."[40]

Louis XV and his magistrates agreed that the Constitution should

39. On August 13, 1732, the Parlement condemned the *Judicium francorum,* which had been published in François-Eudes de Mézeray, *Mémoires historiques et critiques . . .* (2 vols. in 1; Amsterdam, 1732), II, 114–32.

40. *Les Remontrances,* I, 372, 369, 370; *Arrêté du parlement,* February 28, 1741, in FF, Vol. 10908, fol. 213 v.

not be regarded as a "rule of faith" and that untroublesome Catholics should not be interrogated about *Unigenitus*, but they disagreed about the means of dealing with uncooperative clerics and, of course, about the status of the bull in France. The crown continued to discipline prelates who utilized the unauthorized denomination in pastoral instructions. This policy caused cardinal de Rohan to complain in 1735, "It is unprecedented and of very pernicious consequence that the secular power should impose silence on the bishops" in this manner. At the same time, the monarch consistently checked the Parlement's efforts to subvert the authority of the Constitution while enlarging its role in public affairs. When the magistrates ventured to prohibit the refusal of sacraments in 1740, the royal council condemned their meddling in "purely spiritual concerns."[41] Seven years later they audaciously objected to the denominations "judgment of the universal Church in matter of doctrine" and "law of the Church and of the state." They claimed that these denominations contradicted the qualifications of 1714, which the crown had accepted, and threatened to renew the controversies it had charged them with preventing. The clergy protested defensively that "only the same authority that issued a judgment can qualify it" and denounced this devious attempt to make the king contradict himself on the subject of *Unigenitus*. Louis XV quickly dismissed the Parlement's misrepresentation of his intentions and reaffirmed the terminology endorsed in the declaration of 1730. Restating its defense of royal as well as ecclesiastical authority, the crown reminded its magistrates that the prerogative of legislation belonged to the monarch, who never presumed to legislate on "matters of doctrine concerning religion until after those whom God has appointed as judges over them and only in imposing adoption of their terms."[42]

Louis XV eventually silenced the noisy disputes about the Constitution, but only temporarily. The conflicts of the 1730s left behind a legacy of unresolved questions about the fundamental laws of the realm and the relationship between the two powers. Theological con-

41. Rohan to La Fare, November 3, 1735, in Ser. 257 AP, Vol. 15, dossier I, no. 8, AN; *Arrêt du conseil*, September 6, 1740 (Paris, 1740), 1. For the text of the suppressed parlementary decree see *Suite du supplément à la nécrologie des défenseurs de la vérité*, 326.

42. PV, VIII, 61; *Arrêt du conseil*, February 21, 1747, in *Mémoires sur la cour*, VIII, 396. For the text of the suppressed parlementary decree, see 392–94.

troversy surrounding *Unigenitus* spawned decades of constitutional dissension because the clergy, the parlements, and the crown identified their stands on issues raised by the bull with the defense of their own prerogatives in the corporate kingdom. Their disagreements about the denominations of the bull and the administration of the sacraments added up to something more than empty "disputes over words," for they argued not only about the definitions of words but also about the right to define them.[43] All three parties claimed the right to interpret the conventional principles of the religious and political order. These principles hardly described the reality of eighteenth-century France, yet they constituted the ideological field of battle on which the bishops, the magistrates, and the king played out their momentous contests of authority in the form of endless squabbling over the meaning of traditions they all claimed to uphold. They collectively undermined these same traditions by interpreting them in such a way as to serve their own purposes.

Clergy and parlementaires alike insisted upon their loyalty to the monarch and their fidelity to the past, while accusing each other of subverting the sovereignty of the crown and violating the traditions of the kingdom. The bishops, who complained about unprecedented meddling in spiritual affairs, reminded the king that his throne rested upon the foundation of religion, which God had assigned to their jurisdiction. They insinuated that the magistrates, who abused the authority he had entrusted to them and repeatedly defied his efforts to confine them to their proper functions, embraced the "republican" errors of the forty lawyers. The parlementaires, who condemned the arbitrary evocations of the council as well as the uncanonical innovations of the clergy, warned the monarch that the maintenance of order in his realm depended upon the preservation of the laws, which he himself had charged them to defend. They suggested that the prelates, who harassed his subjects and refused to submit to his judges, shared the ultramontane sentiments they attributed to the bishop of Nîmes. Both parties, in other words, linked their interests to those of the monarchy in order to refute the accusations of their adversaries and to justify resistance to the monarch himself when necessary.

43. Michel-Celse-Roger de Rabutin de Bussy, bishop of Luçon, to Fleury, in Vol. 3053, fol. 294, Arsénal.

In his attempts to adjudicate these disruptive controversies, Louis XV sometimes resorted to legerdemain and obfuscation in order to avoid conflict with the prelates and the judges. When he did venture to define the meaning of words, he attempted to impose his own interpretation of contested traditions and thereby reaffirm his sovereignty over quarrelsome subjects who respected it in theory but challenged it in practice. Politically conscious contemporaries expressed concern about the consequences of the internecine dissension involving the authorities responsible for the preservation of the traditions of the Christian kingdom. Barbier feared that the disputes about *Unigenitus* and the two powers would undermine "submission and subordination to the Church, which are the result of ignorance but which are necessary for the *police* of a sizable state." The *maître des requêtes* François Richer d'Aube worried that the constitutional debates provoked by the bull might have similarly detrimental effects on the authority of the crown. "Everything seems to be becoming uncertain in the realm," he lamented presciently in 1731, such that no one can "rely with confidence on its most incontestable laws and maxims."[44]

Debates about these "incontestable laws and maxims" continued in different form in the wake of the costly War of the Austrian Succession. Lines of confrontation shifted temporarily as Louis XV, who had repeatedly defended ecclesiastical jurisdiction against the parlements, endeavored to subject ecclesiastical property to the *vingtième* tax of 1749. Under the reforming comptroller general Machault the crown pressured the clergy more vigorously than it had in the case of the abortive *cinquantième* of 1725. At that time the bishops had remonstrated that the royal levy "directly attacks exemptions which appertain to religion," and the king had retreated. Casting the retraction of 1726 in the form of an "interpretation" of the edict of the previous year, he reconfirmed the irrevocable immunities of the First Estate.[45] Twenty-five years later he nonetheless expressed dismay that the clergy, "so zealous in defense of the sovereign and independent au-

44. Barbier, *Chronique*, II, 148; François Richer d'Aube, "Réflexions sur le gouvernement de France" (1731), in NAF, Vol. 9511, fol. 348.

45. PV, VII, 82. For the texts of the declarations of June 5, 1725, and October 8, 1726, see *Recueil général*, XXI, 289–93 and 301–303.

thority of kings in temporal matters," seemed paradoxically to wish to exempt their worldly possessions from the obligation "to contribute to the needs of the state to which they belong."[46]

In opposing the *vingtième*, the clergy again identified their fiscal exemptions with the sacred cause of religion and defended these privileges "belonging to the Catholic faith" on constitutional grounds as well. Contending that property had, in effect, changed in nature under ecclesiastical ownership, the bishops informed the crown that conscience prevented them from consenting to the sacrilegious despoiling of revenues consecrated to God for the maintenance of public worship and the relief of the poor. They denounced the imposition of the *vingtième* as a dangerous innovation that violated not only the declaration of 1726 but also the coronation oath. They insisted that Louis XV could not arbitrarily revoke legitimate immunities that the Church had possessed since the time of Clovis and that it regarded as "essentially connected with the form and constitution of the government." Since "all corporate bodies in the state enjoy privileges which distinguish them," the clergy warned the king that the new tax threatened the social order of the kingdom as a whole by reducing them "to the condition of the rest of your subjects."[47]

The Parlement of Paris criticized the burdensome tax in its remonstrances of May 18 but subsequently registered the legislation. While intendants struggled to overcome widespread opposition in the provinces, the Parisian parlementaires applauded Louis XV's efforts to humble the unsubmissive clerics. One magistrate suggested that "it was very dangerous and more so than ever to suffer the clergy to color their pretensions with the pretext of religion." Another declared that renunciation of the royal prerogative of taxing the Church would amount to abdication of the crown. The Parlement rejected a motion to condemn Daniel Bargeton's trenchant letters, commissioned by Machault and published under the epigraph *Ne repugnate vestro bono*,

46. Louis XV to the assembly of the clergy, September 15, 1750, in Mention (ed.), *Documents*, 148–49.

47. D'Allencourt to Jean-Baptiste de Machault d'Arnouville, August 20, 1749, in *Mémoires sur la cour*, X, 463; Letter from seventeen bishops to Louis XV, August 2, 1749, quoted in Marcel Marion, *Machault d'Arnouville: Étude sur l'histoire du contrôle général des finances de 1749 à 1754* (Paris, 1891), 232.

which denied the sacred character of Church property. Bargeton argued that ecclesiastics, those "more opulent and less useful" members of society, had no justification for disregarding the New Testament injunction to render unto Caesar that which was Caesar's. Always alert for inklings of ultramontanism, Joly de Fleury warned that the clergy, having invoked conscience to block the exercise of a royal prerogative so obviously sanctioned by Scripture, "might plead this motive in other matters" as well.[48]

A multitude of pamphleteers seconded Bargeton's indictment of clerical independence by demonstrating that taxation of the Church did not constitute an unprecedented innovation and that it did serve the best interests of the kingdom. Contending that no French monarch could have granted perpetual fiscal exemptions that violated the principle of the inalienability of sovereignty, they supported Louis XV's rescinding of privileges accorded in centuries of ignorance in order to meet pressing financial needs of the present. They charged that the First Estate, by its subversive defiance of royal authority in the name of religion, made itself "a republic in the midst of the realm." The clergy's misplaced appeal to conscience in this strictly temporal matter indicated that they wished "to be of no usefulness to the king, the state, and their fellow citizens." One overtly anticlerical pamphleteer reviewed the various functions of ecclesiastics—delivering tedious sermons, listening to nonsense in the confessional, praying for those who did not want their prayers—only to scorn these duties as "wretched pretexts with which they adorn themselves to escape the greatest of obligations, which is unquestionably to make oneself useful to the state."[49]

Opponents of the *vingtième* denied the accusation that resistance to royal taxation amounted to renunciation of the "sacred obligations" of citizens and rebutted the insinuation that the First Estate consti-

48. Lambert parlementary journal, in Vol. 800, fol. 144 v., Sénat; [Daniel Bargeton], *Lettres Ne repugnate vestro bono* . . . (Hague, 1751), 11; Joly de Fleury, Memoir excerpted in Chrétien-Guillaume de Lamoignon de Malesherbes, *Mémoire sur le mariage des protestants* (N.p., 1785), 171.

49. [François-Vincent Toussaint], *Essai sur le rachat des rentes* (London, 1751), 25; *Mémoire concernant le clergé et la déclaration du mois d'août 1750* . . . (N.p., 1753), 21; *Les Commentaires des Lettres Ne repugnate* . . . (Peking [sic], 1750), 48.

tuted a useless and "foreign nation" in France. Catholicism, after all, sanctified the throne and preserved the social order of the ancien régime. Clerics therefore contributed significantly to the welfare of the Christian kingdom through the administration of public worship, which was "vitally related to the proper *police* of the state." Responding to critics who denounced the linking of "the possessions of this life" to "the advantages of the next life" as "a self-interested trick," apologists for the clergy reminded their contemporaries that "the thought of the next life regulates the conduct of this life."[50] Given this relationship between conscience and conduct, they insisted that the worldly benefits of religion amply justified the temporal privileges of the Church. Utility as well as history, according to these pamphleteers, consecrated ecclesiastical property and condemned the *vingtième.*

Although Machault had not only commissioned Bargeton's letters but also solicited Voltaire's participation in the public campaign in favor of the new tax, the crown did not endorse the anticlerical sentiments of its overzealous advocates. In keeping with his obligations as Most Christian King, Louis XV joined the bishops in condemning *Ne repugnate,* declaring that "under the pretext of upholding the prerogatives of royal authority," Bargeton wrongly questioned the utility of the clergy, "as if to serve religion and the Church were not to render the most useful service to the king and the state." The crown, in other words, defended the ecclesiastical order while subverting its fiscal immunities. The bishops, likewise, defended the principles of absolutism they resisted in practice. They censured propositions in Bargeton's letters that they regarded as subversive of divine right as well as his attacks on their privileges. The magistrates and pamphleteers who championed royal authority by supporting the new tax, meanwhile, also impugned it by dismissing the declaration of 1726 as "contrary to the rights of sovereignty" and invalid.[51] By the time the crown yielded

50. [Bargeton], *Lettres,* 8; [Antoine Duranthon], *Réflexions sur un écrit intitulé Lettre d'un imprimé de Londres* (N.p., n.d.), 56; Jean de Caulet, *Lettres ou réponse aux Lettres Ne repugnate* (3 vols.; n.p., n.d.), I, 24; [Henri-Philippe Chauvelin], *Examen impartial des immunités ecclésiastiques . . .* (London, 1751), 74.

51. *Arrêt du conseil,* June 1, 1750, in *Mémoires sur la cour,* X, 276; [Etienne Mignot], *Traité des droits de l'état et du prince sur les biens possédés par le clergé* (6 vols.; Amsterdam, 1755–57), VI, 227.

to the clergy in 1751, the conflicts about the *vingtième*, like the quarrels about *Unigenitus*, had raised confusing and compromising questions about the traditional order of the realm.

Disputes over Jansenism and taxation in the first half of the eighteenth century strained the conventional identification of the corporate kingdom with the divinely ordained kingship. Throughout these decades of politico-religious strife the crown endeavored to preserve both orthodoxy and sovereignty by commanding compliance with royal interpretations of contested traditions. The Most Christian King thwarted the Parlement's efforts to "temporalize" the sacraments in order to expand secular jurisdiction and opposed the First Estate's attempt to "spiritualize" ecclesiastical property in order to escape civil obligations. Both parties acknowledged the absolute authority of the monarch who reigned "by the grace of God," but they also undermined divine-right absolutism, not by challenging divine ordination in principle but by denying royal unaccountability in practice. The magistrates condemned evocations, as well as refusals of sacraments, as violations of the laws of the realm, which they claimed to interpret. The bishops denounced taxation of clerical property, like temporal meddling in spiritual affairs, as a threat to Catholicity, which they claimed to define. Both parties excoriated independence and innovation, ransacked Scripture and history, invoked the constitution and the coronation in order to defend their own privileges and the French people as a whole not only against each other's depredations but also against the misguided policies of the crown. By appealing to legal and religious standards that transcended the royal will, they not only justified their own resistance to the king but also suggested that he did not faithfully represent the interests of the kingdom.

Prolonged dissension concerning the differentiation of spiritual and temporal concerns and jurisdictions also underscored the problematic character of the conjunction of citizenship and Catholicity. Opponents of the Constitution argued that the clergy could not deprive citizens arbitrarily of sacraments, regarded as spiritual property, to which they were entitled as Catholics. Proponents of the *vingtième* insisted that the clergy, like other citizens, must contribute to the common welfare by paying taxes on their temporal property. The ideology of absolutism and the corporate structure of French society deprived the word *citizen* of any specific juridical meaning in the traditional vocabulary, but the word took on polemical connotations in the eighteenth century. The controversialist who complained about the way in which critics of the clergy paraded "the title of citizen" recognized that the word already suggested expansion of secular at expense of ecclesiastical authority before 1750. Threatened by encroachments upon its prerogatives, the First Estate clung to the customary argument that "it is religion alone which makes humans thoroughly reasonable and produces true citizens." Magistrates and pamphleteers did not question the conventional assumption that the ancestral faith of the realm constituted "the strongest bond of civil society."[52] They nonetheless bared the subject of the role of religion in the public order to less respectful scrutiny after midcentury, when the disputes about Jansenism resumed with even more sound and fury.

52. *Examen des observations sur l'extrait du procès-verbal de l'assemblée générale du clergé tenue en l'année 1750* (Brussels, 1751), 25; Caulet, *Lettres,* II, 111; *Les Remontrances,* I, 340.

4

Politico-Religious Strife from the Billets de confession *to Damiens, 1751–1757*

Even before the crown reluctantly abandoned its attempt to subject the First Estate to the *vingtième* toward the end of 1751, politico-religious strife reverted to the familiar pattern of the 1730s. Louis XV had silenced the debates about Jansenism temporarily, but the clergy and the parlementaires had not exhausted their disagreements about the denomination and application of *Unigenitus* by midcentury. The bull provoked controversy regarding the relationship between the two powers and the fundamental laws of the realm for another fifteen years. Dissension concerning the role of religion in the public order and the disposition of authority in the kingdom intensified during the 1750s. Bishops systematized the refusal of sacraments and magistrates expanded their constitutional claims, while pamphleteers inundated the capital with unauthorized commentaries on their disputes. As in the time of cardinal Fleury, the monarchy attempted to impose silence on its unruly subjects, appointed commissioners to study the issues, promulgated declarations, and resorted to coercive measures in order to stop the strife that had plagued the country for decades. The conflicts of the 1750s challenged traditional conceptions of the religious character and obligations of the monarchy more dramatically than the quarrels of the 1730s. These conflicts induced the crown to suspend its customary support of the clergy against the magistrates and prompted Damiens to attack the sacred person of the king.

"Devout" prelates led by Christophe de Beaumont, the new archbishop of Paris, precipitated another round of hostilities with the parlementaires by aggressively withholding the sacraments from reputed Jansenists. As refusals of sacraments multiplied in dioceses within the jurisdiction of the Parlement of Paris, the watchful magistrates renewed their campaign "to confine the clergy within the true limits of their ministry and ensure that all subjects of the king enjoy all the spiritual and temporal privileges which they are entitled to claim." As in the 1730s, they argued that "canons recognized and authorized by the laws of the realm" regulated "the external and public administration of the sacraments."[1] They denounced the exclusion from the last rites of persons who refused to accept *Unigenitus* as an uncanonical innovation that disrupted public order and deprived citizens of their privileges by excluding them arbitrarily from the communion of the faithful. The judges called upon the king to defend the privileges of his people, the canons of the Church, and the peace of the kingdom by putting a stop to this abuse of ecclesiastical prerogatives. When Louis XV ignored their protests, the magistrates eventually ordered priests to administer the sacraments. When he overruled these interventions in religious matters, their opposition to the Constitution again involved them in resistance to the crown itself.

For much of 1751, the confrontation over the royal declaration of March 24 overshadowed the ongoing disputes about the bull and refusals of sacraments. This declaration consolidated Christophe de Beaumont's control over the general hospital of Paris and effectively sanctioned his exclusion of Jansenists from the administration of the institution. The Parlement registered the declaration with extensive modifications intended to limit the archbishop's influence over the hospital. Louis XV's suppression of these modifications, which challenged his monopoly of legislative authority, resulted in months of wrangling, in the course of which the parlementaires repeatedly disobeyed his orders. They justified themselves by explaining that genuine obedience to the crown consisted not in unquestioning submission to royal commands but in "never consenting to anything which might violate the public order, the laws and principles of the kingdom, and the rights

1. Durey de Mesnières parlementary journal, in Vol. 800, fol. 38, Sénat; *Les Remontrances*, I, 418.

of sovereignty." One of the magistrates told his colleagues that God Himself had installed them in their offices and "marked our duty by the voice of our conscience," which would not allow them to betray the true interests of the monarchy.[2] Others suggested deviously that Louis XV could resolve the tug-of-war by "interpreting" his declaration in the sense of their modifications, in much the same way as he had yielded to the clergy in the matter of the *cinquantième* in 1726. The judges yielded in the end, but without retracting their appeal to standards of lawfulness that transcended the will of the divinely ordained monarch.

The magistrates retreated on the issue of the general hospital by the end of 1751 but escalated their offensive against *Unigenitus* in the following year. Tired of resorting to what Gilbert de Voisins called "measures peculiar to each case," they prohibited uncanonical refusals of sacraments altogether on April 18, 1752. They specifically condemned the use of *billets de confession*, issued by priests in good standing to certify submission to the bull, to exclude persons who rejected the Constitution from the last rites. Chancellor Lamoignon warned that "the clergy cannot fail to protest against the Parlement's decree, which decides important questions concerning refusals of sacraments and *billets de confession* which the king himself does not feel entitled to decide."[3] As if in fulfillment of this prediction, Beaumont promptly composed a pastoral instruction in which he denounced the decree and directed the faithful to regard *Unigenitus* as a "rule of faith." Louis XV had never endorsed this denomination and therefore ordered the plates of the archbishop's inflammatory instruction broken in the printer's shop.

Describing the Constitution in the language of 1720, 1730, and 1731 as a "judgment of the universal Church in matter of doctrine" and as a "law of the Church and of the state," the monarch subsequently rebuked the parlementaires for meddling in "purely spiritual matters such as the dispensation of the sacraments."[4] His decree of April 29 required the judges to refer cases involving "spiritual mat-

2. *Les Remontrances*, I, 475; Lambert parlementary journal, in Vol. 800, fol. 181, Sénat.
3. Ser. K, Vol. 698, no. 139, fol. 1, AN; Ser. 177 Mi, Vol. 74 [Ser. 154 AP, Vol. 9], no. 54, AN.
4. *Arrêt du conseil*, April 29, 1752, in *Mémoires sur la cour*, XII, 267.

ters" to ecclesiastical courts but also reminded the clergy to abide by the canons recognized in the kingdom. When the king forwarded this decree to the bishops, he enclosed the circular letter of 1731, which advised them to refrain from troubling his subjects concerning submission to the bull.[5] Having scolded extremists in both camps, he announced his intention to appoint a commission of prelates and magistrates to investigate what he referred to disingenuously as "the new troubles."

A dozen disgruntled bishops protested to Louis XV in June that he had not adequately defended their prerogatives, and the agents-general of the clergy called for outright suppression of the parlementary decree in July. At the end of November the crown formally condemned the decree of April 18, like the modifications of the declaration of March 24, on the grounds that the magistrates had usurped "the power which belongs to His Majesty alone to make laws." Royal efforts between April and November to restrain the clergy and the parlements alike left both parties dissatisfied. Clerics grumbled that the king seemed "to appropriate legislative power in spiritual matters" because he disapproved of the denomination "rule of faith" and discouraged refusals of sacraments.[6] Magistrates, meanwhile, complained that he left his subjects and his sovereignty undefended by not allowing them to prosecute clerics who violated the injunctions contained in the circular letter of 1731.

When Louis XV named the members of the royal commission at the end of May, he charged them to deliberate on those thorny issues concerning the use of *billets de confession* that, according to Lamoignon, he did not feel entitled to decide. As the secretary of foreign affairs Antoine-Louis Rouillé noted, the king had no intention of promulgating another declaration on religious matters "without having negotiated with both parties and assured himself of the broadest possible support."[7] More polarized than their predecessors of 1731, the commissioners of 1752 found it impossible to work out a compromise between

5. Royal letter to bishops, April 30, 1752, in Ser. 177 Mi, Vol. 74, no. 59, AN; Vol. 2453, fol. 138, Arsénal; FF, Vol. 20958, fol. 194.

6. *Arrêt du conseil*, November 21, 1752, in *Mémoires sur la cour*, XII, 301; Ser. 177 Mi, Vol. 75 [Ser. 154 AP, Vol. 10], no. 29, fol. 1, AN.

7. Antoine-Louis Rouillé to Guillaume-François Joly de Fleury, July 1, 1752, in JF, Vol. 1493, fol. 101.

the episcopal and parlementary positions represented, on the one hand, by cardinal Armand de Rohan de Soubise, the intemperate bishop of Strasbourg, and, on the other, the indefatigable opponents of *Unigenitus*, Gilbert de Voisins and Joly de Fleury.[8] After one unproductive session the former attorney general complained with some exasperation that "it requires a good deal of patience to listen to the cardinal de Soubise contest the authority of the king over the discipline of the Church." Joly de Fleury was equally annoyed, however, by reports of "His Majesty's scruples and his fear of intruding upon ecclesiastical jurisdiction by prescribing rules concerning the administration of the sacraments."[9]

Divided among themselves, the commissioners failed to formulate the pacificatory recommendations that Louis XV had hoped for. Before disbanding in the spring of 1753, they drafted conflicting statements that manifested irreconcilable differences of opinion about the status of the bull, the refusal of sacraments, and the competence of secular authority. The prelates and one dissenting magistrate urged the king to authorize the denomination "rule of faith" but contended that he could not settle spiritual questions regarding the use of *billets de confession*.[10] They justified interrogations concerning submission to *Unigenitus* and defended broad interpretation of the grounds for exclusion from the sacraments. The remaining commissioners not only rejected the "rule of faith" but even advised against invocation of the declaration of 1730, which had provoked such violent opposition in the Parlement. The magistrates argued that all Catholics not specifically disqualified by misconduct attested by judicial sentences were entitled to the sacraments of the Church. They condemned deathbed interrogations about the bull and claimed that Louis XV had the authority to forbid the exaction of *billets de confession*. All of the commissioners, with the exception of Gilbert de Voisins and Joly de

---

8. The other commissioners were Frédéric-Jérôme de Roye de La Rochefoucauld, archbishop of Bourges, Nicolas de Saulx de Tavannes, archbishop of Rouen, Jean-François de Rochechouart, bishop of Laon, Daniel-Charles Trudaine, and Julien-Louis Bidé de Grandeville.

9. Joly de Fleury to Rouillé, September 10, 1752, in JF, Vol. 1493, fol. 160 v., and April 22, 1753, Vol. 1494, fol. 216.

10. The dissenting magistrate was Bidé de Grandeville.

Fleury, agreed that it would be improper or at least imprudent for the sovereign to attempt to legislate on such matters.

While the commissioners quarreled behind closed doors, pamphleteers rehashed familiar accusations about the independence of the clergy and the disobedience of the parlementaires. Opponents of the Constitution attacked the bishops, who had resisted taxation of ecclesiastical property, for seditiously depriving French citizens of the spiritual privileges they possessed as Catholics. These critics of the clergy exploited the juridical conjunction of citizenship and Catholicity in order to shelter Jansenists from persecution. Insisting that "the possession of the most spiritual thing in the world is purely temporal," pamphleteers like the prolific Jansenists Maultrot and Mey denounced the withholding of sacraments as a violation of property rights that the king and his judges were obliged to protect. Their polemical adversaries, of course, rejected this confusion of spiritual and temporal matters, civil and religious status, secular and ecclesiastical jurisdictions. "It is as Catholics," not citizens, the abbé Bon pointed out, "that we have the right to the sacraments."[11] Apologists for the clergy denied that the civil consequences and external character of participation in the rites of the Church automatically gave subjects access to, and magistrates jurisdiction over, the sacraments. They accused the judges of promoting religious indifference and encouraging political insubordination by contesting the king's efforts to defend the Church and preserve orthodoxy.

The well-publicized disputes over the refusal of sacraments culminated in the constitutional crisis of 1753. Thwarted by the crown in their attempts to bring the intractable archbishop of Paris to trial before the peers of the realm, the parlementaires approved preliminary articles for their "great remonstrances" against abuses of ecclesiastical and royal authority in January. Lamoignon characterized these articles as a collection of subversive misrepresentations intended to undermine the jurisdiction of the Church and the sovereignty of the

11. [Gabriel-Nicolas Maultrot and Claude Mey], *Apologie de tous les jugements rendus par les tribunaux séculiers contre le schisme* . . . (2 vols.; En France, 1752), II, 88; [Bon], *Lettres d'un homme du monde au sujet des billets de confession et de la bulle Unigenitus* (N.p., 1753), 22.

crown.[12] When Louis XV subsequently refused to receive the completed remonstrances, adopted on April 9, the judges suspended their services. Strewn with quotations from Frankish charters, Church councils, and Gallican jurists, the "great remonstrances" explicated "the genuine principles of government" in such a way as to justify parlementary opposition to refusals of sacraments and evocations by the royal council. The magistrates acknowledged that "the king, the state, and the law form an indivisible whole," but they interposed themselves between the king and the state by identifying themselves as the guardians of the law. They appropriated Montesquieu's characterization of the parlements in *De l'Esprit des lois* (1748) as intermediary bodies essential to the preservation of the monarchy. They cited a seventeenth-century treatise commissioned by Louis XIV himself to remind his great-grandson that the fundamental laws supposed "a sort of contract" between the sovereign and his people.[13] The parlementaires warned Louis XV that his "irregular" interventions in the administration of justice violated the obligation contracted at his coronation to reign lawfully. They attempted to convince the king that reigning lawfully meant collaborating in their efforts to preserve the "legitimate liberty" of his subjects, the peace of the Church, and the security of the realm by checking the uncanonical conduct of the clergy, who had masked their dangerous ambitions with religious pretexts for centuries.[14]

Louis XV hoped to subdue the judges by exiling them, as he had in 1732, but controversialists quickly took up the contentions of the "great remonstrances." In his monumental *Lettres historiques sur*

12. Guillaume de Lamoignon de Blancmesnil, "Réflexions sur le projet des remontrances arrêtés par le parlement le 25 janvier 1753," in Ser. 177 Mi, Vol. 75, no. 68, AN.

13. Barthélemy-Gabriel Rolland d'Erceville, "Histoire des remontrances du 9 avril 1753," in NAF, Vol. 8496, fol. 1; *Les Remontrances*, I, 525, 522. On the *Traité des droits de la reine* (Paris, 1667) and its uses in the eighteenth century, see Herbert H. Rowen, *The King's State: Proprietary Dynasticism in Early Modern France* (New Brunswick, 1980), 98–102; John Lough, "The *Encyclopédie* and the Remonstrances of the Parlement of Paris," *Modern Language Review*, LVI (1961), 393–95; Dale Van Kley, "The Jansenist Constitutional Legacy in the French Pre-Revolution, 1750–1789," *Historical Reflections/Réflexions historiques*, XIII (1986), 411.

14. *Les Remontrances*, I, 522.

les fonctions essentielles du parlement the Jansenist polymath Louis-Adrien Lepaige catalogued the subversive enterprises of the First Estate and traced the prerogatives of the Parlement to Frankish assemblies in which "the nation parleyed with the king concerning various public matters." Lepaige and other apologists for the exiled magistrates maintained that the absolute monarch preserved the plenitude of his authority by commanding "nothing but in conformity with the laws. His power is the image of the omnipotence of God, who can do all that he wishes, because He does only the just." They insisted that the parlementaires had a sacred duty to resist unjust commands that violated the traditions of the kingdom and endangered the sovereignty of the crown. When critics of the Parlement invoked divine ordination, they emphasized the Almighty's "independence in the exercise of His power" so as to underscore the obligation of obedience to the monarch who reigned "by the grace of God."[15] These pamphleteers consulted French history in order to recount the offenses of the unruly magistrates who seditiously claimed to represent the public interest. They rejected the suggestion that the legality of royal policies depended upon the endorsement of judges appointed only to execute the ordinances of the sovereign, who alone made and interpreted laws for the benefit of his subjects.

When the crown exiled the parlementaires, it did not repudiate the conventional maxim that "one of the principal obligations of kings is to dispense justice to the people whom providence has entrusted to them." Asserting his authority more forcefully than in 1732, Louis XV established a plenary court commonly called the *chambre royale* to assume the functions of the disgraced magistrates. The judges of the Châtelet court refused to recognize the new tribunal. Like their exiled colleagues, they argued that "it is permitted to resist the will of the sovereign when the obedience he demands is incompatible with duty." Gilbert de Voisins regarded this case of Frondish insubordination as a sign of "a kind of revolt in the minds" of his contemporaries. "Today," he observed, "it is the very foundation of the constitution and the order of the state that is called into question. The different degrees of

---

15. [Louis-Adrien Lepaige], *Lettres historiques sur les fonctions essentielles du parlement . . .* (2 vols.; Amsterdam, 1753), I, 17, II, 89; *Lettres sur les remontrances des parlements* (N.p., 1753), 161.

authority and power, the rules and extent of obedience, the mysteries of state are discussed indiscreetly before the eyes of the common people," whom the traditions of the ancien régime excluded from political consciousness.[16] The disobedience of the Châtelet occasioned a noteworthy polemical exchange concerning the meaning of divine right that exemplified the indiscreet discussions reported by Gilbert de Voisins. The theologian Bertrand Capmartin de Chaupy assumed that the authority of the French kings derived immediately from God and that "the plenitude of power is inseparable from and inalienably attached to their sacred person." The monarch had obligations to his subjects, summarized in his coronation oaths, but he remained accountable only to God, who had bestowed the crown upon every French sovereign since Clovis. He was obliged to respect divine and fundamental law, but his will constituted "the supreme law of the realm." Capmartin de Chaupy denied that the Parlement played an essential role in the making of the laws and scorned the "English" notion that it somehow "represented" the "nation." Insisting that "no subject may resist in France," he denounced the judges of the Châtelet for embracing the condemned principles of the forty lawyers and the *Judicium francorum.*[17] He consigned them, along with rebellious Jansenists and Encyclopedists, to the ranks of "anti-French" malcontents.

The vicomte Pierre-Alexandre d'Alès de Corbet responded to this

16. *Lettres patentes*, November 11, 1753, in *Recueil général*, XXII, 258; *Mémoire de M. A. en réponse à celui qui lui avait été envoyé par M. le procureur-général ancien*, dated June 25, 1753, in FF, Vol. 7573, fol. 218; Gilbert de Voisins, quoted in Philippe Godard, *La Querelle des refus de sacrements, 1730–1765* (Paris, 1937), 277. On the polemics occasioned by the refusal of sacraments, see J. M. J. Rogister, "The Crisis of 1753 in France and the Debate on the Nature of the Monarchy and the Fundamental Laws," in Rudolf Vierhaus (ed.), *Herrschaftsverträge, Wahlkapitulationen, Fundamentalgesetze* (Göttingen, 1977), 105–20; Carroll Joynes, "Parlements, Peers, and the *Parti janséniste*: The Refusal of Sacraments and the Revival of the Ancient Constitution in Eighteenth-Century France," in *Proceedings of the Eighth Annual Meeting of the Western Society for French History* (1981), 229–38; Dale Van Kley, "The Refusal of Sacraments Controversy and the Political Crisis of 1756–57," in Richard Golden (ed.), *Church, State, and Society Under the Bourbon Kings of France* (Lawrence, 1982), 284–326.

17. [Bertrand Capmartin de Chaupy], *Observations sur le refus que fait le Châtelet de reconnaître la chambre royale* (En Europe [*sic*], 1754), 11, 9, 53.

restatement of the conventional principles of absolutism in unconventional terms. Denying that God had established kings "immediately" by means of visible miracles, he suggested that the divine ordination of the crown referred instead to the social instincts, inspired by Providence, which led peoples to pledge their obedience to rulers in return for the protection of royal justice. "To interpret the texts of Saint Paul otherwise," the vicomte declared, "is to say unintelligible things." He described the coronation as a contractual ceremony designed to remind the monarch that he derived his power "from the nation." Alès de Corbet conceded that the king was accountable only to God, who "authorized" his reign, but he divested this axiom of its traditional political meaning. Intent upon defending corporate privileges and the "sacred rights of citizens" against despotic abuses of absolute authority, he applauded the magistrates for opposing "illegitimate" royal commands that contravened the fundamental laws of the realm. Like the editors of the *Encyclopédie*, he coyly quoted the passage from the seventeenth-century text cited in the "great remonstrances" to demonstrate the orthodoxy of his contractualism and vindicate himself from accusations of "republicanism."[18]

    While pamphleteers debated the character and limits of monarchical authority, the crown groped toward resolution of its awkward standoff with the exiled parlementaires. Joly de Fleury declared that the magistrates would not accept any denomination which implied that *Unigenitus* had been properly accepted in France. He reported that the bishops agreed privately "that the Constitution is not a rule of faith and that it cannot have the effects of one," but lamented that they asserted publicly "that it is not for the king to pronounce on this." Apprehensive as always about trespassing upon spiritual jurisdiction, Louis XV prohibited further disputes by the "law of silence" of September 2, 1754, without taking a legislative stand on the status of the bull and the refusal of sacraments. He recalled the judges, reproached them for their misconduct, but also charged them to ensure that "nothing is done, attempted, undertaken, or innovated" contrary to

18. [Pierre-Alexandre d'Alès de Corbet], *Examen critique des principes du gouvernement qu'a voulu établir l'auteur des Observations sur le refus que fait le Châtelet de reconnaître la chambre royale* (N.p., 1754), 64, 155, 24, 52.

the peace of the kingdom.[19] This last article marked a significant shift in royal religious policy. Unlike the declaration of 1730, it did not exempt the clergy from silence and therefore left them vulnerable to parlementary prosecution.

Considering that "it was less a matter of modifying this new law than of interpreting it and defining its meaning," the magistrates disregarded the imputation of disobedience and renewed their ban on "innovations in the external and public administration of sacraments" when they registered the declaration.[20] Annoyed because the prelates maintained "that their consciences did not permit them to observe the silence imposed upon them," Louis XV exiled the obdurate Christophe de Beaumont and permitted the impatient judges to prosecute troublesome priests who persisted in requiring *billets de confession* from their parishioners. As Barbier commented, the Parlement seemed to have gained *de facto* recognition from the crown of "everything it had always claimed." The king drew the line, however, when the magistrates on March 18, 1755, boldly prohibited enforcement of the bull *Unigenitus* itself on the pretext of strict enforcement of the "law of silence." In suppressing their decree he reprimanded them, as he had in 1752, for presuming that "it rested with others than His Majesty to interpret the laws which have emanated from him."[21] On paper, at least, the Constitution remained a "law of the Church and of the state" because the crown said so.

Alarmed by Louis XV's concessions to the Parlement, the assembly of the clergy of 1755 reminded him that "the duty of protecting religion is the most essential duty of kings" and proceeded to lecture him on the subject of "protecting religion." The bishops acknowledged their

19. "Extrait d'une conversation avec l'archevêque de Narbonne," dated June 3, 1753, in JF, Vol. 2103, fol. 119; *Déclaration du roi*, September 2, 1754, in *Mémoires sur la cour*, XIII, 341.

20. FF, Vol. 20958, fol. 344; *Mémoires sur la cour*, XIII, 342. Luynes complained in *Mémoires sur la cour*, XIII, 343, that the Parlement interpreted the declaration otherwise than the king had intended.

21. NAF, Vol. 3335, fol. 141; Edmond-Jean-François Barbier, *Chronique de la régence et du règne de Louis XV, 1718–1763* (8 vols.; Paris, 1866), VI, 54; *Arrêt du parlement*, March 18, 1755, in *Mémoires sur la cour*, XIV, 87; *Arrêt du conseil*, April 4, 1755, *ibid.*, 105. Unless otherwise specified, the word *parlement* in texts entitled *Arrêt du parlement* refers to the Parlement of Paris.

own obligation as subjects to obey their sovereign but also stressed his obligation as Most Christian King and Eldest Son of the Church to preserve the authority of the clergy in doctrinal and disciplinary matters. Insisting that unmistakable spiritual and temporal ends defined the jurisdictions of the two powers, they denounced the larcenous standard of externality invoked by the magistrates, who presumed to fix the language of the faith and interpret the will of the king. Although the bishops granted that *Unigenitus* did not deserve the denomination "rule of faith," they denied the suggestion that citizens were somehow automatically entitled to participation in the sacraments. They petitioned the monarch to disavow the parlementary reading of the declaration of 1754 by reconfirming the ecclesiastical prerogatives guaranteed by the declarations of 1695 and 1730. "Extremely troubled" by Louis XV's discouraging reply that he would clarify his legislation "if necessary," the assembly concluded its sessions by referring the problem of the refusal of sacraments to Rome. [22]

The bishops had agreed in March to suspend the use of *billets de confession* until the meeting of the assembly of the clergy in October. Differences of opinion within the assembly resulted in the submission of two sets of articles to the pope for his consideration. [23] Both sets of articles characterized *Unigenitus* as a "dogmatic and irreformable judgment of the universal Church," claimed exclusive jurisdiction over the administration of the sacraments for the Church, and condemned appeals to the magistrates. Both justified the refusal of sacraments on grounds of opposition to the bull not only in cases of "notoriety in law," attested by voluntary confession or judicial sentence, but also in cases of "notoriety in fact," attested simply by public opinion. The so-called "ten articles" of the majority, which required priests to consult with the bishop, described "notoriety in fact" more restrictively than the "eight articles" of the minority, which allowed priests more latitude in withholding the sacraments.

The magistrates, of course, frowned on further papal intervention in the disputes engendered by the papal bull of 1713. Continuing their campaign against *Unigenitus* through enforcement of the "law of silence," they took action in 1756 against the aggressively orthodox

22. PV, VIII/1, *Pièces justificatives*, 190; VIII/1, 553.
23. PV, VIII/1, 555–58.

doctors of the Sorbonne and archbishop of Paris. In May they struck down the Sorbonne ordinance of 1729, which had been ratified by the royal declaration of 1730 and required unqualified acceptance of the bull from all candidates in the faculty of theology. Louis XV overruled this attack upon the Constitution, but he did not object to the suppression of Beaumont's intemperate pastoral instruction of September 19. This instruction condemned a series of parlementary decrees (including those of April 18, 1752, and March 18, 1755) issued, according to Beaumont, upon "the specious pretext of maintaining public tranquillity." The archbishop recognized, on the one hand, that "the Church is in the state," in the sense that "the clergy as citizens, as members of the state, are obliged to obey the laws of the state." He pointed out, on the other hand, that "the ruler is in the Church," such that "the laws of the Church in spiritual matters bind the ruler" and his magistrates. Beaumont denounced the magistrates for making "problematic questions" of doctrine and the sacraments, assigned by the laws of the realm and by God Himself to ecclesiastical jurisdiction.[24]

Soon after the public burning of the archbishop's instruction, the magistrates suppressed the papal letter *Ex Omnibus*, which had been published in France without royal authorization. Composed in response to the petition of the assembly of the clergy, this pacificatory encyclical involved months of negotiations between Rome and Versailles. Intent upon stifling controversy once and for all, Louis XV initially asked the pope to refrain from assigning *Unigenitus* any denomination unacceptable to the Parlement, to enforce the prescription of silence, and to limit punishment for resistance to the bull to penalties of conscience without exclusion from the sacraments. Benedict XIV reportedly found these proposals "rather difficult." While granting that the Constitution was not a "rule of faith," he wished to confirm its status as a dogmatic judgment in terms repeatedly sanctioned by the crown. He eventually agreed, however, to characterize its authority indirectly by indicating that no Catholic could withhold submission to *Unigenitus* "without endangering his eternal salvation."[25]

24. Christophe de Beaumont, *Mandement*. . . , September 19, 1756 (Paris, 1756), 4, 56, 98.

25. Maurice Boutry (ed.), *Choiseul à Rome, 1754–1757* (Paris, 1895), 75; *Ex omnibus*, in Boutry (ed.), *Choiseul à Rome*, 321.

Having already criticized the declaration of 1754 and the decree of March 18, 1755, the pope declined to countenance the silencing of the bishops and sanctioned the refusal of sacraments in cases of "notoriety in fact" as well as "notoriety in law." He defined "notoriety in fact," however, with more qualifications than the "ten articles" of the majority in the assembly of the clergy.

Drafted as an encyclical rather than a bull in order to avoid the necessity of formal acceptance by the French bishops and registration by the Parlement, *Ex Omnibus* emboldened Louis XV to legislate on spiritual questions that he had declined to decide unilaterally in 1754. Instead of releasing the papal letter, the king communicated it confidentially to the prelates for their instruction and incorporated its provisions selectively into his declaration of December 10, 1756. While commanding his subjects to respect the Constitution, he ventured to announce for the first time that it could not have "the denomination, the character, or the effects of a rule of faith." [26] Louis XV responded to the protests of the clergy and amended the declaration of 1754 by exempting them from silence and by reaffirming ecclesiastical jurisdiction over cases involving the sacraments. He did not impose statutory limits on the *appel comme d'abus*, but he did bar the magistrates from ordering the administration of the sacraments and nullified their proceedings against refractory priests since 1754. The king, at the same time, disregarded Benedict XIV's directives regarding "notoriety in fact." He authorized the withholding of the sacraments only in cases of "notoriety in law," from persons formally convicted of disobedience to the bull and from moribund individuals who professed opposition to *Unigenitus* of their own volition.

Louis XV's adaptation of *Ex Omnibus* for his own conciliatory purposes not only failed to placate the bishops but also antagonized the magistrates. Bishops complained that the king had defined the grounds for the refusal of sacraments more narrowly than the pope. Magistrates criticized departures from the "law of silence" that effectively repudiated their contention "that all the faithful are entitled to participation in the sacraments." The king forced them to register the declaration in the *lit de justice* of December 13, along with a disciplinary

---

26. *Déclaration du roi*, December 10, 1756, in *Suite du supplément à la nécrologie des défenseurs de la vérité* (N.p., 1764), 409.

edict designed to check parlementary agitation. The magistrates had provoked the crown not only by their endless attacks on the Constitution but also by their opposition to royal attempts to expand the jurisdiction of the rival Grand Conseil in 1755 and their resistance to the imposition of the second *vingtième* in 1756. During the confrontation over the Grand Conseil the judges aggressively restated and expanded the constitutional arguments they had articulated in the course of their campaign against *Unigenitus*. They staked out an essential role for themselves in the political order of the kingdom by describing the Parlement as "an august sanctuary where the sacred engagements which constitute the monarchy are forever sealed, where the sovereign customarily resides, where the state is centered, where the law is prepared, defined, consummated, deposited, and executed."[27] Having secured their place in the constitution and their roots in history, thanks to Montesquieu and Lepaige, they claimed that all of the parlements composed a single body devoted to the preservation of the laws. Provincial magistrates, not much involved in the battle over the refusal of sacraments, joined their Parisian colleagues in opposing the Grand Conseil and resisting the second *vingtième*. They insisted that the crown could neither dispense with parlementary registration nor compel them to register laws contrary to the traditions of the monarchy.

In 1756, as in 1753, debates about the bull and the two powers were subsumed by conflicts over the disposition of authority in the realm. When Louis XV demolished their political pretensions in the *lit de justice* of December 13, the magistrates promptly resigned their offices. In 1757, as in 1754, the crown eventually backed down. By the fall of 1757, the king not only suspended the organizational and procedural reforms imposed on the Parlement at the end of 1756 but also conceded vaguely that the declaration of December 10 should be executed in conformity with the laws of the kingdom and the canons recognized and authorized in France. This amendment amounted to capitulation on the part of the crown, because it allowed the parlementaires to enforce the declaration according to their own interpretation of these laws and canons. Louis XV informed the Sorbonne in October

---

27. "Objets des représentations de la grande chambre du parlement," dated January 19, 1757, *ibid.*, 415; *Les Remontrances*, II, 34.

that, "as a result of his last declaration," he considered "all the disputes and controversies which had arisen regarding the affair of the Constitution *Unigenitus* as concluded."[28] Contestation about the sacraments abated after the "disputes and controversies" of 1756–1757, but the outcome of this episode hardly satisfied the doctors of the Sorbonne. The monarchy, in the last analysis, reconsidered the extent of its obligations to the clergy and subdued the magistrates by letting them have their own way.

Describing himself in a letter to the pope as "the protector and the father of both the clergy and the magistrates," Louis XV declared in 1755 that he "must not allow either of these two orders to undertake any enterprise prejudicial to the other," or, he might have added, to his own sovereignty. What the kingdom needed, Barbier observed, was "an absolute and impartial authority to forbid the clergy, on the one hand, to cause any trouble with respect to the sacraments, so as to devote themselves entirely to divine service, and to forbid the Parlement, on the other, to exercise any surveillance over the clergy, so as to occupy itself with rendering justice." The bishops and the judges made it exceedingly difficult for the king to play this mediatory role in the politico-religious conflicts of the 1750s. Whether he temporized by imposing silence, sidestepped thorny issues through ambiguous expressions, pronounced himself unequivocally on paper and in public, or tacitly repudiated his own policies, he could not pacify both parties. "The Parlement," as d'Argenson despaired, "will always find the power of the state too restricted, and the clergy that of the Church irreligiously restrained."[29] No matter how emphatically he insisted upon his authority to define the jurisdictions of the two powers, no matter how carefully he sorted out the proper concerns and legitimate prerogatives of the adversaries, no matter how vigorously he attempted to compel his subjects to accept his interpretation of contested traditions, Louis XV could not close the gap between the ideology of absolutism and the reality of French politics after midcentury.

Magistrates and bishops alike refused to confine themselves to the

28. Louis XV to the Sorbonne, October 30, 1757, in NAF, Vol. 3335, fol. 250.

29. Louis XV to Benedict XIV, December 18, 1755, in Boutry (ed.), *Choiseul à Rome*, 38; Barbier, *Chronique*, V, 445; René-Louis de Voyer d'Argenson, *Journal et mémoires*, ed. E.-J.-B. Rathéry (9 vols.; Paris, 1859–67), VII, 347.

modest roles outlined for them by Barbier. The magistrates not only dispensed justice but also claimed, in the words of the Parlement of Brittany, "to judge the equity and utility of new laws, the cause of the state and of the public, to preserve order and tranquillity in the realm, to exercise a sovereign jurisdiction for the general *police* which extends over all matters, over all subjects, and over all persons."[30] As guardians of the standard of lawfulness, they protested both the clergy's abusive withholding of the sacraments and Louis XV's failure to protect the French people from uncanonical deprivation of their religious possessions. Describing their remonstrances as those of the "nation," the parlementaires interposed themselves between the king and his subjects as well as between the clergy and their parishioners.[31] The bishops, meanwhile, concerned themselves not only with the administration of divine service but also with the preservation of orthodoxy. They condemned Jansenist errors and denounced what they called "Protestant" claims of temporal jurisdiction in spiritual matters. They specifically denied the proprietary argument that the withholding of sacraments from a citizen who refused to respect the doctrinal decisions of the Church deprived this individual of "any rights which belong to him as a citizen." The prelates did not hesitate to remind Louis XV of his obligation to defend the privileges of the Church and promote the salvation of his subjects when he seemed to allow the magistrates to have their way through "criminal silence, scandalous indifference, and monstrous neutrality."[32]

"How long," lamented the royal historiographer Moreau in 1755, "will we take questions of theology for affairs of state?" As Moreau himself recognized, controversies about the denomination and application of *Unigenitus* involved much more than theology by the 1750s. "In 1714," he explained, "it was a matter of knowing whether Father

---

30. Arthur Lemoy (ed.), *Remontrances du parlement de Bretagne au XVIIIe siècle* (Paris, 1909), 55.

31. See d'Argenson's well-known comments about the usage of the word *nation* in his time, in his *Journal*, VI, 320, VII, 271, VIII, 315. See also J. H. Shennan, "The Political Vocabulary of the Parlement of Paris in the Eighteenth Century," in *Diritto e potere nella storia europea: Atti in onore di Bruno Paradesi* (Florence, 1982), 953–64.

32. *Lettre à Madame la marquise de *** en lui envoyant des réflexions au sujet de l'assemblée du clergé de 1755* (N.p., n.d.), 24; Pierre-François Lafitau, "Sermon pour l'ouverture de l'assemblée du clergé," in *Collection intégrale*, LII, 395.

Quesnel had explained the nature and effects of grace well in a very devout and rather boring book. In 1753 it was a matter of knowing whether the king was master in his realm. All authority was compromised, all order was disturbed." While accusing each other of ultramontanism and republicanism, the magistrates and the clergy challenged the authority of their sovereign by resisting his efforts to settle conflicts concerning the relationship between the two powers and the fundamental laws of the realm. Both parties justified their resistance to the divinely ordained monarch within the framework of the political and religious traditions of the ancien régime, which they interpreted in such a way as to serve their own interests. They regularly cited the "sacred and inviolable engagement" of the coronation in order to defend their corporate prerogatives as well as the standards of lawfulness and orthodoxy the king had promised to respect. Neither parlementaires nor prelates seconded Alès de Corbet's reinterpretation of the principle of divine right, but both parties undermined divine right by exploiting it to legitimize their disobedience. By discrediting royal unaccountability they obscured "the indelible imprint of divine majesty" upon the authority of the crown and made politics a more public matter in France. After decades of politico-religious strife, one pamphleteer wondered how "one can be a Christian and a citizen without taking an interest in the disturbances troubling the Church and the state."[33]

The conflicts involving the magistrates, the bishops, and the crown also made religion a more private matter in France. They subverted the conjunction of citizenship and Catholicity as well as the identification of kingdom and kingship. The parlementaires manipulated the juridical fiction of confessional uniformity in order to protect subjects accused of doctrinal deviations against the loss of "the most precious part of their estate, that is to say their Catholicity." They did not condone heresy or advocate disestablishment of the national Church.

---

33. Jacob-Nicolas Moreau, *Lettre du chevalier de *** à Monsieur *** conseiller au parlement ou réflexions sur l'arrêt du parlement du 18 mars 1755*, dated April 6, 1755, in his *Variétés morales et philosophiques* (2 vols.; Paris, 1789), I, 38; Jean de Caulet, *Mandement . . .* , December 18, 1752 (Grenoble, 1752), 10; PV, VIII/1, 195; [Henri-Philippe Chauvelin], *Tradition des faits qui manifestent le système que les évêques ont opposé dans les différents siècles aux principes invariables de la justice souveraine du roi* (N.p., n.d.), 3.

But their assimilation of religious and civil privileges effectively divorced the sacramental signs of conformity, now transformed into property, from conformity in conscience, now sheltered from uncanonical interrogations concerning abusive definitions of orthodoxy. According to the parlementary reading of the canons regarding the administration of the sacraments, "only outward dispositions are necessary not to be refused publicly." As long as citizens behaved like good Catholics, in other words, their beliefs eluded arbitrary scrutiny and the clergy could not exclude them from the religious rites that secured their civil identity. If the clergy objected, as one pamphleteer added, "that appellants conceal error in the heart, this is to admit that the mouth is Catholic, and it is then not humans but God alone who should be their judge."[34] Opposition to the bull *Unigenitus*, not philosophic indifference, turned Jansenists and magistrates against religious persecution.

The politico-religious disputes that undermined the ideology of kingship "by the grace of God" also prompted one dramatic challenge to the inviolability of the king. Shortly before six o'clock on the evening of January 5, 1757, less than a month after the *lit de justice* that resulted in the resignations of the magistrates, a shiftless domestic from Artois by the name of Robert-François Damiens shoved his way through the royal guards and stabbed Louis XV in the side as the king descended the steps to his coach in the Marble Court at Versailles. The monarch, wounded superficially, asked apprehensively for the last rites and apologized remorsefully for his misconduct. Having recovered in a matter of days, he expressed his gratitude by distributing 100,000 écus to the poor through the parish priests of Paris. Abortive or not, Damiens' attack upon the person of the royal father amounted to regicide, described by one jurist as "the most serious and most punishable of all crimes which concern society." Since the unity of the realm resided in the crown, the sacrilegious and parricidal transgression against the body of the monarch threatened the disintegration of the body politic he represented. "To strike a king," as Louis-Sebastien Mercier put it years later, "is to assassinate a nation."[35]

---

34. Lemoy (ed.), *Remontrances du parlement de Bretagne*, 59; Daniel-Charles Trudaine, Memoir in JF, Vol. 1496, fol. 112 v.; *Lettre d'un théologien aux évêques qui ont écrit au roi pour se plaindre de l'arrêté du parlement . . .* (N.p., 1752), 7.

35. Pierre-François Muyart de Vouglans, *Les Loix criminelles de France dans leur*

As a Christian, Louis XV stated that he felt inclined toward clemency for his assassin. As the king, however, he admitted that he felt compelled to yield to his subjects' demands for vengeance against the criminal who had wounded all of them in striking him. The weeks of interrogations and investigations that preceded the inevitable execution revealed that Damiens was, as many of them might have expected, a confirmed reprobate who had repeatedly violated traditional standards of order and orthodoxy. He had disobeyed his father, abused his wife, and robbed his last master. He had mocked the piety of his Jansenist relatives, committed blasphemy, neglected confession, and even attempted suicide. In spite of his multiple infractions of the Ten Commandments, Damiens identified himself as a Catholic and lapsed into religious language more than once in the course of his testimony. He predicted, for example, that he would die "like Jesus Christ in pain and agony."[36] Spectators crowded the Place de Grève, as well as the windows and rooftops surrounding the square, for the execution on March 28. More than a dozen executioners from around the realm reenacted the punishment inflicted upon Ravaillac in 1610, which celebrated the preservation of the king through dismemberment of his assassin. Having doused the hand with which Damiens had struck the monarch in molten sulphur, they tore chunks of flesh from his chest, arms, and legs, and poured a mixture of boiling oil, lead, pitch, resin, wax, and sulphur into the wounds. After attaching horses to the limbs and severing the muscles in the joints, they eventually succeeded in quartering the sturdy body of the criminal, who had piously reproached them for swearing out of frustration. They then burned the remains and scattered the ashes. In order to exorcise all memory of the criminal and his crime, his judges ordered the demolition of the house in which he had been born, exiled his father, wife, and daughter, and directed them and his siblings to change their name.

The gruesome ritual of purification in the Place de Grève reaffirmed the authority and sanctity of the monarchy by destroying the monster who had profaned the crown, but it left disturbing questions

---

ordre naturel (Paris, 1780), 132; [Louis-Sebastien Mercier], *Le Tableau de Paris* (12 vols.; Amsterdam, 1782–88), IX, 141.

36. *Pièces originales et procédures du procès fait à Robert-François Damiens* (4 vols.; Paris, 1757), I, 217.

unanswered. Although Damiens died without revealing any tangible evidence of conspiracy, "it was never doubted that he had accomplices."[37] Contemporaries blamed the crime of January 5 not only on the notoriously "republican" English, with whom the French were at war, but also on Jansenists and magistrates, bishops and Jesuits.[38] They obviously sensed that the attempted assassination resulted somehow from the politico-religious conflicts of the 1750s, which shaped the circumstances in which it took place as well as the polemics it engendered. "One would have to blind oneself," as one pamphleteer exclaimed, "in order not to see its connection with the tragic events which have been taking place before our eyes for several years." Many of the parlementaires, who might otherwise have judged the regicide, had resigned their offices to protest the declarations of December 10. Christophe de Beaumont, who had the responsibility of summoning Parisans to public prayers for the sovereign's recovery, was in exile for violating the "law of silence" by publishing inflammatory pastoral instructions. Damiens' attack on Louis XV prompted the magistrates to offer to resume their functions without conditions and roused prelates like Beaumont to issue jeremiads on the Pauline injunction of submission to divinely ordained rulers. Both parties hastened to anathematize the criminal and trumpet their own allegiance to "the most virtuous, the most benevolent, the most faultless" of kings in effusive terms, as if to alleviate anxiety provoked by years of public criticism of his policies.[39] If only because Damiens had served as a domestic at the Jesuit school of Louis-le-grand and in the homes of several magistrates, suspicion nonetheless fell on judges and clergy alike.

The records of the Damiens case, published within months of his execution, show that he acted alone, that he was troubled by the res-

37. Emmanuel-Henri de Grouchy (ed.), "Livre-journal des événements remarquables, 1757–1765," *Nouvelle revue retrospective*, X (1899), 84.

38. An imaginative ship captain charged that the English had bribed French priests to withhold the sacraments from their parishioners in order to trouble the kingdom during the Seven Years' War.

39. [Pierre-Jean Grosley], "Lettre d'un solitaire sur le mandement de M. l'archevêque de Paris du 1 mars 1757," in *Les Iniquités découvertes ou recueil de pièces curieuses et rares qui ont paru lors du procès de Damiens* (London, 1760), 146; César-

ignations of the magistrates and motivated by hostility toward the bishops, and that he was not a fanatic in the mold of Clément and Ravaillac. Président Hénault exaggerated in declaring that "religion played no part in this execrable deed," but Damiens baffled his judges by his repeated assertions that he had struck the king "on account of religion." When they reminded him that Christianity forbade this unspeakable crime against God and society, he indicated "that he took the misery in which three-quarters of the kingdom found itself as a principle of religion." Distressed by "the complaints of the people and the provinces who were perishing" from excessive taxation, Damiens was even more indignant "that the sacraments were refused to respectable folk worthy of receiving them, who were buried like dogs." Dismayed by Louis XV's failure to heed parlementary expostulations against these fiscal and ecclesiastical injustices, the impressionable domestic had become obsessed with the project of "touching him and making him more disposed to listen to the remonstrances, to act justly, and to listen no longer to the bad advice of his ministers," who favored the clergy. Damiens recognized the sacredness of the monarch, but "he thought, perhaps erroneously, that religion did not stand in the way of his laying hands violently upon his king when he saw that he constantly spurned the truth and did not wish to listen to it."[40]

Damiens claimed that he would not have "touched" his king "if there had been no refusals of sacraments," "if the archbishop of Paris had not been so stubborn," "if the king had had four or five bishops beheaded," "if justice had been rendered to the Parlement," or "if he had never set foot in the Palais [de Justice]," where he had absorbed the provocative rhetoric of the judges. If moved by fanaticism of any sort, he was, as Barbier realized, a "parlementary fanatic."[41] Hardy claimed that the regicide had planned to strike down the monarch in the courtyard of the Palais immediately after the *lit de justice* of De-

---

Guillaume de La Luzerne, "Sur les effets de l'incrédulité," in *Collection intégrale*, LXXIII, 890.

40. Charles-Jean-François Hénault, *Mémoires*, ed. François Rousseau (Paris, 1911), 243; *Pièces originales*, I, 133, II, 149, 25, III, 321, 178–79, 175. Damiens added the conventional qualification: "Perhaps it is less the fault of the king than of his ministers."

41. *Pièces originales.*, III, 388, 317, I, 217, III, 313, 295; Barbier, *Chronique*, VI, 509.

cember 13![42] Prodded by one of his jailers, Damiens did dictate a list of seven magistrates known to him by name, but he subsequently denied that they had had anything to do with his crime, and the Parlement cleared them after resuming its functions in September. A month later a placard appeared in the Palais congratulating Beaumont on his own return from exile and rejoicing that "the Parlement had not succeeded in the assassination of the king." Louis XV himself exonerated the seven magistrates in November, but he reportedly regarded the Parlement as "an assembly of republicans" whose mutinous talk had "disturbed" the mind of Damiens.[43]

Beaumont likewise pointed his finger at the Palais de Justice in his pastoral instruction of March 1 on the miraculous preservation of the Most Christian King. Three weeks later, the bishop of Soissons blamed the attempted assassination on the abominable, monstrous, diabolical teachings of the Jesuits, long regarded as agents of ultramontanism and apologists of regicide. The "Jansenist" lawyer Pierre Grosley of Troyes made the same accusation in several pamphlets published anonymously during the month of March. Intent upon whitewashing the magistrates, Grosley maintained that the regicide's "alleged character of a zealous citizen or rather of a mind excited by the disorders in the government is in no way admissable in the person of a thieving lackey." He denied that consciousness of political issues extended to lowly domestics and "other persons of this sort," who had no reason or right to take an interest in matters of state. He insisted, at the same time, that "a man without name and status in civil society could not have any kind of personal dissatisfaction which might have armed him against his king."[44] Having dismissed the possible motives of a private as well as public nature, he endorsed the widespread conviction that Damiens must have acted at the instigation of enemies of the crown.

42. Siméon-Prosper Hardy, *Mes loisirs: Journal d'événements tels qu'ils parviennent à ma connaissance, 1764–1773*, ed. Maurice Tourneux and Maurice Vitrac (Paris, 1912), 229.

43. JF, Vol. 2078, fol. 6; Nicole Collesson du Hausset, *Mémoires* (Paris, 1824), 95, 169.

44. [Grosley], "Déclaration de guerre contre les auteurs du parricide tenté contre la personne du roi," in *Les Iniquités*, 83; [Grosley], *Lettre d'un patriote où l'on rap-*

Grosley attempted to exculpate the Parlement, which, according to him, had never advocated disobedience, by implicating the clergy, who had opposed the *vingtième* and the "law of silence." He denounced the rendition of Romans 13 in Beaumont's pastoral instruction, in which the archbishop spoke ominously of submission to "legitimate" authority. He challenged Beaumont and other prelates who had defied the crown "to define the distinction they made between the authority of the king and legitimate authority." While playing on apprehensions concerning episcopal disloyalty in this way, he also appealed to popular hostility toward the Jesuits. Damiens confessed under torture that he had imagined he performed "a deed deserving of Heaven" when he struck Louis XV, but he denied that anyone in particular had led him to believe "that there were cases in which it was allowed to make an attempt upon the life of one's sovereign."[45] Grosley insinuated nonetheless that the Jesuits had promised the sinful domestic salvation in return for murdering the king who had thwarted their subversive designs by denying the character of "rule of faith" to the bull *Unigenitus*. He charged that the magistrates chosen to interrogate Damiens were sympathetic to the Jesuits and therefore suppressed damning evidence or at least failed to investigate the case thoroughly.

Damiens claimed to have overheard muttering against Louis XV not among the Jesuits but "in the streets and cafés."[46] In the months (and

---

porte les faits qui prouvent que l'auteur de l'attentat commis sur la vie du roi a des complices . . . , dated March 11 (N.p., 1757), 46; [Grosley], "Réflexions sur l'attentat commis le 5 janvier contre la vie du roi," in *Les Iniquités*, (N.p., 1757), 4.

45. [Grosley], "Lettre d'un solitaire," in *Les Iniquités*, 145; *Pièces originales*, III, 397, II, 149.

46. *Pièces originales*, II, 25. On public opinion as reflected in the records of the Damiens case, see Van Kley, *The Damiens Affair and the Unraveling of the Ancien Régime, 1750–1770* (Princeton, 1984), chapter 5. On public opinion more generally, see Keith Michael Baker, "Politics and Public Opinion Under the Old Regime: Some Reflections," in Jack Censer and Jeremy Popkin (eds.), *Press and Politics in Pre-Revolutionary France* (Berkeley, 1987), 204–46; Sarah Maza, "Le Tribunal de la nation: Les mémoires judiciaires et l'opinion publique à la fin de l'ancien régime," *Annales*, XLII (1987), 73–90; Mona Ozouf, "L'Opinion publique," in Keith Michael Baker (ed.), *The Political Culture of the Old Regime* (Oxford, 1987), 419–34, vol. I of Baker, François Furet, and Colin Lucas (eds.), *The French Revolution and the Creation of Modern Political Culture*, 3 vols.

years) following his attack upon the king, the police received scores of denunciations and detained dozens of persons for making threatening remarks about the monarch. They arrested Claude Horsel in July, 1757, for declaring that "by stabbing His Majesty" Damiens "gained entry to Heaven." He defended himself by protesting that only an Englishman was capable of uttering such dreadful words. Gaspard Ferlin, detained in August for bantering about shooting the king, likewise insisted that he was "too good a Frenchman to stray from the respect and love he owed His Majesty." During his interrogation he responded to a leading question about Romans 13 by acknowledging that his religious beliefs sustained these loyal sentiments. The police dismissed most accusations, including those against Horsel and Ferlin, on grounds of inebriation, misunderstanding, or personal animosity, but not all suspects got off so lightly. Jean Moriceau de la Motte was executed in 1758 for posting placards defaming the magistrates who judged Damiens and for denying over dinner in a Parisian tavern the obligation of obedience to rulers. Barbier, who reported grumbling in the Place de Grève about the severity of the sentence, recognized that the authorities intended to intimidate "fanatics who speak too boldly about the government" by making an example in this case. Auguste-Charles Tavernier, who had boasted that "if Damiens had missed [the king], he would not miss him," remained incarcerated in the Bastille until July 14, 1789, by which time he had lost his sanity.[47]

In the wake of the attempted assassination, the police investigated reports concerning unknown men in black on the Pont Neuf, suspicious horsemen in the Bois de Boulogne, surly beggars, prophetic children, mysterious foreigners, seditious messages in Latin and hieroglyphics. The dossiers of the cases involving alleged threats against the king contain some hostile complaints about burdensome taxes, inflated grain prices, and Louis XV's debauchery but include few specific allusions to politico-religious controversies. Explicit references to these disputes materialized much more often in the form of placards, such as the laconic triplet posted in the capital late in January:

47. JF, Vol. 2076, fol. 97; JF, Vol. 2074, fol. 238 v.; Barbier, *Chronique*, VII, 91; *Archives de la Bastille* (19 vols.; Paris, 1866–1903), XVII, 351.

Lit de justice à Paris.
Lit de justice à Versailles.
Lit de justice à Saint Denis.[48]

These menacing lines made Damiens' crime of January 5 at Versailles sound like retribution for Louis XV's "crime" of December 13 in Paris and sentenced the king to join his ancestors in the royal necropolis at Saint-Denis as soon as possible. D'Argenson and Barbier, who regarded the proliferation of scurrilous placards and satires as evidence of disaffection toward the king, read the same message into the apparent indifference of the Parisian populace to the news of the attack upon his sacred person. The records of the Damiens affair suggest that Gilbert de Voisins had reason to worry in 1753 about the consequences of political discussions "before the eyes of the common people." Damiens was not the only "man without name and status" exposed to and affected by the acrimonious strife over matters that such subjects supposedly knew nothing about. Public contestations during the decade of the "great remonstrances" and the "law of silence" provoked more widespread interest and concern, at least in some milieus, than Grosley wanted to admit in 1757.

The crime of Damiens dramatically illustrated the extent to which the Most Christian King had become entangled in conflicts he had been unable to resolve in his capacity as sovereign arbiter of the public order of the realm. These conflicts underscored the disparity between the theoretical absolutism of the crown and the actual vulnerability of the monarch. The magistrates and the bishops reacted to the attempted assassination by reaffirming the conventional maxim that the king "by the grace of God" was "not accountable to anyone for what he commands," but they themselves had already discredited this principle. In resisting their divinely ordained ruler within the framework of traditions that disallowed such resistance, they inadvertently "disturbed" the mind of the regicide whose offense they subsequently condemned with predictable defensiveness. Unlike the parlementaires and the clergy, Damiens had no voice in the corporate kingdom and made no effort to justify himself by appealing to conscience. He acted

48. Quoted in Pierre Rétat *et al.*, *L'Attentat de Damiens* (Paris, 1979), 193.

alone, without calling, but in the name of "the public," who could, as Barbier realized, "read its own condemnation" in the published transcripts of his testimony. Eager to dissociate themselves from the regicide, contemporaries dismissed his invocations of their welfare as a "mask" and insisted that he "was neither of his century nor of our country."[49] Anxious to explain away his crime as an alien and anachronistic misadventure, they wrote him off as a pawn in the hands of foreigners or a fanatic in the mold of Clément and Ravaillac and thereby gainsaid the historical significance of his attack on Louis XV. The assassinations of 1589 and 1610, prompted by criticism of allegedly heretical and tyrannical rulers, had encouraged seventeenth-century ideologists to insist that divine ordination not only sanctified the person of the king but also invested him with absolute authority and exempted him from criticism. Damiens' graphic denial of the inviolability of the monarch, provoked by the conflicts of the 1750s, demonstrates the extent to which parlementary and ecclesiastical denials of the sovereign's unaccountability had undermined this amalgamation of religion and politics by the middle of the eighteenth century.

49. Caulet, *Discours prononcé par M. l'évêque de Grenoble dans son église cathédrale le 30 janvier 1757* . . . (N.p., 1757), 9; Barbier, *Chronique*, VI, 535; Vol. 548, no. 43 bis, PR; Jean-Pierre Mailhol, *Oraison funèbre . . . de Louis XV* . . . (Carcassonne, 1774), 25.

5

Politico-Religious Strife from the Expulsion of the Jesuits to the Reforms of Turgot, 1757–1776

"Every good citizen must respect by his silence the important affairs of state which do not concern him," declared an apologist for the refusal of sacraments in the year of the "great remonstrances." "There are no discussions more interesting for every good citizen than those concerning public affairs," countered a parlementaire at the time of the assembly of the clergy of 1765. Refusals of sacraments abated in the wake of *Ex Omnibus*, and conflicts over *Unigenitus* finally subsided after the assembly of 1765, but these conflicts left their mark on the political consciousness of the kingdom. By transforming "affairs of state" into "public affairs," they challenged the authority of the absolute monarchy and undermined the principle of the divine ordination of the crown. These "quarrels regarding the Constitution *Unigenitus*," as Moreau lamented, "led us by degrees to the frightful disputes over our constitution."[1] Louis XV closed the endless controversies about the bull by endorsing the magistrates' interpretation of the relationship between the two powers in 1766. Their obstinate resistance to his fiscal policies and assertions of their political claims in the name of the fundamental laws of the realm led him to

---

1. [Bon], *Lettres d'un homme du monde au sujet des billets de confession et de la bulle Unigenitus* (N.p., 1753), 83; Brunville parlementary journal, Vol. 802, fol. 1, Sénat; Jacob-Nicolas Moreau, *Mes souvenirs*, ed. Camille Hermelin (2 vols.; Paris, 1898–1901), I, 44.

take the drastic step of suppressing their offices in 1771. This "revolution" prompted "patriotic" defenses of the rights of the "nation" and attacks on the ideology of divine-right absolutism. When Louis XVI came to the throne in 1774, he inherited unresolved constitutional issues along with silence on the subject of *Unigenitus*.

Parlementaires and prelates alike were genuinely horrified by Damiens' regicidal attack on Louis XV, but this crime did not deter them for long from criticism of the declarations of 1754 and 1756 in the name of lawfulness and orthodoxy. The magistrates extorted concessions from the monarch before the end of 1757, but the assembly of the clergy found it necessary to reiterate their complaints about royal edicts "which manifestly exceed the powers of secular authority" in 1760. Although "civil authority may not impose silence upon those whom God Himself has chosen to preach His faith," Louis XV had muzzled the bishops in 1754. Two years later, he had disallowed the denomination "rule of faith," "as if civil authority could ever fix the character of holy decrees." The assembly urged the Most Christian King to ratify Pope Benedict XIV's guidelines for the refusal of sacraments and denounced the more restrictive standards promulgated in 1756, which seemed to second the parlement's confusion of "the rights of citizens with the benefits that religion offers to the Christian." Assuring the bishops that he never intended "to pronounce upon purely spiritual matters," Louis XV reaffirmed the stature of the Constitution as "a law of the Church and of the state," yet refused to publish the papal encyclical.[2]

The clergy expressed their dissatisfaction with the king's noncommittal response to their remonstrances by publicly exhorting him to defend ecclesiastical privileges "effectively." Attacks on the Jesuits in the wake of the attempted assassination of Louis XV only intensified their misgivings about the efficacy of royal protection. "The public," according to one pamphleteer, blamed the crime of Damiens on the Jesuits, who "wished to drown in the blood of the king" the declaration that deprived *Unigenitus* of the denomination "rule of faith." The Parlement of Toulouse condemned the reprinting in 1757 of the Jesuit

2. PV, VIII/1, *Pièces justificatives*, 237; VIII/2, *Pièces justificatives*, 365, 367; VIII/2, 1121; VIII/1, *Pièces justificatives*, 239.

Busembaum's *Theologia moralis,* which sanctioned regicide in some cases, as "a crime of *lèse-majesté.*" The attempt upon the life of Joseph I of Portugal in the following year seemed to justify Gallican suspicions that the disciples of Loyola were committed to the liquidation of rulers "who firmly resist ultramontane pretensions." When the Jesuits appealed a verdict against one of their foreign missions to the Parlement of Paris in 1760, the charge of regicide figured prominently in the indictment their enemies formulated against them. Jansenist magistrates turned the case into a comprehensive review of the conduct and constitutions of the order. Christophe de Beaumont condemned the judicial proceedings against the Jesuits as a flagrant transgression upon ecclesiastical prerogatives in his pastoral instruction of October 28, 1763, which the judges promptly suppressed. "After all," one pamphleteer scoffed, "is it not the height of idiocy to maintain that the officers of the king, the ministers of his sovereign justice, are not competent to determine whether the statutes of a religious order are compatible with the laws of the state?"[3] Louis XV did not ignore the protests of the prelates, but he managed only to delay the expulsion of the Jesuits from the realm until 1764.

In the controversy surrounding the Jesuits, as in the conflicts over the *vingtième* and the refusal of sacraments, the question of the respective jurisdictions of the two powers became mired in acerbic polemics concerning sacerdotal independence. Foes of the Jesuits described them as "blind and passive instruments of the arbitrary and despotic will of a foreign general," and as dangerous aliens whose "enthusiastic" obedience to their Italian superior precluded submission to the laws of the kingdom and allegiance to the king. Such "slaves," contended the attorney general of the Parlement of Rennes, "have no

---

3. PV, VIII/1, 890; [Jacques Tailhé], *Abrégé chronologique de l'histoire de la société de Jésus* . . . (En France [*sic*], 1760), 88; *Arrêt du parlement de Toulouse,* September 9, 1757, in Pierre-Toussaint Durand de Maillane, *Les Libertés de l'église gallicane . . .* (5 vols.; Lyon, 1771), V, 152; *Les Jésuites criminels de lèse-majesté dans la théorie et dans la pratique* (Hague, 1758), 3; *Lettre de Jean-Jacques Rousseau, citoyen de Genève à Jean-François Montillet, archevêque et seigneur d'Auch . . .* (Neufchâtel, 1764), 8. (This letter was not really written by Rousseau.) On the debates concerning the Jesuits and the Jansenist campaign against them, see Dale Van Kley, *The Jansenists and the Expulsion of the Jesuits from France, 1757–1765* (New Haven, 1975).

country." "They will be citizens when they are no longer Jesuits."[4] Jesuits themselves denied the accusations of fanaticism and disloyalty and stressed the legitimacy of their constitutions by characterizing them as "monarchical" rather than "despotic." They protested that magistrates with no jurisdiction over spiritual matters, such as religious vows, could not deprive the order of privileges it had enjoyed in France for two centuries. Critics dismissed these claims of exemption from secular intervention—like ecclesiastical claims of immunity from taxation and exclusive control of the sacraments—as insidious attempts to undermine royal authority by "spiritualizing" the external manifestations of religion in this world.

The assembly of the clergy of 1765 in turn denounced the "temporalization" of religion implied by the declarations of 1754 and 1756 and the expulsion of the Jesuits. The bishops summarized their grievances against the magistrates and the crown in the form of three articles published in unprecedented fashion as the *Acts* of the assembly. In the first article they invoked their "duty to remind the people of the principles of the obedience which they owe to their sovereign" and implicitly criticized the laxity of parlementary and royal censorship. They condemned ten books (most of them, in fact, already condemned by the judges and/or the king) that they considered subversive of monarchy as well as religion. The prelates introduced the second and most extensive of the articles, in which they expounded their interpretation of the relationship between the two powers, with strikingly inaccurate versions of two well-known passages commonly cited in discussions of this knotty problem. In quoting Pope Gelasius I to the effect that "two powers are instituted to govern mankind, the sacred authority of the popes and that of kings," they obscured his distinction between pontifical "authority" and royal "power." They also altered the sense of the second half of the first verse of Romans 13, according to which God ordained all powers: "non est enim potestas nisi a deo: quae autem sunt, a deo ordinatae sunt." By placing the comma after *a deo*,

---

4. Henri-Philippe Chauvelin and Jean-Omer Joly de Fleury, *Comptes rendus par un magistrat et par Messieurs les gens du roi au parlement au sujet des constitutions, de la doctrine, et de la conduite des jésuites . . .* (Paris, 1765), 8; Louis-René de Caradeuc de La Chalotais, *Compte rendu des constitutions des jésuites . . .* (N.p., 1762), 137, 188.

rather than before these words, as in the common reading of the Vulgate, the assembly made Saint Paul say that all "well-ordered" powers emanated from God.[5]

Because God Himself had established the Church as well as the monarchy, the bishops argued, the Church "owes nothing to human institution." Since "that which falls under the competence of each power is distinguished by its nature," they claimed exclusive jurisdiction in religious matters and repudiated "Gallican" arguments about their accountability to the secular authorities in the exercise of their divinely appointed prerogatives. They obeyed the civil laws of the realm as subjects, but they also expected the monarch, as a Christian, to enforce the doctrinal and disciplinary decisions of the Church as explained by the Church. "It is therefore acting against the canons to claim to interpret them as one pleases on the pretext of defending them," as the magistrates had done for several decades out of "feigned zeal for the reputation of citizens."[6] According to the second article of the *Acts*, the secular authorities could not silence the clergy, define the character of ecclesiastical pronouncements, or intervene in the administration of the sacraments. The assembly completed its indictment of temporal transgressions in the third article by describing *Unigenitus* as a "dogmatic judgment of the universal Church," as Louis XV had done in 1730 but not in 1755, or "an irreformable judgment of the universal Church in matter of doctrine," a denomination the king had never sanctioned.

The royal councillor Jean-François Joly de Fleury, convinced that the bishops had parlementary remonstrances as well as "philosophic" books in mind in their first article, remarked that they "did not anticipate or did not want to anticipate that in accusing the parlements of attacking the authority of the king they exposed themselves to the same reproach by trying to fix the limits of the two powers." Angered by the insinuation of negligence in censorship, alarmed by the subversive readings of Gelasius and Paul, and outraged by the defiant characterization of the bull, the Parisian magistrates repeated Joly de

5. PV, VIII/2, 1353; VIII/2, *Pièces justificatives*, 420, 421. The collected PV corrected the misplaced comma in the original edition of the *Acts* (Paris, 1765), 16–17.
6. PV, VIII/2, *Pièces justificatives*, 426, 430, 424, 460.

Fleury's accusation when they suppressed the *Acts* in September. Declaring sanctimoniously that "our kings have no need to have their rights defined by any of their subjects," they accused the clergy of claiming independence from their sovereign by denying his jurisdiction over external matters wrongly characterized as "divine things."[7] Insisting upon the legitimacy and necessity of secular intervention in such matters, they defended the imposition of silence, branded the use of unauthorized denominations as an act of rebellion against the crown, and reiterated their case against the refusal of sacraments.

The Parlement of Aix joined in the defense of secular prerogatives by accusing the bishops of "spiritualizing the temporal on the pretext of the interest of religion." Like their Parisian colleagues, the Provençal magistrates condemned the assimilation of the two powers in the misreading of Gelasius, which wrongly implied that God had endowed ecclesiastics with "external and coercive jurisdiction." The Church, as the judges had argued in the 1730s, had no such jurisdiction "other than that which the ruler imparts to it," for which it was accountable to him.[8] They also attacked the misreading of Paul, which implied that *only* "well-ordered" powers were ordained by God and that the clergy had the right to determine which powers were "well ordered." They denounced this distortion of the text as one more attempt to reassert the pernicious ultramontanism of the ninety-first article of *Unigenitus*, the office of Gregory VII, and the address of the bishop of Nîmes. The same misconstruction of Romans 13 occurred not only in the infamous bull *Unam sanctam* (1302), the most extreme statement of the principle of papal supremacy, but also in the article "Political Authority" in the *Encyclopédie*, one of the works anathematized in the first article of the *Acts*.

When the clergy protested to the king about the suppression of the *Acts*, they made explicit the criticism of parlementary pretensions discerned by Joly de Fleury in the same article. They accused the magistrates of usurping the corporate privileges of the First Estate by

---

7. Guillaume-François-Louis Joly de Fleury, "Réflexions sur les actes du clergé de 1765," in JF, Vol. 1479, fol. 79; *Les Remontrances*, II, 600; "Registres de la première chambre des enquêtes du parlement de Paris," in Vol. 730, fol. 259, Sénat.

8. *Arrêt du parlement d'Aix*, October 30, 1765 (Aix, 1765), 58, 22.

meddling in ecclesiastical affairs and of claiming independence from the throne by conducting themselves "as if the depositories of the laws could interpret them as they pleased," often contrary to royal commands. Louis XV, intent upon "conserving the rights of the two powers," overruled the judicial condemnations of the *Acts* and suspended the assembly of the clergy while his councillors drafted a decree defining those rights. Joly de Fleury, who characterized the *Acts* as "a sort of league of the whole clergy of France against the declarations of 1754 and 1756," advised the king to defend his sovereignty by restricting the authority of the Church to *purely* spiritual (internal) matters. Gilbert de Voisins, likewise committed to the preservation of royal jurisdiction in (external) religious matters, warned that "the efforts the assembly of the clergy is making to contest it are a compelling reason for His Majesty to maintain it firmly." He assumed that "our principles on the distinction of the two powers are certain and immutable" and concluded that these principles, based on Scripture itself, supported parlementary arguments about silence, the bull, and the sacraments.[9]

Recognizing (as in 1731 and 1752) that the prelates and the judges disagreed "not only about terms, which can be understood differently, but also about the very substance of things," the crown stated its own interpretation of the relationship between the two powers—this time without having appointed an advisory commission to study the issues—in the decree of May 24, 1766. Louis XV, attempting to resolve "the diversity of opinions" through definition of problematic traditions, reaffirmed ecclesiastical prerogatives in principle but qualified the assembly's exposition of these prerogatives in the same sense as the parlements. He acknowledged that the Church had spiritual *authority* over doctrine and discipline, including the right, claimed by the bishops in the 1730s, to impose "real spiritual penalties" that took effect on the souls of offenders regardless of resistance. At the same time, only temporal *power*, ordained by God and accountable to the

9. PV, VIII/2, 1374; *Arrêt du conseil*, September 15, 1765, in *Recueil général*, XXII, 448; Joly de Fleury, "Réflexions sur les actes du clergé," in JF, Vol. 1479, fol. 82; Pierre Gilbert de Voisins, "Considérations sur les actes de l'assemblée du clergé de 1765," in Ser. U, Vol. 865, unpaginated, AN.

Divinity alone, could inflict temporal penalties. Subjects, furthermore, could not be released, "under any pretext whatsoever," from obedience to their sovereign, whose jurisdiction included "everything that concerns the public order and the welfare of the state."

Since "it is for the Church alone to determine what must be believed," the king and his magistrates could not meddle in "*purely* spiritual matters." They could, however, assess the compatibility of ecclesiastical decisions with the laws of the realm, silence disputes "unessential to the faith," and prohibit the use of unauthorized denominations. Because the "external jurisdiction" of the Church derived from royal concession, the clergy remained answerable to the monarch in the exercise of their "external functions belonging to the public order." They alone administered vows and formulated canons, but the sovereign was entitled to correct abuses in the religious orders and to protect "the reputation of citizens" by arresting departures from the canons recognized and authorized in France. Louis XV invoked the "invariable principles" of 1682, 1695, and 1731, but he interpreted these principles differently in 1766 than he had in the past. The king had always disavowed any intention of trespassing upon ecclesiastical jurisdiction, but he had adopted a more parlementary interpretation of royal prerogatives in religious matters in the 1750s. When, in 1766, he forbade further controversy concerning "the limits which God Himself has established between the two powers," he gave divine sanction to the argument from externality that he himself had previously repudiated. [10]

The injunction of silence, as usual, proved ineffectual. The bishops complained that Louis XV, far from abrogating the offensive declarations of 1754 and 1756, had publicly endorsed the offensive language of the magistrates. Attributing the misquotation of Romans 13 to "mistakes in punctuation," they protested that their sovereign seemed to accuse them of disloyalty by restating Gallican maxims so emphatically. [11] While denying that the *Acts* constituted a presumptuous at-

10. *Arrêt du conseil*, May 24, 1766, in *Recueil général*, XXII, 451–53.

11. PV, VIII/2, *Pièces justificatives*, 443. The *Nouvelles ecclésiastiques*, March 27, 1765, pp. 54–55, explicitly charged that the assembly of 1765 had renounced the Gallican articles of 1682. On the polemics provoked by the assembly see Van Kley, "Church, State, and the Ideological Origins of the French Revolution: The Debate over

tempt "to fix the limits of the two powers," the clergy took exception to many clauses in the decree of May 24, such as the broad definition of "public order." After the assembly disbanded in July, the judges resumed the offensive by condemning the mandements of individual prelates who subscribed to the *Acts*, but the king overruled these sentences. For once Louis XV had the last word. He reminded the magistrates in December (as in 1755) that *Unigenitus* remained "a law of the Church and of the state" (but nothing more), and directed the clergy to abide by the declaration of 1756. Having warned ecclesiastics (more pointedly than in 1731 and 1752) not to trouble his subjects about submission to the bull and commanded parlementaires not to countenance disrepect to the Church, the monarch indicated that he would tolerate no further contraventions of his decree.

The disputes surrounding the assembly of 1765 prompted the publication of a host of works that reiterated the magistrates' indictment of the *Acts* and, in some cases, drew lessons that they themselves had not drawn from the controversy. In the most striking of these works, François Richer, a lawyer in the Parlement of Paris, combined "philosophic" rhetoric with Gallican, Jansenist, and parlementary criticism of the clergy. Having consulted "nature," Richer suggested that humans formed societies for "the preservation and the amenities of earthly life" and not out of any religious motivation. Because they did not need "to live in society to fulfill the duties required by the Creator," religion remained a private concern rather than a collective imperative. Since the state antedated the Church, one could "be a citizen without being a Christian, but one cannot be a Christian without being a citizen."[12] Religion, inherently personal in character, became a public matter only through the conditional concession of worldly privileges to the Church. Inasmuch as the Church derived these privileges from the state, the state retained jurisdiction over the external aspects of religious life. Richer concluded that the king and his magistrates must exert their temporal "power" to arrest clerical abuses of spiritual

the General Assembly of the Gallican Clergy in 1765," *Journal of Modern History*, LI (1979), 629–66.

12. [François Richer], *De l'autorité du clergé et du pouvoir politique sur l'exercise des fonctions du ministère ecclésiastique* (2 vols.; Amsterdam, 1766), I, 13, 110.

"authority." He justified parlementary condemnations of the abusive vows of the Jesuits and of ultramontane pronouncements (from the ninety-first article of *Unigenitus* to the second article of the *Acts*) that threatened the sovereignty of the crown. He denied the sanctity of ecclesiastical property and contended that the clergy could not deprive citizens of their "spiritual possessions" by excluding them arbitrarily from communion and the last rites. He divorced citizenship and Catholicity more aggressively than other critics of the clergy by insisting upon the validity of the civil contract of marriage without the sacrament of matrimony administered by the Church.

Jean-Georges Le Franc de Pompignan, bishop of Le Puy, denounced Richer's book as a blasphemous attempt "to reduce a divine religion to the rank of a merely political institution." "It is insulting Providence," he argued, "to imagine either that civil societies were formed without it or that its principal object in influencing their formation was not to gather men in order to render to the Sovereign Author of their destinies the common duties He required of them." Dismissing Richer's secularized conception of the origins of society as "philosophic" nonsense, the bishop restated the traditional characterization of religion as a collective obligation rather than a private option. Religion, after all, united humans in society and sanctified the sovereignty of their rulers. God accordingly required rulers "to make genuine Christians" of their subjects by supporting public worship and enforcing the doctrinal and disciplinary decisions of the Church. Because the Church derived its authority from God Himself and devoted itself to the dissemination of His word in this world, "religion and all affairs concerning it are not within the competence of secular power."[13] The bishop denounced Richer's transformation of the sacraments into "possessions" and his use of the abusive standard of externality in order to justify temporal encroachments upon spiritual jurisdiction. Pompignan, like the assembly of 1765, repudiated Gallicanism in the parlementary style because it entailed the wholesale subordination of the Church to the secular authorities.

---

13. Jean-Georges Le Franc de Pompignan, *Défense des actes du clergé concernant la religion,* in his *Oeuvres complètes,* ed. Jacques-Paul Migne (2 vols.; Paris, 1855), I, 1151, 1023, 1027, 1119.

As the polemics engendered by the assembly of 1765 abated, the monastic reforms initiated by the assembly provoked further debate about the prerogatives of the two powers. The prelates had requested royal permission to solicit the pope's assistance in correcting corruption and restoring discipline in the religious orders. Reluctant to sanction papal intervention and anxious to avoid any involvement on the part of the magistrates, who had forced him to expel the Jesuits, Louis XV responded by naming a commission of bishops and councillors to make recommendations in this matter. He subsequently raised the minimum age for claustral vocations and established minimum quotas for conventuality. He appointed the so-called *Commission des réguliers*, composed of prelates and councillors (including both Joly de Fleury and Gilbert de Voisins), to enforce these quotas by consolidating houses whose enrollments had dwindled. A few pamphleteers contested the competence of the commission, and assemblies of the clergy subsequently complained that these innovations endangered the survival of monasticism in France.[14] The crown, however, ignored this criticism of its application of the broad definition of temporal jurisdiction it had expounded in 1766.

While the commission implemented its reforms, the Most Christian King became involved in an international incident that likewise involved issues agitated by the assembly of 1765. Ferdinand, duke of Parma, grandson of Louis XV and pupil of the philosophe Condillac, had antagonized the Holy See by curtailing ecclesiastical jurisdiction, taxing Church property, and suppressing the Jesuit order within his domains. When Clement XIII annulled these measures and threatened the duke with excommunication in 1768, the Parlement of Paris renewed its outcry against ultramontanism, and the king ordered the military occupation of the papal enclave of Avignon. Working in concert with other Catholic monarchs, Louis XV induced the next pope, Clement XIV, to discontinue the annual publication of the fourteenth-century bull *In coena domini*, which imposed the penalty of excommunication for offenses including taxation of ecclesiastics and appeal

14. On the pamphlets see Suzanne Lemaire, *La Commission des réguliers, 1760– 1780* (Paris, 1926), 203–205, and Pierre Chevalier, *Loménie de Brienne et l'ordre monastique* (2 vols.; Paris, 1959–60), II, 271–74.

of spiritual cases to secular courts. Before withdrawing his troops from Avignon, the king also pressed the pope to ratify the expulsion of the Jesuits from France as well as Parma by dissolving the Society in 1773. These papal concessions, like the reform of the monastic orders, confirmed the crown's authority in religious matters.

Although the agents-general of the clergy continued to complain about secular encroachments upon ecclesiastical jurisdiction, the relationship between the two powers no longer provoked public contestation by the time Jean Pey, canon of Strasbourg, published his bulky treatise on the subject in 1781. In this elephantine footnote to the assembly of 1765, Pey assailed Jansenists, magistrates, and pamphleteers along with Protestants and philosophes for contesting the privileges of the Church. He also chided Louis XV for deviating after midcentury from his policies of the 1730s and embracing the "English" interpretation of temporal prerogatives in spiritual affairs. The late king, according to Pey, failed to recognize that it was not the First Estate but rather the common enemies of altar and throne identified in his three volumes who threatened the sovereignty of the crown. "The two powers," both ordained by God, "are so closely connected by the common sources which establish their authority that one cannot attack either of them except by means of principles which tend to the destruction of the other." Pey declared that the "republicans" who disputed the authority that the Church derived from God also challenged the plenitude of royal power. These subversives, he warned, not only dissociated "the interest of citizens and the welfare of religion" but also divorced "the interest of subjects from that of rulers."[15]

Pey's strident defense of ecclesiastical prerogatives sounded anachronistic in 1781, inasmuch as fiscal and administrative conflicts had eclipsed religious controversies in France even before the death of Louis XV. His warnings about "republicanism," however, rightly called attention to the continuity between "Jansenist" resistance to episcopal "despotism" and "patriotic" opposition to ministerial "despotism." The fifty years of dissension about *Unigenitus*, the sacraments, and the two powers autopsied by the canon of Strasbourg raised the constitutional questions about the disposition of authority in the kingdom

15. Jean Pey, *De l'autorité des deux puissances* (3 vols.; Strasbourg, 1781), III, 285, 347.

involved in the ongoing political debates of the 1760s and 1770s. After 1757, the parlementaires clashed with the crown about taxes and the limits of absolutism rather than religious matters, but the essential issue of the accountability of the divinely ordained monarch remained the same. In the 1730s and 1750s, Jansenist magistrates and pamphleteers standardized criticism of royal declarations, *lits de justice*, and evocations that subverted the fundamental laws of the realm, violated the prerogatives of the parlements, and threatened the privileges of the French people. After midcentury they also radicalized the ideology of opposition to absolutism by their application of conciliar ecclesiology to the state. Eighteenth-century Jansenists, like sixteenth-century conciliarists, located authority within the Christian community in the body of its members, who delegated this authority to the ecclesiastical hierarchy. The disputes about refusals of sacraments prompted them to translate this religious model into political terms. The resulting conception of the sovereignty of the "nation" figured prominently in the debates provoked by Maupeou's reform of the parlements in 1771, by which time Jansenism, according to the *nouvelliste* Pidansat de Mairobet, had "transformed itself into the patriotic party."[16]

The parlementaires, so quick to reprimand the bishops for disobedience to the declarations of 1754 and 1756, opposed the fiscal policies of the crown much more belligerently in the 1760s than they had during the Regency or the disputes surrounding the *vingtièmes* of 1749 and 1756. Elaborating upon constitutional claims articulated during the religious conflicts of the preceding decades, they complained that the royal system of imposing and collecting taxes not only burdened the people but also violated the laws of the realm. When the

16. [Matthieu-François Pidansat de Mairobet], *Journal historique de la révolution opérée dans la constitution de la monarchie française par M. de Maupeou, chancellier de France* (7 vols.; London, 1774–76), II, 351. On Jansenist uses of conciliarism in particular and the evolution of Jansenist ideology in general, see Van Kley, *The Damiens Affair*, 173–202, and his article "The Jansenist Constitutional Legacy." On the political meaning of eighteenth-century Jansenism, see also Monique Cottret, "Aux origines du républicanisme janséniste: Le mythe de l'église primitive et le primitivisme des lumières," *Revue d'histoire moderne et contemporaine*, XXXI (1984), 99–115, and Yann Fauchois, "Jansénisme et politique au XVIIIe siècle: Légitimation de l'état et délégitimation de la monarchie chez G.-N. Maultrot," *Revue d'histoire moderne et contemporaine*, XXXIV (1987), 473–91.

king resorted to *lits de justice* and other "arbitrary" measures to stifle widespread resistance in the provinces, the magistrates protested against the infringement of their "sacred prerogative" of registration, which they described as "the sacramental solemnity of French legislation." They denounced ministers and censured intendants who attempted "to substitute a despotic for a monarchical government" by subjecting citizens to unregistered taxes and thereby depriving them unlawfully of their property. Louis XV rebuked the magistrates in 1759 for pretending to protect his people against the "irregular proceedings of despotic power" and reminded them that he did not rule arbitrarily but in the spirit of "council, justice, and reason." The king invoked the same trinity of royal attributes in the dramatic "Session of the Flagellation" on March 3, 1766, when he made an unannounced appearance in the Palais de Justice and berated the judges for "mistaking the real and fundamental laws of the state." His councillors, according to Joly de Fleury, carefully weighed every word of this address.[17] Louis XV proscribed the "novel," "foreign," "independent," and "erroneous" claims about representation of the nation and interpretation of the laws that made the Parlement "judge between the king and his people." Dismissing this "imaginary" disjunction of kingship and kingdom, he restated the absolutist version of the "sacred and immutable principles" of the monarchy in memorable terms. "The entire public order emanates from me," he declared, and "the rights and interests of the nation, which some dare to describe as a body separate from the monarch, are necessarily united with my own and rest only in my hands."[18]

In the address of March 3, as in the decree of May 24, 1766, the king attempted to terminate prolonged strife by imposing his interpretation of disputed traditions on obstinate corporate bodies. When the magistrates complained that the publication of his censorious remarks in the official *Gazette de France* disparaged them in the eyes of the

---

17. *Les Remontrances*, II, 417, 346, 435, 204, 557; JF, Vol. 2104, fol. 155. On the drafting of the royal address, see Michel Antoine, "Le Discours de la flagéllation (3 mars 1766)," in *Recueil de travaux offerts à M. Clovis Brunel* (2 vols.; Paris, 1955), I, 33–37.

18. *Les Remontrances*, II, 557–58. On the issue of representation see Keith Michael Baker, "Representation," in Baker (ed.), *Political Culture*, 469–92.

country, he replied sharply that "my wishes and decisions," unlike their remonstrances, "are made to be known and public." Gilbert de Voisins suggested that Louis XV intended to address his manifesto "even more to the public" than to the Parlement, so as to "show the whole kingdom, all subjects of whatever order and station they may be, what the king believes, as it belongs to him to say, regarding the character of and attributes inseparable from his royal authority and what they must believe inviolably according to him."[19] In the Session of the Flagellation, as in the decree concerning the jurisdictions of the two powers, the crown defined the implications of kingship "by the grace of God" in order to silence the rival discourses of the magistrates and the clergy to which the kingdom had been exposed for decades.

When the delegates from the Parlement of Rouen presented its remonstrances of February 2 to the king at Versailles on March 5, he reportedly interrupted them to condemn the allegation that he had taken an oath to the nation at the time of his coronation. He declared "that he had taken the oath only to God and was accountable to Him alone." Although both Joly de Fleury and Gilbert de Voisins had invoked the principle of the derivation of sovereignty from God in their drafts, Louis XV mentioned it only in passing in the address of March 3. His councillors undoubtedly realized that the traditional rhetoric was ineffectual in itself without explicit delineation and vigorous defense of royal prerogatives. The magistrates, after all, had always acknowledged that the monarch "is accountable only to God for the exercise of the supreme power," as they did in their representations of March 20. "The parlements," as Joly de Fleury explained, "have never dared and let us hope they never will dare to contest openly the fundamental principles of our constitutional law, but they have often contested the consequences." The Divinity did not figure prominently in the monarch's indictment of the Parlement on March 3, but his fortuitous encounter with a procession of the holy sacrament on the Pont Neuf immediately after the Session of the Flagellation seemed to give God's blessing to his version of the fundamental laws. Louis XV, who

19. *Les Remontrances*, II, 561–62; Gilbert de Voisins, Draft for *arrêt du conseil* (1765), Ser. U, Vol. 872, unpaginated, AN.

had just humbled the presumptuous magistrates, hastily descended from his coach and kneeled in the mud before the Host. Onlookers, according to the duc de Croy, cried, "'Long live the king!' which had not happened in a long time."[20]

The royal decree of 1766 concerning the two powers heralded the conclusion of a half-century of dissension provoked by *Unigenitus*, but the Session of the Flagellation of the same year did not settle Louis XV's differences with his magistrates. They continued to oppose his fiscal legislation and remonstrated against repeated attempts to resolve the acrimonious "Brittany Affair" involving the Parlement of Rennes by means of "despotic" evocations that violated "what they called the fundamental principles of the monarchy." After the crown again repudiated their constitutional pretensions in the *lit de justice* of December 7, 1770, the Parisian magistrates went on strike. When they refused to resume their functions, the king made good his threat of 1766 "to exert all the power I have received from God to protect my people from the fatal consequences" of such insubordination by exiling them and suppressing their offices in 1771. Chancellor Maupeou, who engineered this "revolution," replaced them with a new tribunal composed of councillors and *maîtres des requêtes*, divided the territory of the former parlement among six *conseils supérieurs*, and abolished judicial venality and fees. He also purged or reorganized many of the provincial parlements and abolished the Cour des aides (the court with jurisdiction over tax cases) of Paris because of its criticism of these reforms. Maupeou had reminded the disgraced parlementaires to no avail that the sovereign held his crown "only from God." He invoked divine ordination again when he instructed their successors, obliged to register royal edicts and forbidden to publish remonstrances, to remember that the king was "accountable only to God for the administration of his kingdom."[21]

20. Comptroller general Charles-François de Laverdy to Armand-Thomas Hue de Miromesnil, first president of the Parlement of Rouen, March 5, 1766, in Miromesnil, *Correspondance politique et administrative*, ed. Pierre-Jacques-Gabriel Leverdier (5 vols.; Rouen, 1899–1903), IV, 160; *Les Remontrances*, II, 563; Jean-François Joly de Fleury, "Mémoire sur les évocations" (1766), in JF, Vol. 1051, fol. 74; Anne-Emmanuel-Ferdinand-François de Croy, *Journal inédit*, ed. Emmanuel-Henry de Grouchy and Paul Cottin (4 vols.; Paris, 1906), II, 227.

21. *Lit de justice*, December, 1770, in *Recueil général*, XXII, 506; *Les Remon-*

The chancellor's "revolution" engendered a flood of polemics that made the discussion of "public affairs" more "public" than ever before. Maupeou's apologists applauded him for checking the "English" independence of the parlementaires and upholding the plenitude of power that the king derived from God. They reiterated the traditional argument that the absolute authority of the crown preserved the order of the kingdom and constituted "the bulwark of the liberty of subjects." As for accusations of despotism, one pampleteer claimed that "the people do not know this word. They know that the king should be the master." "Patriots," on the other hand, charged that Maupeou had subverted the liberty of subjects and overthrown the constitution of the monarchy by confiscating the magistrates' offices. They condemned his lawless violation of property rights and attacked the principle of divine right more directly than the parlementary pamphleteers of the 1750s. "When Scripture says that resistance to the authorities is resistance to God," one critic of the judicial reforms protested, "it does not mean to give the monarch the power of a despot." He stripped divine ordination of its political meaning by suggesting that royal authority derived from the Almighty only in the loose sense that "it is God as the master of events who disposes of all things."[22] Jansenists, who regarded the judicial "revolution," like the *Acts* of 1765, as the work of the Jesuits, directed their conciliar argument about the sovereignty of the nation against Maupeou's despotism. The "patriotic" opposition combined this Jansenist legacy with more conventional invocations of the fundamental laws and more "philosophic" appeals to natural law.

Events took an unexpected turn when Louis XV died suddenly of smallpox on May 10, 1774. The parish priest of Saint-Genevieve,

---

trances, II, 558; *Lit de justice*, December, 1770, in *Recueil général*, XXII, 506; *Les Remontrances*, III, 189.

22. "La Tête leur tourne," in *Le Code des Français ou recueil de toutes les pièces intéressantes publiées en France relativement aux troubles des parlements* (2 vols.; Brussels, 1771), II, 129; *Ils reviendront, ils ne reviendront pas ou le pour et le contre* (N.p., n.d.), 8; [André Blonde], "Le Parlement justifié par l'impératrice de Russie," in *Les Efforts de la liberté contre le despotisme . . .* , (6 vols.; London, 1775), I, 120, 122. On the controversy surrounding Maupeou's reforms, see Durand Echeverria, *The Maupeou Revolution: A Study in the History of Libertarianism, 1770–1774* (Baton Rouge, 1985).

when questioned about the patron saint's apparent deafness to Parisians' prayers during the monarch's illness, allegedly replied, "He died, didn't he?" One of many mock epitaphs summed up popular disaffection with a malicious play on the royal motto: "Here, by the grace of God, lies Louis XV."[23] Sartine, the lieutenant general of police of Paris, reportedly informed Louis XVI that he could only stop the circulation of such insolent epigrams by arresting the entire population of the capital. Wits travestied the traditions of the crown, which ecclesiastics, charged with the responsibility of eulogizing the Most Christian King for the edification of his ungrateful subjects, reaffirmed with transparent defensiveness in their funeral orations. Most of them chastised the French people for judging him too harshly, but many mixed pastoral reprobation with reverent mythification in their assessments of the late king. A few alluded to the sensitive issue of ecclesiastical prerogatives in reviewing his six decades on the throne.

Brochier, for one, remembered Louis XV as a "citizen monarch," a striking juxtaposition of terms that violated customary political dichotomies and underlined the monarch's devotion to the welfare of his people. Insisting that he had ruled in a fatherly, not an "asiatic" manner, the euologists attributed any abuses that marred his reign to wicked councillors and despotic lieutenants. They strove to outdo one another in relating the pathetic episode of his illness at Metz, which had moved his adoring subjects to acclaim him as "the Beloved," the only title, Boismont noted, "which authority cannot usurp." "Of all his titles," Géry added, "the dearest to his heart was that of Most Christian King." Louis XV had not only inherited but also earned this title, according to the ecclesiastics, by defending the faith of his ancestors. He had renewed the draconian penalties for publication of irreligious books and rejected Protestant appeals for acceptance of confessional pluralism. He had not only refused to pardon the impious chevalier de La Barre but also provided a graphic counterexample for his subjects on the Pont Neuf after the Session of the Flagellation. A number of the eulogists fixated upon this edifying incident, but almost all of them

---

23. *Mémoires secrets pour servir à l'histoire de la république des lettres en France depuis 1762 jusqu'à nos jours* . . . (36 vols.; London, 1777–89), VII, 183; Nicolas Baudeau, "Chronique secrète de Paris sous le règne de Louis XVI en 1774," *Revue retrospective*, III (1834), 68.

had to acknowledge some discrepancy between the checkered reality of Louis XV's rule and the mythology of kingship in which they shrouded his memory. Beauvais, who had recently pleaded the cause of overtaxed and undernourished subjects in his Holy Thursday sermon at court, granted in his funeral oration that "the people doubtless do not have the right to grumble." He cautioned, however, that "they undoubtedly have the right to remain silent, and their silence is the warning of kings."[24] Beauvais and other ecclesiastics, whose pastoral offices endowed them with liberty denied to ordinary French men and women, broke this silence in addressing the subjects of the monarch's profligacy and the politico-religious strife that had troubled his reign. They acknowledged that Louis XV had yielded to "the most criminal passions," yet maintained that he "never ceased to be, by the sincerity of his faith, as by the prerogative of his crown, the Most Christian King," as his stunning deathbed penitence testified. The moribund Louis XV had apologized publicly for having offended God and scandalized his people, and this *amende honorable* "atoned for everything."[25]

Coger indulged in wishful thinking when he reported that the dying monarch had reproached himself not only for his sins but also for "having neglected the cares of kingship and for not having protected religion with all the zeal he owed it." Some eulogists ignored the facts and

24. Brochier, *Oraison funèbre . . . de Louis XV . . .* (Vienne, 1774), 4; Corréard, *Oraison funèbre de Louis le bien-aimé . . .* (Lyon, n.d.), 8; Nicolas Thyrel de Boismont, *Oraison funèbre de Louis XV . . .* (Paris, 1774), 4; André-Guillaume de Géry, *Oraison funèbre de . . . Louis XV* (Paris, 1774), 37; Jean-Baptiste-Charles-Marie de Beauvais, *Oraison funèbre . . . de Louis XV . . .* (Paris, 1774), 26. Joseph-Antoine de Véri alluded to this striking passage when he commented on the silence in the churches at the time of the death of Louis XV. See Véri, *Journal*, ed. Jehan-Caspar-Marie de Witte (2 vols.; Paris, 1928), I, 85.

25. Jean-Félix-Henri de Fumel, *Oraison funèbre de . . . Louis XV . . .* (Paris, 1775), 46; Beauvais, *Oraison funebre*, 16; Guillaume-Germain Guyot, *Oraison funèbre de Louis XV . . .* (Soissons, 1774), 23. According to Siméon-Prosper Hardy, "Mes loisirs ou journal des événements tels qu'ils parviennent à ma connaisance" (1764–1789), in FF, Vol. 6681, fol. 332, the cardinal de La Roche-Aymon, speaking for the incapacitated king, announced that Louis XV "asks God's pardon for having offended Him and for the scandalous example which he has given his people." Hardy reported that "ill-intentioned persons" had circulated another version of this *amende honorable*, in which the king prefaced his apology by haughtily reminding his subjects that he was accountable only to God.

praised Louis XV for having heeded the remonstrances of the assemblies of the clergy and checked encroachments upon ecclesiastical jurisdiction. Dessauret exclaimed that the king "protected the faith to the extent that he nearly became a martyr to his zeal," assuming that Louis XV's "resoluteness in defending our holy religion" had provoked Damiens to attack him in 1757. Beauvais, more realistically, recognized that the king "sometimes seemed to falter in his protection." Beauvais' funeral oration, which implicitly condemned secular meddling in spiritual matters, more accurately recalled clerical criticism of Louis XV's policies during the last decades of his reign. According to one shocked contemporary, this eulogy, read at the official service at Saint-Denis on July 27, contained but "a few words of praise and whole pages of animadversion."[26] *Nouvellistes* assumed that its delayed publication resulted from censorship of offensive passages.[27] Beauvais' disparaging comments about the parlements, along with La Luzerne's transparent denunciation of what he called "an audacious sect," aroused the wrath of Jansenist pamphleteers, who reiterated the substance of arguments elaborated by opponents of *Unigenitus* throughout the reign of Louis XV.[28] Buisson de Beauteville, one of the four bishops who did not subscribe to the *Acts* of the assembly of 1765, seconded their criticism of Beauvais, who had delivered the customary panegyric of Saint Augustine at the same assembly. Buisson de Beauteville had deplored the sins of Louis XV in no uncertain terms in his mandement on the king's death. He again distanced himself from his episcopal colleagues by applauding the expulsion of the Jesuits and welcoming the dismissal of Maupeou and the reestablish-

26. François-Marie Coger, *Oraison funèbre de . . . Louis XV . . .* (Paris, 1774), 24–25; Isaac-Alexis Dessauret, "Oraison funèbre de Louis XV," in *Collection intégrale,* LXIX, 503; Beauvais, *Oraison funèbre,* 38; *Lettres sur quelques oraisons funèbres* (Bouillon, 1774), 26.

27. *Mémoires secrets,* VII, 192, 199, XXVII, 271; Baudeau, "Chronique secret," 386; Maurice Tourneux (ed.), *Correspondance littéraire et critique par Grimm, Diderot, Raynal, Meister, etc.* (15 vols,; Paris, 1877), X, 447; Hardy, "Mes loisirs," in FF, Vol. 6681, fol. 394; *Lettres sur quelques oraisons funèbres,* 23; *Correspondance secrète, politique, et littéraire . . .* (18 vols.; London, 1787–90), I, 68; *Nouvelles ecclésiastiques,* October 3, 1774, p. 157.

28. César-Guillaume de La Luzerne, *Oraison funèbre de . . . Louis XV . . .* (Paris, 1774), 7.

ment of the parlements in his mandement on the coronation of Louis XVI. When he died in 1776, Buisson de Beauteville left behind a spiritual testament, one of the last episcopal echoes of the disputes over the Constitution, in which he recorded his refusal to recognize the bull as a decision of the Church binding the consciences of Catholics.[29]

Anticlerical "patriots" read the funeral orations of 1774 not only as eulogies of Louis XV but also as self-interested pronouncements in which the clergy gave his successor a piece of their minds upon his accession to the throne. The *Mémoires secrets* regarded "this stir in all the pulpits" as the result of "a sort of confederation of ecclesiastical power to make its wishes known in such opportune circumstances." *Nouvellistes* reinterpreted Beauvais' bold Holy Thursday sermon well after the fact as an attempt to subject the crown to clerical influence. They claimed that the demeaning *amende honorable* extorted from the late king on his deathbed had "scandalized" the "public." The *nouvellistes* alleged that "the priests are exerting themselves to regain the ground they have lost by the exile of the chancellor," who had amnestied clerics forced to flee the country in order to escape prosecution by the Parlement.[30] They reported with satisfaction that Louis XVI, who had already released imprisoned convulsionaries from the Bastille and warned Christophe de Beaumont not to trouble his subjects about the bull, banished the parish priest of Saint-Séverin for withholding the sacraments from a Jansenist parishioner in April, 1775.[31]

The young king, to the dismay of many ecclesiastics, disbanded the Maupeou courts and recalled the parlements only months after his grandfather's death. He vowed "to keep each of his subjects within the bounds of his duties," but the reinstated magistrates quickly declared that their duties included the protection of "the constitution of the state, the existing laws, the maxims and principles of the monarchy, the rights of the different orders or different classes of subjects." They criticized the deregulation of the grain trade, for example, as tantamount to abdication of the sovereign's obligation to ensure that

29. "Testament spirituel de feu M. l'évêque d'Alais," in Vol. 576, no. 2, PR.
30. *Mémoires secrets*, VII, 197; Baudeau, "Chronique secret," 38, 407.
31. On Beaumont and the priest of Saint-Séverin, see *Correspondance secrète*, I, 133, and *Mémoires secrets*, XXX, 200–201, respectively.

his people could obtain their daily bread at a reasonable price. When poor harvests led to rioting in the spring of 1775, Louis XVI asked the bishops to remind his subjects that such disruptions of public order constituted "a crime before God and men alike." Beaumont obliged by condemning the riots on May 18 as "rebellion against God Himself," but some ecclesiastics regarded the royal request as a transgression upon spiritual jurisdiction.[32] The hostile *Mémoires secrets* charged that the priests themselves had instigated the disorders so as to embarrass the reforming comptroller general Turgot, no friend of the First Estate.[33] The same source denounced Beaumont's pastoral instruction of June 2 on the subject of the coronation of Louis XVI as written "altogether from the viewpoint of the clergy, which ascribes the authority of the ruler wholly to God, which is to say to itself."[34]

Turgot provoked the Parlement by responding to its objections concerning the liberty of the grain trade with a *lit de justice.* He also antagonized the clergy by urging Louis XVI to dispense with the traditional coronation altogether or at least to move it to Paris in order to economize on expenses. The king rejected his advice, and the ceremony took place at Reims, as it had for centuries, on June 11, 1775. Contemporaries did report one significant alteration in the ritual: the officiating bishops did not even make the gesture of asking the spectators in the cathedral if they accepted Louis XVI as their sovereign. The *Mémoires secrets* acknowledged that this last vestige of the Germanic custom of election was perfectly meaningless. The authors noted that the omission nonetheless "roused the indignation of patriots," because the clergy had not seen fit to abridge the proceedings, so as to avoid overtaxing the young king as well as the aged archbishop of Reims, by eliminating other formalities that involved ecclesiastical interests. La Roche-Aymon, archbishop of Reims, had the distinction of crowning the monarch on June 11. The evening before, the spotlight belonged to Turgot's friend Boisgelin, the "enlightened" archbishop of Aix, who delivered a somewhat unorthodox sermon on the eminently

32. *Lit de justice,* November 12, 1774, in *Recueil général,* XXIII, 50; *Les Remontrances,* III, 256; "Lettre royale aux archevêques et évêques," May 9, 1775, in Anne-Robert-Jacques Turgot, *Oeuvres,* ed. Gustave Schelle (5 vols.; Paris, 1913–23), IV, 436–37; Christophe de Beaumont, *Lettre pastorale . . .* (Paris, 1775), 4.

33. *Mémoires secrets,* XXX, 227.

34. *Ibid.,* VIII, 64.

appropriate subject of the duties and perils facing the king of France. His conventional rhetoric about the divine origins of royal authority and the religious responsibilities of the crown made less impression on his listeners than his emphatic remarks about the sovereign's obligation to rule only according to the laws. Boisgelin had previously criticized the Maupeou reforms and extolled the magistrates, in their own terminology, as "interpreters of the laws" in an address to the Parlement of Provence on the occasion of its reestabishment.[35] His coronation sermon, unlike Beauvais' funeral oration, was never printed because of its political content.

Some commentators praised Boisgelin's "patriotic" sentiments, but the *nouvelliste* Pidansat de Mairobet criticized the archbishop for endorsing the assumption that the king derived his power from God and remained accountable to Him alone.[36] The coronation prompted the publication of a number of undisguised attacks on the principle of divine right, recently invoked by Maupeou, including reeditions of several indictments of despotism occasioned by the chancellor's reforms. The lawyer Martin de Mariveaux, the self-styled *Ami des loix*, condemned Maupeou's use of divine right to justify the unlawful suppression of the parlements and insisted that the sovereign held his crown not from God but from the "nation." "The laws entrust the people to him" *not* unconditionally but only "on the condition that he will be the father of his subjects." The nation participated in the making of the laws and delegated to him the authority to execute them. The dangerous "fable" of monarchical unaccountability, which denied any such contractual obligations on the part of the ruler, encouraged royal misrule and resulted in popular servitude. Martin de Mariveaux traced the "fable" back to the eighth century, when Pepin had himself consecrated by the pope in order to legitimize his dispossession of the Merovingians. Locating the origins of French kingship in Germanic election rather than divine ordination, he dismissed the canonical version of the coronation as a romance "hardly worthy of belief among the Iroquois."[37]

---

35. *Ibid.*, VIII, 87; Tourneux (ed.), *Correspondance littéraire*, XI, 16.

36. [Pidansat de Mairobet], *L'Espion anglais* . . . (4 vols.; London, 1779), I, 447.

37. [Jean-Claude Martin de Mariveaux], *L'Ami de lois ou les vrais principes de la monarchie française* (N.p., n.d.), 4, 14, 13 (first published in 1771).

Jansenist critics of Maupeou's "revolution" did not, like Martin de Marivaux, dispense with God and paraphrase Rousseau, but they too repudiated the traditional constitutional consequences of divine ordination. The lawyer Martin Morizot assumed that God had consigned sovereignty to the nation and therefore interpreted the coronation in contractual terms. The motto "Vox populi vox Dei" issued from a radiant cloud in one corner of the frontispiece of his *Sacre royal,* which depicted the moment in the ceremony when the bishops asked the audience for its consent before they crowned the monarch. Insisting that "a king without the approbation of his subjects would be no less a prodigy than a man with neither father nor mother," he condemned the suppression of the ritual of assent as a crime of *lèse-patrie.* According to Morizot, the people in effect elected their ruler and then invited the Almighty to ratify their choice. They promised to obey the sovereign conditionally, only as long as he abided by the standard of justice that God Himself had prescribed. The authors of the monumental *Maximes du droit public français* (Claude Mey and others) agreed that "it would be an absurd system to conclude from [the principle] that the power of kings derives from God that they are permitted to do everything." They insisted that divine right was meant "to establish the independence of the crown and not to fix the prerogatives of the king relative to his people."[38] They also rejected the conventional assimilation of royal and paternal authority, because subjects, unlike children, chose their sovereign. The king acknowledged his accountability to the nation at the time of his coronation. He promised explicitly to respect the fundamental laws of the realm and agreed implicitly to submit his own laws to the parlements for registration. Elected by the people, consecrated by God, the monarch could no longer command their obedience or claim His blessing if he reigned in a lawless manner. Romans 13, according to Mey and his collaborators, did not preclude resistance to rulers who violated their contracts with their subjects and thereby forfeited their sacred character.

38. [Martin Morizot], *Le Sacre royal ou les droits de la nation reconnus et confirmés par cette cérémonie* (2 vols.; Amsterdam, 1776), II/3, 15 (first published in 1772 in one volume under the title *Inauguration de Pharamond . . .*); [Claude Mey *et al.*], *Maximes du droit public français . . .* (6 vols.; Amsterdam, 1775), II/2, 164, II/1, 389 (first published in 1772 in two volumes).

These revised and expanded critiques of Maupeou's despotism discarded the absolutist myth of divine ordination along with the absolutist fiction of the unaccountability of the crown, which the magistrates and the clergy had supported in principle but contested in practice. Inasmuch as it renewed the public discussion of constitutional issues provoked by the chancellor's reforms, the coronation of Louis XVI may well have furthered the waning of traditions it was supposed to reaffirm.[39] Turgot's friend the abbé de Véri reported in June, 1775, that ordinary French subjects had become accustomed to "regarding the sovereign merely as the agent of the nation" and that they no longer had "the veneration for royalty that our ancestors had for its divine origin." Pidansat de Mairobet, who dismissed the ceremony that took place at Reims that month as a farce and denounced the Holy Ampulla as a fraud, referred to Louis XVI's exercise of the royal touch as an "indecent act" that exposed the king to "public ridicule." Théveneau de Morande summarized the "patriotic" repudiation of divine right as the window dressing of despotism in his hyperbolic complaint that any subject who dared to question the monarch's thaumaturgic powers ran the risk of being "thrown in a dungeon, castrated, garroted, broken on the wheel. What a splendid constitution!"[40]

The trouble with France, Turgot informed Louis XVI, was that the kingdom "has no constitution," in the sense that it was composed of heterogeneous corporate bodies devoid of "public spirit," such that the king "is obliged to decide everything himself." The "philosophic" comptroller general, like the "patriots," hoped to make the administration of the realm less arbitrary and more public in character. Unlike the "patriots," however, he put little stock in parlements and estates as guardians of the rights of subjects and the welfare of the country. He called for the establishment of assemblies of property-owning citizens to make decisions about the assessment of taxes and implemen-

39. For a different perspective on the coronation, see Hermann Weber, "Das Sacre Ludwigs XVI. vom 11. Juni 1775 und die Krise des Ancien Regime," in Ernest Hinrichs, Eberhard Schmitt, and Rudolf Vierhaus (eds.), *Vom Ancien Regime zur Französischen Revolution: Forschungen und Perspektiven* (Göttingen, 1978), 539–65.

40. Véri, *Journal*, II, 8; [Pidansat de Mairobet], *L'Espion anglais*, I, 454; [Charles Théveneau de Morande], *La Gazette noire . . .* (A cent lieues de la Bastille [*sic*], 1784), 4.

tation of public works. This rationalized administrative structure, based on earthly interests rather than divine purposes, would allow the monarch "to govern like God through general laws" instead of intervening in the details of local affairs.[41] Louis XVI dismissed the comptroller general's plan as a dangerous dream but took many of his other proposals more seriously.[42] Ecclesiastical and parlementary opposition to these innovations demonstrated once again the extent to which the "grand chieftain" of the French, no matter how independent in principle, was in fact "dependent" on "the priests of his faith" and the judges who "claim to share authority with him."[43]

The quinquennial assembly of the clergy, which convened a month after the coronation, reminded the new king of his obligation "to protect religion." "The vow pronounced at the foot of the altar" at Reims, they declared, "makes it your most sacred duty."[44] Consecration by God required the monarch to serve God, and the bishops did not hesitate to explain just what God expected of his royal lieutenant. God expected him, among other things, to respect ecclesiastical jurisdiction in doctrinal and disciplinary matters and to arrest the circulation of irreligious books. Louis XV had disappointed them on both counts, and they hoped for more compliance from his successor. Louis XVI responded to most of their remonstrances with little more than vague assurances of his devotion to the faith of his ancestors, but he listened more attentively to their strident warnings that the Most Christian King could not tolerate religious pluralism. Clerical opposition played a large part in the failure of Turgot's efforts to restore the civil rights of Protestants during his tenure in the ministry.

Three weeks after the ceremony at Reims, solicitor general Séguier denounced *L'Ami des loix* to the Parlement of Paris as "prejudi-

41. Turgot, "Mémoire sur les municipalités" (1776), in his *Oeuvres*, IV, 576, 577, 576. On this important text see Baker, "French Political Thought at the Accession of Louis XVI," *Journal of Modern History*, L (1978), 279–303.

42. "Observations marginales de Louis XVI sur un mémoire de Turgot relatif à l'administration," dated February 15, 1778, in Louis XVI, *Oeuvres* (2 vols.; Paris, 1864), II, 28–35.

43. *Lettres iroquoises ou correspondance politique, historique, et critique entre un iroquois voyageur en Europe et ses correspondants dans l'Amérique septentrionale* (2 vols. in l; London, 1781), I, 25.

44. PV, VIII/2, 2084.

cial to the sovereignty of the king and contrary to the fundamental laws of the nation." He sanctimoniously wished that the subject of sovereignty and the fundamental laws had remained concealed "beneath the veil with which the prudence of our ancestors shrouded everything concerning government and administration." The magistrates displayed no such reticence about discussing constitutional matters in their remonstrances against Turgot's Six Edicts in the spring of 1776. Having reminded Louis XVI that "justice is the first duty of kings," they charged that the comptroller general's innovations violated the sovereign's coronation oath and the sacred rights of property. They warned that the edicts concerning the grain trade, the guilds, and the *corvée* encouraged license, independence, and equality and thereby subverted the venerable traditions of paternalism, subordination, and privilege that the monarchy was expected to defend. Alarmed by the spectacle of administrative "revolutions" and the news of unrest in the countryside, the parlementaires reasserted their conception of their public role as guardians of the traditional order in the decree of March 30, by which they directed all French subjects to abide by the "ancient and immutable principles" the crown itself seemed to have betrayed.[45]

Turgot, who lasted only twenty months in office, frankly rejected the custom of "deciding what should be done by the study and example of what our ancestors did in times of ignorance and barbarism." He repudiated the conventional argument from history and the familiar language of the past that figured so prominently in the chorus of clerical and parlementary criticism of his ministry. Throughout the prolonged ecclesiastical and constitutional disputes of the eighteenth century, the clergy, the magistrates, and, more often than not, the crown as well condemned the "itch for innovating." They all claimed to defend the traditions of the corporate, Catholic kingdom, yet they all contributed to the undermining of these traditions before the Revolution. The monarchy tampered with tradition by sponsoring the controversial reforms of Machault, Maupeou, and Turgot and by imposing

45. *Arrêt du parlement*, June 30, 1775 (Paris, 1775), 5; *Les Remontrances*, III, 278; *Arrêt du parlement*, March 30, 1776, in *Recueil général*, XXIII, 526. Unless otherwise specified, the word *parlement* in texts entitled *Arrêt du parlement* refers to the Parlement of Paris.

its interpretations of the relationship between the two powers and the fundamental laws of the realm on its unruly subjects at the expense of their corporate prerogatives. Bishops defended their jurisdiction and parlementaires expanded their pretensions by advancing their own interpretations of the principles of the politico-religious order. The former, as the abbé de Véri noted, hastened "to involve the interests" of God "in everything which concerns them," while the latter appealed to "the public interest" in opposing reforms that threatened their privileges. Both demanded their rights in the corporate kingdom, as the Cour des aides explained to Louis XVI, "because they are the rights of your people," in the sense that the preservation of the status of Catholics and citizens depended upon the preservation of the prerogatives of the prelates and magistrates who could speak for them in exhorting the monarch to fulfill his divinely ordained obligations to protect orthodoxy and rule lawfully.[46] Both parties discredited the traditional identification of kingdom and kingship by challenging their sovereign's departures from the usages of his predecessors and protesting his apparent disregard for the welfare of his subjects.

The bishops consecrated the king, and the judges burned books that impugned his sacred character. Both acknowledged in principle that he was answerable only to God but disowned this axiom of absolutism in practice by exploiting it to justify their resistance to the crown. Divine right survived until the end of the ancien régime in ecclesiastical and parlementary discourse and in the works of royal publicists like Moreau, who adjured his fellow subjects on the eve of the Revolution "to believe what our ancestors believed."[47] It had already become politically dysfunctional, however, by the accession of Louis XVI, even before "patriots" attacked it outright. Royalist pamphleteers, like "patriotic" ones, accordingly appealed to history and utility as well as divine right. The politico-religious strife that spanned the reign of Louis XV exposed the constitutional tensions lurking within the traditional rhetoric of kingship "by the grace of God." It

46. Turgot, "Mémoire sur les municipalités," 575; PV, VIII/1, 629; Véri, *Journal*, II, 334, I, 64; *Mémoires pour servir à l'histoire du droit public de France en matière d'impôt . . .* (Brussels, 1779), 12.
47. Moreau, *Maximes fondamentales du gouvernement français . . .* (Paris, 1789), 6.

revived sixteenth- and seventeenth-century debates about customary restraints upon royal prerogatives and regularized opposition to royal authority within the traditional structures of the ancien régime. It nurtured corporate arguments about the *de facto* accountability of the crown, which the Maupeou crisis catalyzed into "patriotic" claims of contractual accountability to the nation. When the Jansenist lawyer Gabriel-Nicolas Maultrot punctuated Romans 13 in 1789 as the prelates had done in 1765, in order to prove that God did not require obedience to the unjust commands of rulers, he left the king answerable not to Rome but to the sovereign nation, rescued from the political minority to which Moreau had relegated it.[48]

Maultrot, like the magistrates, had denounced the *Acts* of 1765 as further evidence of the ecclesiastical threat not only to the sovereignty of the king but also to the privileges of his subjects. Without presuming to "confine the religion of Christ to internal acts," Maultrot and other critics of the clergy made "an object of *police* of everything external about religion." In transforming the sacraments into property, parlementaires and pamphleteers expanded the scope of temporal jurisdiction in spiritual affairs and, at the same time, restricted the scope of public concerns to what they defined as the outward aspects of religion. They claimed cognizance of religious conformity, based on externalized evidence and judged by doctrinal norms formally recognized in France, and insisted that the clergy could not negate the civil status of French men and women by depriving them of their spiritual possessions because of deviations from doctrinal norms not authorized by the secular authorities. Opponents of *Unigenitus* stressed the juridical linking of legal and confessional identities in order to arrest refusals of sacraments but also underscored the fictional quality of the ideal of religious uniformity by sheltering nonconformists from persecution and nudging the crown out of the business of enforcing ecclesiastical standards of orthodoxy. They not only invoked but also discredited the conjunction of citizenship and Catholicity, like the principle of divine ordination, by the way in which they exploited it to serve their own purposes. Disputes about Jansenism and taxation sug-

48. [Gabriel-Nicolas Maultrot], *Origine et étendue de la puissance royale suivant les livres saints et la tradition* (3 vols.; Paris, 1789–90), I, 183.

gested that citizenship involved a shared status underlying confessional identity and corporate distinctions. By the time of Louis XVI, citizenship implied not only loyalty to the crown, which commanded the obedience of the French people as a whole, and devotion to the national welfare, which concerned them all, but also their common right to the security of their persons and their property, which "makes of man a citizen," the magistrates declared, "and of all citizens a state."[49] Their arguments against the uncanonical deprivation of sacraments, as well as their protests against the unlawful imposition of taxes, played a role in the making of this right of man and citizen.

49. *Du droit du souverain sur les biens fonds du clergé . . .* (Naples, 1770), 97; PV, VIII/2, 1609; *Les Remontrances*, III, 613.

6

Citizens in the Wilderness: The Problem of Toleration

The Protestant chevalier de Jaucourt, who managed to compose more than seventeen thousand entries for the *Encyclopédie*, did not attempt to catalogue the many defects of the ancien régime in his brief and inoffensive article entitled "France." Instead he coyly referred readers to his subsequent articles "Tax" and "Toleration," which criticized the fiscal and religious policies of the monarchy. "Toleration," a reforming slogan in the vocabulary of the *Encyclopédie*, carried pejorative connotations in more conventional dictionaries published during the century between the revocation of the Edict of Nantes and the promulgation of the edict of 1787, which restored the civil status of Protestants. In conventional usage the term implied not approbation or even authorization but merely reluctant "sufferance, indulgence for that which cannot be prevented."[1] The Most Christian King, who vowed at his coronation to expel heretics from the realm, "tolerated" the unlawful existence of Protestants in France, just as he "tolerated" prostitution and the trade in illicit books, only in the sense that he simply could not suppress these abuses.[2]

1. "Tolérance," *Dictionnaire de l'Académie française* (2 vols.; Lyon, 1776), II, 586. For the text of Jaucourt's article on toleration, suppressed by the publishers of the *Encyclopédie*, see Douglas H. Gordon and Norman L. Torrey, *The Censoring of Diderot's Encyclopédie and the Re-established Text* (New York, 1947), 95–106.
2. Nicolas-Toussaint-Lemoyne Desessarts mentioned the "toleration" of prostitution in his *Dictionnaire universel de police . . .* (7 vols.; Paris, 1786–89), III, 567.

Eighteenth-century disputes concerning the problem of "the so-called Reformed faith," like the contemporaneous strife over Jansenism, furthered the disjunction of religion and politics in the public order of the ancien régime.[3] Both controversies involved conflicting interpretations of the fundamental laws of the kingdom and of the relationship between spiritual and temporal authority. The campaign for toleration, unlike opposition to *Unigenitus*, did not represent a constitutional challenge to the crown, but it did raise questions about the religious obligations of the monarchy. Proponents of toleration, like critics of the bull, differed with defenders of orthodoxy about the definition of royal prerogatives in religious matters and the implications of the conjunction of citizenship and Catholicity. For decades, the clergy exhorted the successors of Louis XIV to realize his vision of "one faith, one king, one law" by compelling both groups of nonconformists to submit to the discipline of the established Church. In spite of these exhortations, Louis XV yielded repeatedly to the parlements on the subject of *Unigenitus*, thereby compromising his own sovereignty, and Louis XVI eventually conceded civil toleration to the Protestants on the eve of the Revolution in one of the last gestures of royal absolutism.

The contest between tradition and innovation played itself out in far less ambiguous terms in the case of the heretical Protestants than in that of the schismatic Jansenists. Jansenists, to use the contemporary terminology, sought "ecclesiastical toleration," which protected dissidents against exclusion from the communion of the Church, whereas Protestants advocated "civil toleration," which guaranteed the rights of citizens to persons who did not share the national faith. With the backing of the crown, the clergy endeavored to deprive the former, who wished to be considered Catholics, of sacraments they demanded, while attempting to force the latter, who asked for recognition as non-

---

Chrétien-Guillaume de Lamoignon de Malesherbes described the "toleration" of unauthorized books in his *Mémoires sur la librairie et la liberté de la presse* (Paris, 1809), 101 (written in 1759 and 1788).

3. "La religion prétendue réformée" (often abbreviated "R.P.R."), was the official designation for Protestantism. Eighteenth-century sources refer to its adherents variously as "the Reformed," "Protestants," "Calvinists," "Huguenots," and, most pejoratively, "religionaries."

Catholics, to participate in sacraments they rejected. Opponents of the bull accordingly formulated their case largely within the conventional framework by manipulating the juridical fiction of religious uniformity. Adherents of "the so-called Reformed faith," on the other hand, denounced the dependence of legal identity on confessional conformity and proposed nothing less than the public acceptance of pluralism.

French Protestants in the last century of the ancien régime were the objects of a formidable but not altogether coherent body of repressive legislation. In revoking the Edict of Nantes, Louis XIV explicitly directed that "those of the so-called Reformed faith, while awaiting the time when it might please God to enlighten them like the others," should not be bothered on account of their beliefs, as long as they refrained from any exercise of their religion. Thirty years later, however, the aged monarch endorsed the incongruous proposition that no Protestants remained in France. According to the declaration of March 18, 1715, the residence in his domains of "those who *were* of the so-called Reformed faith" constituted "more than sufficient proof" of their conversion, "without which they would not have been tolerated in the kingdom." The presumption of conformity, repeatedly invoked by Jansenists in order to secure the sacraments, had more problematic effects in the case of Protestants. If taken to mean that "no one is allowed to question the Catholicity of any subject of the king," as the former minister of the royal household Malesherbes explained, the legal fiction could enable them to elude persecution in some ways. At the same time, it exposed them to the penalties inflicted upon relapsed heretics if they spurned the sacraments on their deathbeds, even though, "no law," as d'Aguesseau protested, "ever imposed on religionaries the obligation of converting."[4]

Louis XV's declaration of May 14, 1724, consolidated the provisions of a number of his predecessor's decrees that deprived Protestants of civil means of registering births, marriages, and deaths. This "masterpiece of Christian policy," as the Jesuit Novi de Caveirac called it,

---

4. *Déclaration du roi*, November 12, 1685, in *Recueil général*, XX, 534; *Déclaration du roi*, March 8, 1715, *ibid.*, XX, 640 (emphasis added); [Malesherbes], *Mémoire sur le mariage des protestants* (N.p., 1785), 13; Henri-François d'Aguesseau, letter dated March 26, 1715, in FF, Vol. 7046, fol. 38.

required all French subjects to be baptized, married, and buried according to the rites of the Church. It prohibited emigration, banned nonconformist schools and religious assemblies, outlawed heretical pastors, and excluded non-Catholics from public office and various professions. The declaration not only proscribed external manifestations of "the so-called Reformed faith" but also deprived its adherents of legal identity, since, as Malesherbes noted, "the status of citizen is attested in France only by certificates of birth, marriage, and death furnished to Catholics by their priests."[5] The government subsequently considered many proposals for regularizing the status of Protestants, especially after the presidial court of Nîmes set the precedent for the dissolution of their marriages in 1739. It took the first step in this direction in 1736 by providing for the interment of persons who could not be buried in consecrated ground, but it did not generalize the separation of civil from sacramental registration for another fifty years.[6]

Protestants in northern France, less numerous but more prosperous than their southern coreligionists, generally observed the letter of the law by confining their devotions to domestic gatherings and complying outwardly with the formalities of the Church. Since the clergy often required couples to abjure their errors before uniting them in marriage and frequently listed the offspring of recalcitrant parents in the parish registers as illegitimate children, more militant Protestants in the Midi persisted in celebrating weddings and baptisms at clandestine assemblies "in the wilderness," or, more prosaically, in the countryside. As a result of this disregard for the laws, they remained "subjects of the king," in the words of a sympathetic pamphleteer, "without being citizens."[7] According to royal jurisprudence they lived in concubinage, and their progeny were consequently disqualified

5. Jean Novi de Caveirac, *Apologie de Louis XIV et de son conseil sur la révocation de l'édit de Nantes* . . . (Paris, 1758), 49; Malesherbes, "Mémoire sur le mariage des protestants fait en 1779," in FF, Vol. 10625, fol. 13 v. For the text of the declaration of 1724, see *Recueil général*, XXI, 261–70.

6. *Déclaration du roi*, April 9, 1736, in *Recueil général*, XXI, 409. See Guillaume-François Joly de Fleury's notes on the application of this legislation to Protestants, in JF, Vol. 160, dossier 1488, fol. 377 v.

7. [Louis Guidi], *Dialogue entre un évêque et un curé sur les mariages des protestants* (N.p., 1775), 25.

from inheriting their property. The authorities, furthermore, sometimes sequestered Protestant children in Catholic schools to preserve
them from the errors of their parents, in spite of protests that this
practice violated the principle of paternal authority upon which the
crown itself rested.[8]

In the surveillance of "the so-called Reformed faith," as in so many
other aspects of the *police* of the ancien régime, administrative laxity
mitigated the severity of the laws. Alarmed by the prospect of a
wholesale exodus of Protestants in 1724, the intendant of Caen warned
that "it would not be suitable to enforce the law with exactitude, but
only to try to punish that which may be done too flagrantly." The fre-
quency and magnitude of the illegal assemblies "in the wilderness" eventually provoked systematic repression during the uneasy years around
midcentury when the kingdom was at war (1744–1748, 1756–1763),
and Protestants were suspected of collusion with foreign coreligionists. After efforts to enforce the laws strictly resulted in localized violence and renewed emigration, Versailles reverted to the policy of
temporization. The crown instructed the governor of Languedoc in
1758, for example, "to threaten more than punish." The royal council
nonetheless recognized that coercive measures remained necessary,
if only to reassure the bishops that the king had not abandoned the cause
of Catholicism and to disabuse the Protestants of the mistaken belief
that Louis XV intended to legalize what the intendant of Languedoc
called "toleration necessitated by circumstances" during wartime.[9]

The Calas case, the most notorious example of religious persecution in the eighteenth century, took place against this wartime background. The family of the twenty-nine-year-old Marc-Antoine Calas
discovered his body in his father's shop in Toulouse on the evening of
October 13, 1761. Jean Calas, a Protestant clothier, maintained that

8. In *L'Accord parfait de la nature, de la raison, de la révélation, et de la politique . . .*
(2 vols.; Cologne, 1753), II, 97, the chevalier de Beaumont compared the sequestering
of Protestant children with the alleged kidnapping of children by the police, which provoked riots in Paris in May, 1750.

9. François Richer d'Aube to comptroller general Charles-Gaspard Dodun, October
22, 1724, quoted in A. Galland, *Essai sur l'histoire du protestantisme à Caen et en basse
Bretagne de l'édit de Nantes à la Révolution, 1598–1791* (Paris, 1898), 304; "Mémoire
lu et approuvé au conseil pour servir d'instruction à M. le maréchal de Thomond dans
la conduite qu'il doit tenir à l'égard des protestants de Languedoc," dated January 7,
1758, *BSHPF*, XVIII (1869), 435; FF, Vol. 7046, fol. 282.

his son, having abandoned hopes for a legal career because of his religion, had hanged himself, but the authorities accused the family of murdering Marc-Antoine in order to prevent his conversion to Catholicism. Calas *père* was tried for murder, not heresy, but confessional hostility clearly influenced the proceedings. Given the menacing reality of rural unrest around Toulouse during the Seven Years' War, the alleged filicide reanimated the traditional fear of Protestants as rebels and fanatics who threatened the lives as well as the souls of Catholic subjects. Despite the lack of evidence of his intended conversion, Marc-Antoine was buried in consecrated ground as a martyr of the true faith, but his heretical father was convicted, tortured, and broken on the wheel, and his body was burned. The parlementary sentence, like the condemnation of the chevalier de La Barre, reflected local circumstances and attracted the attention of the philosophes because of its exceptional character. The crown placated the philosophes and reprimanded the magistrates of Toulouse by overruling the conviction of Jean Calas on March 9, 1765, exactly three years after his execution.

Not long after the promulgation of the "law of silence" in 1754, the pastor Paul Rabaut remarked enviously that the Jansenists seemed sufficiently numerous and vociferous to have won "the protection of the government and all the parlements of the realm." In the years following the execution and posthumous rehabilitation of Jean Calas, Protestants too gained public sympathy and unofficial recognition. They looked less dangerous and more respectable as bourgeois elements rejoined the largely peasant congregations "in the wilderness" and apprehensions about doctrinal differences waned. The clergy continued to denounce infractions of the declaration of 1724, just as they complained about Sabbath-breaking and prohibited books. "Enlightened" intendants like Christophe Pajot de Marcheval, however, renounced not only coercion but also the fiction of confessional uniformity. "I do not forget," he admitted in 1764, "that there is supposed to be only one religion in France and that all the laws assume so, but in reality there are two. The royal council is not unaware of this."[10] The royal

10. Paul Rabaut, "Discours au synode national tenu dans les hautes Cévennes du 4 au 10 mai 1756," in Albert Monod, *Les Sermons de Paul Rabaut, pasteur du désert, 1738–1785* (Paris, n.d.), 123; Christophe Pajol de Marcheval to Etienne-François Choi-

council, indeed, gradually acquiesced in the parlements' tacit legitimization of Protestant marriages during the 1760s and 1770s. The magistrates, intent upon consolidating their jurisdiction over marital cases and protecting property rights, declared these unions valid by natural law in spite of their nullity according to the statutes of the realm. They therefore dismissed the claims of relatives who contested the legitimacy of Protestant heirs in hopes of expropriating their estates. The pastor Jean Gal-Pomaret, for one, believed that the parlements were so favorably disposed toward his coreligionists that he feared Maupeou's suppression of the courts would result in renewed persecution.[11] Sporadic harassments notwithstanding, Rabaut could report in 1770 that "Protestant worship is tacitly tolerated." Ten years later one optimistic pamphleteer announced that "the cause of the Protestants has become that of all good citizens." Summarizing the situation in 1784, the baron de Breteuil, minister of the royal household, observed that the laws against nonconformity "will apparently never be expressly revoked. There might be drawbacks to doing this, but they will gradually fall or rather have already fallen into disuse, which will have the same effect."[12]

The draconian laws remained on the books, but the temporal authorities no longer enforced them systematically in the second half of the eighteenth century. Controversy during these decades focused

---

seul, March 24, 1764, quoted in Joseph Dedieu, *Histoire politique des protestants français* (2 vols.; Paris, 1925), II, 52. *Cf.* Louis Phélypeaux de Saint-Florentin, the minister responsible for the surveillance of the Protestants from 1725 to 1775, to Choiseul, January 18, 1763, in *BSHPF*, VI (1858), 77–80.

11. See his letters of May 4 and 6, 1771, to Antoine Gal-Ladevèze and Pierre Soulier, respectively, quoted in Emile du Cailar and Daniel Benoît, *Gal-Pomaret, pasteur de Ganges* (Paris, 1899), 152; Benoît, "Les Pasteurs et l'échafaud révolutionnaire: Pierre Soulier de Sauve, 1743–1794," *BSHPF*, XLIII (1894), 579.

12. Rabaut, Memoir dated October, 1770, addressed to Charles Juste de Beauvau, governor of Languedoc, in Rabaut's *Lettres à divers, 1744–1794*, ed. Charles Dardier (2 vols.; Paris, Grassart, 1892), II, 131; "Lettre de M. ***, avocat au parlement de Paris," in Marie-Jean-Antoine-Nicolas de Caritat de Condorcet (ed.), "Recueil de pièces sur l'état des protestants de France," in his *Oeuvres*, ed. A. Condorcet O'Connor and M.-F. Arago (12 vols.; Paris, 1847), V, 562; Louis-Auguste Le Tonnelier de Breteuil to le comte de Périgord, governor of Picardy, January 22, 1784, quoted in Dedieu, *Histoire politique*, II, 235.

not on abstruse doctrinal issues but on the thorny question of abrogating or at least modifying the existing legislation. Meridional Protestants demanded not only confirmation of their civil status, which would have been enough to satisfy their northern coreligionists, but also authorization of public worship, without which, they insisted, "there is no religion." Forbidden both to leave the kingdom and to live in accordance with their beliefs within its borders, they complained that the laws forced them, as the pastor Antoine Court put it, "to be wanting either in obedience to the Supreme Being or in submission to their sovereign."[13] Denouncing the linking of citizenship and Catholicity, Protestants urged the monarch to resolve this dilemma by providing some means of attesting births, marriages, and deaths without recourse to the Church and by allowing some form of collective exercise of "the so-called Reformed faith." They argued that they deserved these concessions because of their utility to the realm, their loyalty to the crown, the obligations of kingship, and the rights of conscience.

Rabaut and other Protestant leaders suspected that if Versailles acted favorably upon their petitions, "it will be out of political motives" and "not out of compassion for our sufferings or scruples of conscience for having violated our rights." They therefore emphasized not only the scriptural legitimacy but also the worldly advantages of toleration. Playing upon contemporary anxieties about depopulation and stagnation, they exaggerated the demographic and economic losses resulting from the emigration prompted by the revocation of the Edict of Nantes and suggested that a more enlightened religious policy would encourage both fecundity and productivity among the numerous subjects of "the so-called Reformed faith" remaining in the kingdom. In detailing these "political" considerations, the Protestant chevalier de Beaumont declared that "the need and welfare of the state are a law to which everything else yields." According to Court, "this spirit of patriotism," rather than the benighted bigotry of the past, "suits every true citizen."[14] When Protestants, like Jansenists, appealed to their fellow

13. "Réflexions sur la lettre que l'on suppose avoir été écrite à un gentilhomme protestant de Languedoc," in *La Nécessité du culte public parmi les chrétiens* . . . (2 vols.; Frankfurt, 1747), I, 402; [Antoine Court], *Lettre d'un patriote sur la tolérance civile des protestants de France* . . . (N.p., 1756), 118.

14. Rabaut, "Discours," in Monod, *Sermons*, 120; [Beaumont], *L'Accord parfait*, II, 200–201; [Court], *Lettre*, 47.

"citizens" in this manner, they effectively subordinated ecclesiastical to civil concerns and jurisdictions.

In their campaign for toleration, Protestants described themselves as loyal as well as useful subjects. They deplored the rebellion of the fanatical Camisards under Louis XIV, denied accusations of treasonous conduct during the midcentury wars, and repeatedly contrasted their own willingness to pay the *vingtième* with ecclesiastical opposition to that tax on grounds of conscience. Rabaut, for one, protested in 1751 "that the clergy do not wish to be constrained in their consciences and that they act against their principles in wishing that the Protestants should be constrained in theirs." Protestants denounced episcopal and Jesuitical ultramontanism while stressing their own obedience to the divinely ordained monarch "in all things in which God and conscience are not offended." Commenting on Romans 13 on the occasion of Louis XVI's coronation, Rabaut endorsed the traditional view that "the obligation of submission to civil authority does not derive merely from human conventions but also originates in the will of God, who created man to live in society and maintains him in a state of subordination."[15] Protestants maintained that the very assemblies that violated the letter of the law inculcated this lesson of fidelity to the Anointed of the Lord. Intent upon vindicating themselves from imputations of "republicanism," they made a point of demonstrating their devotion to the crown at the time of the attempted assassination of Louis XV and the coronation of Louis XVI.[16]

As productive and submissive subjects, Protestants insisted that they deserved the protection of royal justice and the status of French citizens. They regarded the Edict of Nantes as a sacred and perpetual covenant as inviolable as the Salic law governing succession to the throne. Arguing, like the Jansenists, that "no one should be deprived

15. Rabaut to Court, April 16, 1751, in Rabaut, *Lettres à Antoine Court, 1739–1755*, ed. Charles Dardier (2 vols.; Paris, 1884), II, 134; First National Synod (May 16, 1726), in Edmond Hugues (ed.), *Les Synodes du désert: Actes et règlements des synodes nationaux et provinciaux tenus au désert de France de l'an 1715 à l'an 1793* (3 vols.; Paris, 1885–86), I, 54; [Rabaut], *Discours prononcé au désert à l'occasion du couronnement de Louis XVI* (En Languedoc, 1775), 17.

16. See Rabaut's "Lettre circulaire," dated January 15, 1757, *BSHPF*, V (1857), 319–23, and John Woodbridge, "La Conspiration du prince de Conti, 1755–1757," *XVIIIe siècle*, XVII (1985), 97–110.

and stripped of his rights and privileges without some serious cause on his part," they alleged that the clergy had duped Louis XIV into revoking the edict. This unjust and imprudent concession to fanaticism endangered their lives, threatened their property, and burdened their consciences. To rectify the Sun King's blunder, the pastor Jeanbon Saint-André suggested, his successors had only to recognize that in order "to claim the sovereign's protection it is not necessary to share his religion." While invoking the Most Christian King's obligation to rule justly, Protestants exhorted him to enhance his claim to that title by treating adherents of "the so-called Reformed faith" with mercy and charity. In a more subtle reference to his spiritual responsibilities, Beaumont indicated that the monarch could promote the salvation of his non-Catholic subjects more effectively by permitting them to worship the Lord in their own manner than by forcing them "to live without religion in the midst of a Most Christian Kingdom."[17]

Disavowing "philosophic" indifference in religious matters, Protestants endeavored to convince the crown that genuine confessional uniformity was unattainable and that coercion produced only hypocritical conformity. They reminded their sovereign, furthermore, that he had no authority over the consciences of his subjects, who answered to God alone for their beliefs. As the pastor Frédéric-Guillaume de La Broue explained, temporal power could punish misdeeds but not beliefs "unrelated to the duty of citizens." "What does it matter to the state," he asked, "whether I think one way or another, as long as I render to it and to society that which I owe them?" The faith of law-abiding men and women, according to Protestants, remained a private concern immune from public scrutiny. Failure to acknowledge this truth, not the fact of pluralism itself, caused the religious disorders that had troubled the realm since the time of the Reformation. Error, in short, was not a crime, because Catholicity, in the words of the pastor Rabaut Saint-Etienne, was not "the essential and distinctive character of the French kingdom."[18] Because birth, not baptism,

---

17. [Court,] *Le Patriote français et impartial* . . . (N.p., 1751), 48; Jeanbon Saint-André, "Considérations sur l'organisation civile des protestants," in Michel Nicolas, *Jeanbon Saint-André: Sa vie et ses écrits* (Paris, 1848), 280; [Beaumont], *L'Accord parfait*, II, 184.
   18. [Frédéric-Guillaume de La Broue], *Esprit de Jésus Christ sur la tolérance* . . .

made the French citizen a French citizen, Protestants maintained that civil status was distinct from and not dependent on religious conformity. The crown had established the abusive conjunction of citizenship and Catholicity, so the crown, which had previously recognized the rights of Protestants between 1598 and 1685, could and should disestablish it.

While Protestants questioned some of the basic assumptions of the traditional order, their adversaries warned against "tolerationism" conducive to religious indifference and political insubordination. Catholic apologists no longer called upon the Eldest Son of the Church to put heretics to the sword, but they still advocated what Liévin-Bonaventure Proyart described as "that just and prudent intolerance which unites all members of the state in the same worship and laws." They assured the monarch, on the one hand, that he had "as much right as he had interest" in preserving religious uniformity. They reminded him, on the other hand, that "the ancestral faith and received worship are possessions which cannot be tampered with without endangering the constitution of the state." In refuting Protestants, like Jansenists, defenders of orthodoxy emphasized the king's obligation to protect the Church but denied his authority to meddle in spiritual affairs or disregard the religious traditions of the kingdom. They argued that the sovereign—fortunately powerless "to alter the forms consecrated by divine authority" and sanctioned by his predecessors— could not separate the registration of birth, marriage, and death from the sacraments without transgressing upon ecclesiastical jurisdiction and undermining Catholicism.[19]

Opponents of toleration, of course, contradicted all of the arguments advanced in its favor. They accused Protestants of exaggerating the detrimental effects of the policy followed by the crown since 1685 and refused to relinquish religious unity for the sake of utilitarian considerations. It would not be wise, Novi de Caveirac cautioned, "for

---

(N.p., 1760), 95, 98; [Jean-Pierre Rabaut Saint-Etienne], *Le Roi doit modifier les lois portées contre les protestants* (London, 1784), 61.

19. [Liévin-Bonaventure Proyart], *Lettre à un magistrat du parlement de Paris sur l'édit concernant l'état civil des protestants* (Avignon, 1787), 14; *Lettres théologiques, historiques, et politiques sur la forme des mariage* . . . (Paris, 1765), xx; Novi de Caveirac, *Apologie de Louis XIV*, 359.

France to risk losing its faith, its law, and its king for a few more farmers or artisans." The intransigent abbé Bouniol de Montégut, who berated Protestants for "parading the name of citizen," maintained that even if intolerance involved some "political" disadvantages, the Church had every right to demand such a "passing sacrifice" from the state. Catholic apologists also dismissed Protestant professions of "patriotism" and loyalty to the crown. They contended that "the spirit of rebellion which has in all times characterized the Protestants is not yet extinguished among those of this realm," as demonstrated by the seditious assemblies "in the wilderness."[20] "The so-called Reformed faith," they warned, inevitably encouraged rebellion against both of the two powers ordained by God for the ordering of life in this world. It not only sanctioned independent judgment in religious matters but also nurtured "republican" sentiments in its adherents. Hostile pamphleteers commonly charged that the unruly Protestants had extorted the Edict of Nantes from Henry IV and maintained that Louis XIV rightly reasserted royal authority by revoking it.

The case against toleration, in the last analysis, rested upon the conviction that Catholicism was the one true faith and the presumption that the true faith alone was entitled to the privileges of publicity in the Christian kingdom. Opponents of toleration did not acknowledge the extensive rights of "conscience" claimed by Protestants, who "constantly confounded error and truth," according to Novi de Caveirac, "under the auspices of this honorable term." At the same time, they supported the retention of legal sanctions against their misguided fellow subjects, as the same apologist explained, "not because they refuse to believe but because they refuse to remain silent." The king "by the grace of God" could not compel French men and women to accept the doctrines of the national Church, but he could prohibit and punish external manifestations of nonconformity. In doing so, he discharged his sacred vow to expel heretics from the kingdom and fulfilled his paternal obligation to promote the salvation of his people.

20. *Le Secret révélé ou lettre à un magistrat de province sur les protestants* (N.p., n.d.), 38; Novi de Caveirac, *Apologie de Louis XIV*, 267; [Antoine-François Bouniol de Montégut], *La Voix du vrai patriote catholique opposée à celle des faux patriotes tolérants* (N.p., 1756), 1, 59; *Dissertation sur la tolérance des protestants . . .* (France, n.d.), i.

Convinced that two religions could not coexist in France, Charles-Louis Richard concluded that "the Most Christian Kings have the right to repress errors contrary to the faith. To contest this on the pretext that these errors do not offend the civil and political laws is to display a profound ignorance of their authority and their duties."[21] Because they regarded religious orthodoxy as a public necessity directly related to the worldly welfare of society, they considered pluralism unthinkable in the realm of Clovis, Charlemagne, and Saint Louis.

While Protestants, like their Jansenist "first cousins," debated the civil consequences of nonconformity with defenders of orthodoxy, jurists elaborated the views that eventually led the monarchy to unlink citizenship and Catholicity on the eve of the Revolution.[22] Magistrates and administrators alike expressed concern about the flagrant disparity between the laws banning "the so-called Reformed faith" in France and the existence of some half million of its adherents in the kingdom. In assessing the options available to the crown, they explored the uses of the presumption of Catholicity as well as the feasibility of legitimizing Protestant unions. Parlementaires and royal councillors, many of them involved in some capacity in other disputes with the clergy, expounded a broad interpretation of temporal prerogatives in religious matters. In particular, they developed the case for the separation of the contract involved in marriage from the sacrament of matrimony. While supporting the restitution of legal identity to Protestants, most of them nonetheless rejected demands for liberty of worship. They accepted the innovative argument that inward beliefs were irrelevant to civil status but also endorsed the traditional assumption that outward pluralism was contrary to public order.

This compromise concerning the extent of toleration developed out of administrative experience as well as juridical considerations. In return for their vigorous efforts to disperse assemblies "in the wilderness" in the 1750s, royal agents in southern France asked the bishops

---

21. Novi de Caveirac, *Mémoire politico-critique où l'on examine s'il est de l'intérêt de l'église et de l'état d'établir pour les calvinistes du royaume une nouvelle forme de se marier* . . . (N.p., 1756), 126; Novi de Caveirac, *Apologie de Louis XIV*, 450; [Charles-Louis Richard], *Les Protestants déboutés de leur prétentions* . . . (Brussels, 1776), 13.

22. *Mémoires secrets pour servir à l'histoire de la république des lettres en France depuis 1762 jusqu'à nos jours* (36 vols.; London, 1777–89), XXIV, 230.

to abandon the qualifications of legitimacy and the exaction of abjurations that (they assumed) had caused Protestants to refuse baptism and marriage in the Church. Invoking the fiction of confessional uniformity, the intendant Saint-Priest condemned these troublesome practices as indefensible departures from the canons regulating "the external and public administration of the sacraments" to which all French subjects, as Catholics, were entitled.[23] This line of reasoning bore more than accidental resemblance to that advanced by critics of *Unigenitus* during the contemporaneous controversy over the *billets de confession*. Saint-Priest cited parlementary remonstrances of January, 1751, in arguing that the clergy could not prejudice the status of subjects whom the law recognized as Catholics by denying them access to the sacraments that defined civil identity on the grounds that they embraced the errors of a sect which by law no longer existed in France. Bishops retorted, much as they did to parlementaires opposed to the bull, by denouncing secular interference in spiritual affairs.

Although attention focused on the last rites in the case of the Jansenists and on marriage in the case of the Protestants, the question of jurisdiction over the disposition of the sacraments remained, as Malesherbes commented, "absolutely the same." Royal policy toward both groups of nonconformists shifted in the following years, but in the early 1750s, the crown condemned the parlements' efforts to compel ecclesiastics "to give communion to Jansenists without examination" and at the same time pressured the clergy "to marry Protestants without tests."[24] Parlementary resistance to *Unigenitus*, after all, challenged the king's authority, while Saint-Priest's plan, sanctioned by Versailles in instructions of 1752 to the duc de Richelieu, governor of Languedoc, offered a means of resolving the vexing problem of "the so-called Reformed faith" in the Midi.[25] Richelieu himself acknowl-

23. FF, Vol. 7046, fol. 295. For similar differences between bishops and intendants at the end of the seventeenth century, see Jean Lemoine (ed.), *Mémoires des évêques de France sur la conduite à tenir à l'égard des réformés (1698)* (Paris, 1902).

24. [Malesherbes], *Mémoire*, 94; [Claude Carloman de Rulhière], *Eclaircissements historiques sur les causes de la révocation de l'édit de Nantes . . .* (2 vols.; Geneva, 1788), II, 315.

25. Louis-François-Armand de Plessis de Richelieu's instructions, dated October

edged that "religion requires some deference to the sentiments of the bishops with respect to the administration of the sacraments" to Protestants, but he insisted that "the political order, the public welfare, and the most sacred bonds of society demand a certain, invariable, and uniform law to secure the status of such a large number of subjects of the king." As Rabaut suspected, the representatives of the crown understood "as well as we do how important it is for the state that our marriages and our births be authenticated."[26]

Given the inconclusive outcome of Saint-Priest's and Richelieu's negotiations with the bishops, the government asked the former attorney general Guillaume-François Joly de Fleury for his analysis of the Protestant problem. It was Joly de Fleury, according to Malesherbes, who had arranged the incorporation of the presumption of Catholicity into the declaration of 1724, so as "to subject the clergy to the Parlement with respect to the administration of the sacraments." He composed his memoir concerning the Protestants while serving on the royal commission appointed in 1752 to adjudicate differences between the magistrates and prelates over *Unigenitus*. Joly de Fleury argued that the king, as External Bishop, should protect both Protestants and Jansenists against unjust exclusion from the sacraments, those "common possessions which the Church accords to all the faithful." Like Saint-Priest, he contended that priests could neither require uncanonical abjurations before performing marriages nor comment on the legitimacy of infants presented to them for baptism, since they were not by law "judges of the status of men."[27] Since natural law allowed French subjects to marry regardless of their spiritual dispositions, Joly de Fleury suggested that Protestants register their marriages with notaries if the clergy refused to cooperate.

Most jurists agreed with the author of an anonymous memoir of

---

18, 1752, in Charles Coquerel, *Histoire des églises du désert chez les protestants en France* (2 vols.; Paris, 1841), II, 79.

26. Richelieu to Guillaume de Lamoignon de Blancmesnil, November 13, 1752, in FF, Vol. 7046, fols. 325–25 v.; Rabaut to Court, January, 1751, in Rabaut, *Lettres à Antoine Court*, II, 14.

27. Malesherbes, "Développement du système politique de l'auteur de la déclaration de 1724," in FF, Vol. 7047, fol. 647; Joly de Fleury, Memoir excerpted in [Malesherbes], *Mémoire*, 181, 139. For the complete text see JF, Vol. 1671, fols. 144–245.

1752 that "laws founded on illusions are indecent for the legislator and cannot be useful for the people" and therefore did not rely on the fiction of uniformity in the way that Joly de Fleury did.[28] Jean-Pierre-François Ripert de Monclar, attorney general of the Parlement of Aix, shared Joly de Fleury's Gallican sentiments but urged the crown in 1755 to discard the presumption of Catholicity by allowing adherents of the "so-called Reformed faith" to register births, marriages, and deaths before royal judges instead of hostile ecclesiastics. He argued that the king had the authority to alter the formalities for the attestation of marriages, in particular, because the "purely human contract" between man and woman antedated and was consequently separable from the sacrament of matrimony administered by the Church. Insisting that the French monarchs had adequately acquitted themselves of their obligation to exterminate heresy through decades of persecution, Ripert de Monclar urged the government to restore the civil rights of Protestants, who, like other subjects who "labor, trade, populate the realm, and pay taxes to the state, are entitled to the character of fathers, mothers, children, citizens."[29]

The royal councillor Pierre Gilbert de Voisins, who drafted his plan for fixing the legal status of Protestants a dozen years later at the request of the crown, also dismissed the presumption of Catholicity but advised Louis XV against the administrative innovation suggested by Ripert de Monclar. He feared that any formal abrogation of the declaration of 1724 would embarrass the government by making "a striking contrast with what was done in the dissolution of the Society of Jesus." Describing France as a kingdom "where the Catholic faith we profess has been, so to speak, incorporated into the state," he distanced himself from those who ventured to ask "whether it would not be better for society if the political order and religion constituted

28. "Mémoire inédit d'un homme d'état sur la question des mariages protestants et de la tolérance," *BSHPF*, IX (1860), 449. The most ingenious proposal for extending toleration to Protestants by means of juridical fictions involved their naturalization as Alsatians so they could enjoy the privileges conceded to their coreligionists in that province at the time of its annexation by Louis XIV. See the "Mémoire sur l'état des protestants de France," in FF, Vol. 10628, fols. 6–34.

29. [Jean-Pierre-François Ripert de Monclar], *Mémoire théologique et politique au sujet des mariages clandestins des protestants de France . . .* (N.p., 1755), 81, 62.

separate objects." Gilbert de Voisins accordingly recommended that priests should continue to record births and marriages in their capacity as public officers but specified that the monarch should instruct them to discharge this function without regard to the religious affiliation of the subjects who appeared before them. "There is nothing in all this," he declared, "which is not within the power of the king." The archbishop of Narbonne, asked to comment on Gilbert de Voisins' memoir, objected to his interpretation of secular prerogatives in sacramental matters. The governor of Languedoc, on the other hand, not only questioned the practicality of the compromise that Gilbert de Voisins had proposed but also challenged the traditional principles that he had respected: "Why can there not be more than one religion in France? How is the Catholic faith ultimately connected with the constitution of the state?"[30]

Louis XV, in the end, did not secure the legal identity of Protestants by directing the clergy to register their births, marriages, and deaths or by institutionalizing some alternative to clerical registration. It became clear before the end of his reign, however, that Versailles meant to ignore the bishops' tiresome complaints about nonenforcement of the legislation against nonconformity. The monarchy clarified its position somewhat in 1767–1768 when it intervened in the Sorbonne's deliberations concerning the condemnation of Marmontel's *Bélisaire* on the grounds that the novel preached religious indifference. Intent upon checking ecclesiastical pretensions in the aftermath of the contentious assembly of 1765, the crown forced the theologians to accept its own revision of the article in their censure on the subject of toleration, a matter it characterized as "essentially within the jurisdiction of civil administration." Louis XV acknowledged his obligation to protect the Catholic faith but reminded the Sorbonne that it was not for the Church to dictate the manner in which he fulfilled this obligation. Having recently endorsed the parlementary criticism of the dis-

30. Pierre Gilbert de Voisins, "Observations," in Ser. TT, Vol. 463, fol. 2, AN; [Gilbert de Voisins], *Mémoires sur les moyens de donner aux protestants un état civil en France . . .* , (Paris, 1787), 41, 93, 115 (written in 1767); Beauvau, "Observations sur le mémoire concernant les protestants," in TT, Vol. 463, fol. 71, AN. *Cf.* Beauvau's "Mémoires," in Marie-Charlotte de Rohan-Chabot de Beauvau, *Souvenirs* (Paris, 1872), 89–90.

cussion of refusals of sacraments in the *Acts* of 1765, he explicitly renounced temporal prosecution of "errors that are not manifested by any outward indication."[31]

Shortly after his accession to the throne, Louis XVI, acting on the advice of conservative councillors, responded to the complaints of the archbishop of Auch by ordering the destruction of a Protestant church illegally erected in his diocese. The abbé de Véri nonetheless commented optimistically on the progress of toleration "among the administrators charged with the execution of the laws" and noted that "even a great many bishops close their eyes with respect to the Protestants." Encouraged by the appointments of Turgot and Malesherbes to the ministry, Rabaut assured his coreligionists in 1774 that "the system of toleration has been adopted by our new king."[32] The comptroller general, who had written pamphlets in favor of toleration while studying theology at the Sorbonne and had dealt leniently with Protestants as intendant of Limoges, did extend a measure of recognition to pastors for the first time by asking them, as well as parish priests, to preach against disobedience during the subsistence riots of 1775.[33] He failed, however, to persuade Louis XVI to replace the controversial clause in the coronation oath concerning the expulsion of heretics with the words, "All the churches of my realm should count on my protection and justice."[34]

31. Saint-Florentin to the assembly of the clergy, January 24, 1768, in John Renwick, *Marmontel, Voltaire, and the Bélisaire Affair,* Studies on Voltaire and the Eighteenth Century, CXXI (1974), 381; "Governmental Thesis on Intolerance," *ibid.,* 378.

32. Joseph-Antoine de Véri, *Journal,* ed. Jehan-Caspar-Marie de Witte (2 vols.; Paris, 1928), I, 236; Rabaut to Durieux, September 26, 1774, in Vol. 314, fol. 231, PF.

33. See "Première démarche officielle du gouvernement de Louis XVI auprès des pasteurs du bas Languedoc," *BSHPF,* IX (1860), 457–58; Rabaut to Anne-Robert-Jacques Turgot, May 29, 1775, in Rabaut, *Lettres à divers,* II, 187–90.

34. Anne-Robert-Jacques Turgot, *Oeuvres,* ed. Gustave Schelle (5 vols.; Paris, 1913–23), IV, 551. The source of the familiar story about Louis XVI's mumbling of the clause concerning the expulsion of heretics is the biography of Turgot by his friend Pierre-Samuel Dupont de Nemours. The story, however, appears in neither the 1782 original nor the 1788 revision, but only in the version included in Dupont's edition of Turgot's works, published more than thirty years after the fact: *Oeuvres de M. Turgot* (9 vols.; Paris, 1808–11), I, 220. Anne-Emmanuel-Ferdinand-François de Croy, who recorded the most detailed eyewitness account of the coronation, specifically noted in

Resistance within the ministry, disagreement between northern and southern Protestants, and opposition from the assembly of the clergy of 1775 thwarted Turgot's efforts to restore the civil rights of adherents of the "so-called Reformed faith." The bishops reiterated their hostility to "tolerationism capable of weakening the throne and plunging France again into the gravest misfortunes." They admonished the king to discharge the vow he had taken at Reims by completing the work of confessional unification undertaken by Louis XIV and continued by Louis XV. They also condemned the tracts on Protestant marriages, which they suspected Turgot had authorized, in which the Jansenist Louis Guidi argued that "in order to be French it is not necessary to be Catholic." Two years after Turgot's departure from the ministry, Anne-Charles-René de Bretignières exhorted his colleagues in the Parlement of Paris to recommend on behalf of the Protestants the establishment of some "legal means of assuring the status of their offspring." Yielding to clerical pressure, the crown instructed the magistrates to discontinue their deliberations on this sensitive question. Louis XVI, however, subsequently promulgated the edict of May 12, 1782, which forbade priests to record any "personal opinion" regarding the legitimacy of newborn children in the parish registers along with the facts of parentage.[35] The monarchy based this prohibition, which provoked repeated protests from the clergy, not on the fiction of uniformity but rather on the premise that the certification of births was a secular matter distinct from the administration of the sacrament of baptism and therefore subject to royal directives.[36] Be-

---

his *Journal inédit*, ed. Emmanuel-Henry de Grouchy and Paul Cottin (4 vols.; Paris, 1906), III, 183, that the king pronounced his oaths "loudly and deliberately."

35. PV, VIII/2, *Pièces justificatives*, 713; [Guidi], *Suite du dialogue sur le mariage des protestants . . .* (N.p., 1776), 27; "Récit de ce qui s'est passé le 15 décembre 1778 à l'assemblée des chambres du parlement de Paris," in Condorcet (ed.), "Recueil de pièces," in his *Oeuvres*, V, 399; *Déclaration du roi*, May 12, 1782, in *Recueil général*, XXVII, 190.

36. For ecclesiastical protests see *Procès-verbal de l'assemblée générale du clergé de France tenue à Paris au couvent des Grands Augustins en l'année 1782* (Paris, 1783), 186–90; *Procès-verbal de l'assemblée générale du clergé de France tenue à Paris au couvent des Grands Augustins en l'année 1785 et continuée en l'année 1786* (Paris, 1789), 1070–79; "Procès-verbal de l'assemblée générale du clergé de France tenue à Paris

cause the declaration did not divorce the two functions in practice, however, Rabaut Saint-Etienne dismissed it as "an ordinance of priests who do not want to give up their prerogatives."[37]

Malesherbes, who had already secured a decision embodying the substance of the edict of 1782 from the royal council during his tenure in the Turgot ministry, composed a number of memoirs urging the crown to complete the disjunction of civil and religious identities by allowing non-Catholics to marry before royal judges. Aware of Louis XVI's unwillingness to break openly with tradition, he attempted to convince the king that Louis XIV had not intended "that any of his subjects should have as a Protestant a civil status different from that of other citizens." Malesherbes based his case, already outlined by Jansenist pamphleteers, on the decree of September 15, 1685, which allowed pastors to marry Protestants in the presence of royal judges. He noted that the Sun King had not specifically revoked this decree along with the Edict of Nantes and argued that none of the subsequent laws, which invoked the presumption of Catholicity and therefore did not apply to adherents of "the so-called Reformed faith," had invalidated it. He accordingly assured Louis XVI that he could legitimize Protestant marriages in France without offense to his great-great-great-grandfather's memory and without trespassing upon ecclesiastical jurisdiction. Malesherbes urged him to do so without consulting either the magistrates, who had forced Louis XV's hand in the affair of the Jesuits, or the bishops. "It is an illusion," the former minister knew from experience, "to believe that one could ever extort from the clergy as a body a deliberation favorable to the Protestants."[38]

After the publication of Malesherbes' influential memoirs in 1785–1786, other proponents of toleration reiterated his ingenious reading of the legislation regarding "the so-called Reformed faith." The Jansenist magistrate Pierre-Auguste Robert de Saint-Vincent referred to the decree of September 15, 1685, when he raised the question of the civil status of Protestants again in the Parlement of Paris in February,

---

au couvent des Grands Augustins en l'année 1788," in Ser. G8*, Vol. 706, fols. 189–96, AN.

37. Rabaut Saint-Etienne, letter dated August 9, 1782, in Vol. 367, no. 18, PF.

38. [Malesherbes], *Mémoire*, 63; Malesherbes, "Mémoire sur les affaires de religion (1776)," in FF, Vol. 10627, fol. 12.

1787.[39] This veteran of the midcentury disputes about refusals of sacraments, who blamed the revocation of the Edict of Nantes as well as the suppression of Port-Royal on the Jesuits, appealed to the king to regularize the Protestant marriages that the magistrates had tacitly legitimized for twenty years. Louis XVI, according to Rabaut Saint-Etienne, was displeased "that the Parlement wished to dictate to him what he intended to do himself."[40] Several months later, the second committee of the Assembly of Notables passed Lafayette's motion, seconded by Malesherbes' nephew César-Guillaume de la Luzerne, bishop of Langres, calling upon the king to end the unjust and impolitic proscription of Protestants in France.[41] By this time Malesherbes himself had rejoined the ministry without portfolio to draft the long-awaited "edict concerning those who do not profess the Catholic faith," which the crown submitted to the magistrates in November.

Acknowledging that he could not unite all of his people in the ancestral faith of the realm, Louis XVI explained in this edict that considerations of justice and "the interest of our kingdom" had led him to resolve the "dangerous contradictions between the rights of nature and the dispositions of the laws" by assuring the civil status of non-Catholics. Although he did not allow Protestants to assume any collective identity or engage in public worship, as they had under the Edict of Nantes, the king now permitted them to register births, marriages, and deaths before parish priests *or* royal judges. He did not require them to receive pastoral benediction for their marriages and specifically authorized adherents of sects that did not practice baptism to attest the births of their children without reference to that sacrament. Louis XVI still hoped for the eventual conversion of his nonconforming subjects, but he essentially disavowed any responsibility for effecting that spiritual "revolution," which he left in the hands of providence.[42] The crown, in short, discarded the fiction of confessional uniformity

---

39. For the text of Pierre-Augustin Robert de Saint-Vincent's address, delivered on February 9, 1787, see *BSHPF*, V (1857), 423–44.

40. Rabaut Saint-Etienne, "Lettre-rapport à Messieurs les membres du comité de Bordeaux," February 12, 1788, in Rabaut, *Lettres à divers*, II, 400.

41. For the text of the motion see "Correspondance de Lafayette, Paul Rabaut, Rabaut Saint-Etienne, et Poitevin (1785–1788)," *BSHPF*, III (1855), 344.

42. *Déclaration du roi*, November, 1787, in *Recueil général*, XXVIII, 472–73.

along with the conjunction of citizenship and Catholicity but maintained the prohibition of outward manifestations of pluralism, such that the Protestants gained legal recognition but not religious liberty.

The edict disturbed some magistrates, displeased many bishops, and disappointed most Protestants. Chancellor Lamoignon assured the magistrates at the *lit de justice* of November 19 that it only granted "toleration confined to the most incontestable rights of human nature," not to be confused with "culpable indifference for all faiths." During the Parlementary debates, however, the outspoken Jean-Jacques Duval d'Eprémesnil charged that the edict undermined Catholicism. The duc de Mortemart defended the declaration by explaining that it merely recognized non-Catholics as citizens without favoring their beliefs. The abbé Lecoigneux responded to critics who wished to refer the Protestant problem to the Estates General by insisting that the sovereign, as "sole legislator," "can make without the assistance of the nation whatever laws of *police* he deems necessary, and this is one of these." The judges formulated remonstrances concerning some two dozen points in the edict before they registered it at the end of January, 1788, after Louis XVI accepted a number of the modifications they had suggested. He directed Catholics, for example, to register births, marriages, and deaths only through participation in the rituals of the Church and also renewed the exclusion of Protestants from some public offices. At the same time, the crown ignored the magistrates' objection to the dissociation of birth and baptism, which they described as "an absolutely necessary sacrament."[43]

The clergy, too, deplored this innovation, which implied renunciation of the monarch's duty to promote the salvation of his subjects by ensuring their reception of "the most necessary of the sacraments." They likewise protested that it was "unworthy of a Most Christian King" to allow "a wholly profane celebration of marriage" in his realm. Although some bishops applauded the declaration, the extraordinary assembly of the clergy of 1788 complained that it sanctioned "univer-

43. *Gazette de Leyde*, December 7, 1787, and December 21, 1787, supplement; *Les Remontrances*, III, 699. For the royal reply to the remonstrances see pp. 701–702. On the registration of the edict by the provincial parlements, some of which opposed it more vigorously than the Parisian magistrates did, see Léonce Anquez, *De l'état civil des réformés de France* (Paris, 1868), 238–49.

sal tolerationism" in that it permitted every individual "to invent a religion after his liking." Describing Catholicism as "the foundation of the French constitution," the assembly reminded the king that his vow to expel heretics from the kingdom meant that he could not "grant the rights of citizenship in his domains to heretics recognized and condemned by the Church."[44] The prelates insisted that the monarch could and should restrict civil rights to French subjects who embraced the national faith. They accordingly refused to cooperate in recording births, marriages, and deaths in the manner prescribed by the edict. The bishop of La Rochelle ventured to denounce "this law which seems to confuse all faiths indiscriminately" in a pastoral instruction of February 26, 1788. The crown quickly suppressed this instruction for publicly "misrepresenting the purity of His Majesty's intentions for the maintenance of the Catholic faith in his domains."[45]

While the clergy objected that the edict granted Protestants much more than the minimal rights they deserved, Rabaut Saint-Etienne, who had worked closely with Malesherbes during the drafting of the legislation, lamented that it gave them only that which they had already "possessed for many years" through tacit toleration. Dismayed by "the dwarfish steps being taken in the reform of the laws," he cautioned his coreligionists against demanding further concessions too vociferously yet hoped that authorization of public worship would follow the restoration of legal status. In criticizing the limited character of the toleration outlined in the declaration, he rejected the very notion of a national faith, "because the state is not a religious but a civil entity." "No religion," he protested, "should be dominant." While scorning the option of recourse to the established Church, Rabaut Saint-Etienne and other pastors reminded their congregations that

---

44. *Remontrances du clergé de France au roi sur l'édit du mois de novembre 1787 concernant les noncatholiques* (Paris, 1788), 17; "Inconvénients de la permission que le roi accorderait à ses sujets de célébrer leurs mariages devant les magistrats et dans une forme purement civile," in Vol. 8, unpaginated, PF; *Remontrances du clergé,* 12; "Mémoire du clergé contre les protestants," in Ser. TT, Vol. 463, fols. 13, 8, AN; "Procès-verbal" (1788), in Ser. G8*, Vol. 706, fol. 237, AN. For the royal reply to the remonstrances, see Ser. G8*, Vol. 706, fols. 477–78.

45. François-Joseph-Emmanuel de Crussol d'Uzès, *Mandement,* February 26, 1788, *BSHPF,* VII (1858), 158; *Arrêt du conseil,* April 3, 1788, *ibid.* 168.

registration of births and marriages before royal judges did not "release them from the obligations which religion imposes upon them in this regard." The baptism of newborn children remained "absolutely necessary," and couples could not in conscience "neglect the ecclesiastical benediction of their marriages."[46] Protestants welcomed the secularization of civil status but, like the magistrates and the clergy, shunned "philosophic" indifference in religious matters.

The edict of 1787, which failed to fulfill the expectations of the nonconformists whose existence it legalized, engendered one last crop of pamphlets on the subject of toleration. According to critics like the abbé Jacques-Julien Bonnaud, the declaration represented "the complete subversion of the constitution," because it disrupted the linking of religious and civil concerns, which guaranteed the order as well as the orthodoxy of the realm. They not only denounced the Protestants for threatening royal sovereignty but also challenged the crown's authority to "tolerate in his domains errors which the Church condemns." Supporters of the new legislation, meanwhile, repeated the argument that Louis XVI had not sanctioned error as such by recognizing that non-Catholics "cannot be deprived of any temporal possession on the grounds of their belief alone." Applauding the resolution of what the Jansenist lawyer Henri Jabineau called the "absurd contradiction" between "maintaining the law" and "tolerating its violation," they insisted that the king had both the authority and the obligation to assure the civil status of his Protestant subjects. Most of these pamphleteers, at the same time, agreed with their adversaries that "the character of citizen" did not imply the right "to profess publicly a religion different from that which is the national religion."[47] Less

---

46. Rabaut Saint-Etienne, "Instructions aux pasteurs de Languedoc au sujet de l'édit de tolérance," *BSHPF*, XXXVI (1887), 548; Rabaut Saint-Etienne, "Lettre sur l'édit de tolérance de 1787," *ibid.*, XXXIII (1884), 363; Rabaut Saint-Etienne, "Lettre-rapport," in Rabaut, *Lettres à divers*, II, 396; Rabaut Saint-Etienne to Malesherbes, February 10, 1788, quoted in Pierre Grosclaude, "Malesherbes et Rabaut Saint-Etienne: Une correspondance inédite," *BSHPF*, CVI (1960), 9; Rabaut Saint-Etienne, "Instructions," 551.

47. [Jacques-Julien Bonaud], *Discours à lire au conseil en présence du roi par un ministre patriote sur le projet d'accorder l'état civil aux protestants* (2 vols.; n.p., 1787), I, 3; *M. Turgot réfuté par lui-même sur la tolérance civile* (N.p., n.d.), 19; *L'Etat civil pour les noncatholiques de France justifié . . .* (N.p., 1788), 34; [Henri Jabineau], *Lettre*

demanding than the Protestants themselves, they endorsed the distinction between marriages and assemblies that had guided royal policy ever since the midcentury troubles in Languedoc.

While critics and supporters of the edict "concerning those who do not profess the Catholic faith" debated its merits, jurists confronted a number of problems regarding its implementation. Did the declaration, for example, particularly the provisions that liberalized access to trades and offices, apply not only to Protestants but also to Jews, legally expelled from France in 1615? Protestants had some reason to envy Jews before 1787, insofar as the latter not only registered births, marriages, and deaths according to their own rites but also enjoyed communal autonomy and maintained synagogues in some parts of the realm. The situation of the Jews, however, was hardly enviable in other respects, given the economic prohibitions and juridical disabilities that segregated them from the rest of the population. Excluded from citizenship like the Protestants, they were not even considered French subjects, with the exception of the more assimilated Sephardim of southwestern France. While denying the presence of Protestants in the kingdom, the crown recognized the Sephardim as Jews rather than "newly converted Christians" in 1723 and confirmed the commercial privileges of these "good, useful, and loyal subjects" in 1776.[48] When the monarchy recognized the less fortunate Ashkenazim of Alsace as Jews in 1784, it also codified the restrictions defining their separate and unequal condition. Objects of statutory discrimination rather than systematic repression, Jews were not subject to the same sacramental prescriptions or sporadic persecutions as Protestants, but they too played a role in the debates about toleration preceding and surrounding the edict of 1787.

The celebrated case of Borach Lévi, for example, centered on the same sacramental issues involved in the disputes about Jansenism and Protestantism. Lévi, Alsatian by birth, took up residence in Paris in 1751 and sought instruction in the Christian faith. With the backing

---

d'un magistrat de province à M. *** (N.p., n.d.), 14; *Du mariage des chrétiens ou la nouvelle loi sur l'état civil des noncatholiques de France justifié* . . . (N.p., 1788), 134–35.

48. *Déclaration du roi*, June 8, 1776, in *Recueil général*, XXIV, 45.

of archbishop Christophe de Beaumont, the curé of Saint Sulpice refused to baptize him, evidently suspecting that he wished to abandon
Judaism only in order to abandon his Jewish wife. Lévi served the
uncooperative priest with a summons and commissioned an appeal to
the parlement. His lawyers insisted that he had satisfied the canonical
conditions for baptism and accordingly denounced the curé for depriving him arbitrarily of this sacrament and of the civil rights he would
have enjoyed as a Catholic. In France, they pointed out, "it is by baptism that one is made a citizen and made capable of all the effects of
citizenship, such that the refusal of baptism entails exclusion from legal status and the loss of the privileges of citizenship." Unmoved by
this transparent adaptation of parlementary arguments against the
withholding of sacraments from Jansenists, the attorney general Joly
de Fleury gave the bailiff who delivered the summons "a good talking-
to," and the magistrates dismissed the appeal.[49] Having convinced another parish priest to baptize him, Lévi initiated divorce proceedings
in Alsace with the intention of taking a Christian wife. He argued that
the laws of the realm did not recognize his first marriage and appealed
once again for civil intervention when the ecclesiastical court of Strasbourg decided against him. The Parisian magistrates agreed with
Lévi's lawyers that matrimonial cases fell under secular jurisdiction,
but they rejected his suit. They ruled that marriage outside the
Church was both valid by natural law and indissoluble in the Christian
kingdom, the same grounds they later cited in legitimizing Protestant
unions contracted "in the wilderness."

Jews, regarded as aliens, encountered more unmasked hostility and
enjoyed less de facto protection than Jansenists and Protestants.
When Louis XV set aside guild restrictions on the acquisition of mas-
terships in 1767 in order to stimulate commerce, the guilds of Paris
remonstrated that Jews, who lacked "the qualities of citizens," were
not French and therefore were not eligible for these positions, even
though the king had specifically mentioned foreigners in the edict. Insisting that Jews born and resident in the realm who obeyed the laws
and paid their taxes were indeed French subjects, the lawyer Lacratelle suggested that "the real question in this case is whether Jews are

49. *Actes et pièces servant de mémoire à consulter* . . . (Paris, 1752), 30; JF, Vol.
1570, fol. 310.

humans." Louis XVI acknowledged that "Jews are humans" in 1784 when he abolished the toll levied by the city of Strasbourg on Jews, livestock, and merchandise as an affront to humanity and an obstacle to commerce. The Parlement of Paris refused to register the declaration, according to attorney general Joly de Fleury, because it entailed "public recognition that Jews have the right to live in the kingdom" as French subjects. In the same year, however, the court overruled the confiscation of the estate of the Sephardic merchant Abraham Vidal under the right of escheat, which assigned the possessions of deceased foreigners to the crown. Denying the allegation that Vidal's religion made him a foreigner, the lawyers for his heirs argued that "it is not religion but origin, birth which determines whether one is French or of any other nation. Atheist or deist, Jew or Catholic, Protestant or Mohametan, it matters little. If one was [born] in France of French parents, if one has not been expatriated, one is French and enjoys all the rights of citizenship."[50] More willing, as in the cases of Jansenists and Protestants, to protect property than conscience, the magistrates upheld the claims of Vidal's heirs without endorsing this disjunction of citizenship and Catholicity in principle.

Zalkind Hourwitz—one of the laureates of the essay contest sponsored by the Academy of Metz on the question "Are there means of making the Jews more useful and more happy in France?"—assumed that the declaration of 1787 extended the rights of citizenship to Jews as well as Protestants. Pleading the cause of such "useful innovations," he scoffed at intolerance based on "popular prejudices." "Popular prejudices," after all, would have prolonged the customs of ringing bells during storms and burying the dead in churches and banned both lightning rods and inoculation. "Besides," he asserted, "the people are no more favorable to Protestants than to Jews."[51] Jurists apparently were. The edict of toleration allowed Jews to register births, mar-

---

50. *Requête des marchands et négociants de Paris contre l'admission des juifs* (Paris, 1767), 14; Pierre-Louis Lacratelle, *Plaidoyer pour les juifs de Metz* (Paris, 1928), 4 (written in 1767); "Travail de M. le procureur général [Doublet de Persan] pour le ministre des finances sur la nécessité de supprimer les droits de péage corporel sur les juifs," in Ser. H, Vol. 3105, dossier 23, AN; Armand-Guillaume-Marie-Joseph Joly de Fleury to Breteuil, April 14, 1784, in the same dossier; Paul Hildenfinger (ed.), *Documents sur les juifs à Paris au XVIIIe siècle* (Paris, 1913), 43.

51. Zalkind Hourwitz, *Apologie des juifs* (Metz, 1789), 69.

riages, and deaths before royal judges but did not abolish juridical separatism. The magistrates registered the declaration with restrictions or construed it in such a way as to sanction the exclusion of Jews from trades and offices. Louis XVI's ministers approved this restrictive interpretation of the legislation. The edict "concerning those who do not profess the Catholic faith" brought Protestants in from "the wilderness" by dispelling the fiction that all subjects of the Most Christian King were Catholics, but it left the Jews in limbo by perpetuating the fiction that they were not French.

"The French are not like other peoples in religious matters," mused the attorney general Joly de Fleury in 1788, reflecting on the prolonged debates over *Unigenitus* and toleration.[52] These contemporaneous debates involved many of the same issues and some of the same characters. Although the philosophes claimed credit for the decline of "fanaticism" in their time, Jansenist parlementaires and pamphleteers played a significant role in the campaign for toleration.[53] The experience of persecution, not "philosophic" propaganda, prompted them to apply their arguments about conscience and citizenship to the Protestants. Protestants, on the other hand, did not have much to say about the Constitution. They hardly masterminded opposition to the bull, as the beleaguered bishop of Langres charged in 1735.[54] The two groups of nonconformists did not collaborate in a conspiracy against altar and throne, as some of their more intemperate adversaries imagined. They did, however, urge the sovereign to exercise his authority in ways that contracted the scope of his responsibilities as Most Christian King and undermined the linking of religion and politics in the public order. Jansenists and Protestants, along with magistrates and

52. Jean-Omer Joly de Fleury, "Sur l'état civil demandé par les protestants et autres sectes," dated February 12, 1788, in JF, Vol. 1670, fol. 137.

53. On Jansenist support for toleration, see Charles H. O'Brien, "Jansenists on Civil Toleration in Mid-Eighteenth-Century France," *Theologische Zeitschrift*, XXXVII (1981), 71–93; O'Brien, "Jansenists and the Civil Toleration of Protestants in France, 1775–1778: Lepaige, Guidi, and Robert de Saint-Vincent," in Roland Crahay (ed.), *La Tolérance civile* (Brussels, 1982), 183–99; O'Brien, "The Jansenist Campaign for Toleration of Protestants in Eighteenth-Century France: Sacred or Secular?" *Journal of the History of Ideas*, XLVI (1985), 523–38.

54. Etienne-Joseph de La Fare to Armand-Gaston-Maximilien de Rohan, February 2, 1735, in Ser. 257 AP, Vol. 15, dossier I, no. 1, AN.

administrators who opposed *Unigenitus* and supported toleration, dissuaded the crown from enforcing ecclesiastical standards of orthodoxy and thereby made religion a more private matter in France.

The monarchy, as the pastor Olivier Desmons remarked, "prefers a thousand abuses to a revolution in policy." When, after decades of vacillation, the crown endorsed parlementary efforts to protect the Jansenists and restored the civil status of Protestants, it attempted to assert its control of public affairs and at the same time to avoid the appearance of innovation. It characterized the decree of May 24, 1766, as an interpretation of traditional principles and incorporated Malesherbes' reading of Louis XIV's legislation into the preface of the edict of toleration. In both cases, however, the crown subordinated religious to political considerations and furthered the differentiation of spiritual and temporal concerns and jurisdictions. France remained a Catholic country even after the concession of toleration to Protestants, insofar as the ancestral faith of the realm retained its exclusive privileges, but Louis XVI had recognized, much to the satisfaction of the pastor Jay, that "one can be French without being a Catholic." By the end of the ancien régime, pluralism, confined to conscience and denied outward manifestation, seemed less subversive than it had in the times of Bodin and Bossuet. "It matters little to the authority of the ruler whether his subjects are Christians or Moslems," as one pamphleteer proclaimed, "because all religions prescribe the same duties toward him."[55] Protestants, unlike Jansenists, did not question the constitutional implications of divine ordination. The toleration implemented on the eve of the Revolution desacralized the monarchy not by challenging its religious character but by circumscribing its religious obligations.

Like the Edict of Nantes and the declaration that abrogated it a century later, the edict of 1787 manifested the sovereignty of the crown and redefined the character of the kingdom. Whereas Henry IV

55. Olivier Desmons, "Mémoire sur la situation actuelle des protestants de France," dated September 17, 1783, in Emile Doumergue, *La Veille de la loi de l'an X, 1763–1802: Étude sur l'église réformée à la fin du XVIIIe siècle* (Paris, 1879), 113; Jay, quoted in Louis Mazoyer, "L'Application de l'édit de 1787 dans le Midi de la France," *BSHPF*, LXXIV (1925), 151; [Claude-Gaspard Barbat du Closel d'Annery], *Vues sur l'intolérance* (Brussels, 1788), 17–18.

had granted collective privileges to Protestants, Louis XVI assured the natural rights of non-Catholics as individuals. In doing so he warranted that the unity of the realm resided not in the putative Catholicity of his subjects but in their common civil status. This status, explained the lawyer Target, "is in effect ourselves; it is not dependent upon our beliefs." The clergy had complained for decades that Protestants constituted "a body distinct from the rest of the subjects" and exhorted the king to restore homogeneity by enforcing the ideal of conformity. In the end, however, he accepted the jurists' argument that the most just and equitable way to assimilate these nonconformists with the Catholic majority was to make them indistinguishable in law from other citizens. In this sense the promulgation of the edict of 1787, which abolished what Rabaut Saint-Etienne called "the ridiculous distinction between citizens and subjects," marked a momentous step in the unification as well as the desacralization of the French monarchy.[56] Promoting civil at the expense of confessional uniformity, it exemplified the way in which the crown itself contributed to the transformation of the corporate, Catholic kingdom.

56. Guy-Jean-Baptiste Target, *Consultation sur l'affaire de la dame marquise d'Anglure . . .* (Paris, 1787), 3; PV, VIII/1, 343; [Rabaut Saint-Etienne], *Le Roi doit modifier les lois,* 28.

Conclusion

"Everything in the political and religious order has become problematic," lamented the abbé Jacques-Julien Bonnaud in 1787.[1] This outspoken critic of the edict of toleration anathematized Jansenists, Protestants, and philosophes as confederates in a nefarious plot to subvert monarchy and Catholicism in France. The philosophes, of course, participated vociferously in the campaign for toleration, yet they had nothing but contempt for the interminable strife engendered by the bull *Unigenitus*. Montesquieu's Persian travelers made derisive comments about the dissension surrounding the reception of the Constitution in France, Candide chased away the comical priest who pestered him about *billets de confession* during his illness in Paris, and Diderot parodied the tug-of-war between the crown and the parlements in the endless bickering of Jacques le fataliste and his master. Rousseau fatuously suggested that the publication of his provocative letter on the debate over French and Italian music prevented the outbreak of revolution in the troubled 1750s, while d'Alembert naïvely maintained that *philosophie* brought about the expulsion of the Jesuits in the following decade. Even Voltaire, who described the Jansenist controversies at length in his historical works, defensively belittled their significance and ridiculed them as unworthy of his enlightened age.

1. [Jacques-Julien Bonnaud], *Discours à lire au conseil en présence du roi par un ministre patriote sur le project d'accorder l'état civil aux protestants* (2 vols.; Paris, 1787), II, 62.

The philosophes, who wrote the history of their time in their own image, failed for the most part to appreciate the momentous effects of the ecclesiastical and constitutional disputes of the eighteenth century.[2] Inasmuch as these disputes made "everything in the political and religious order" problematic, they allowed Voltaire and his brethren to claim that they, not the monarchy, the clergy, or the magistrates, spoke for "the public interest." The philosophes sometimes agreed with the crown, parlementaires, Jansenists, and/or Protestants about specific ways of serving "the public interest," but they parted company with most of their contemporaries by repudiating the traditional conjunction of religion and politics outright. They scoffed at the coronation ceremony and declared that the monarch reigned not "by the grace of God" but "by the grace of his subjects." By stripping the king of his religious character, the philosophes not only left him accountable to the kingdom but also divested him of his religious obligations. Contending that "religion should no more be the object of the laws than the manner of eating or dressing," they relieved him of the task of avenging offenses against God and required him to treat non-Catholics like the rest of his subjects. They insisted, in the last analysis, that one could be "a decent man, a good citizen, and a loyal subject without going to mass" because they denied that religion ordained authority and unified society.[3]

This kind of deliberate indifference in religious matters, which scandalized Jansenists and Protestants alike, prompted Fréron to protest that the prophets of Enlightenment were "neither subjects nor citizens nor men."[4] Critics of the philosophes exaggerated their radicalism,

2. On the most notable exception see Keith Michael Baker, "A Script for the French Revolution: The Political Consciousness of the Abbé Mably," *Eighteenth-Century Studies*, XIV (1981), 235–63.

3. François-Marie Arouet de Voltaire, "La Voix du peuple et du sage" (1750), in his *Oeuvres complètes*, ed. Louis Moland (52 vols.; Paris, 1877–85), XXIII, 470; [Paul-Henri Thiry d'Holbach], *Système social ou principes naturels de la morale et de la politique . . .* (2 vols.; Paris, 1795), I, 280; [Jean-Antoine-Nicolas de Caritat de Condorcet], *Vie de M. Turgot* (London, 1786), 239; Maurice Tourneux (ed.), *Correspondance littéraire et critique par Grimm, Diderot, Raynal, Meister, etc.* (15 vols.; Paris, 1877), VII, 37.

4. [Elie-Cathérine Fréron *et al.*], *Année littéraire ou suite des lettres sur quelques écrits de ce temps* (8 vols.; Amsterdam, 1768), I, 68.

just as the philosophes exaggerated their own impact on French society. Anxious to take credit for signs of progress toward the ideals of liberty and toleration, they bequeathed to Whiggish historians the mistaken presumption that the weakening of the politico-religious traditions of the ancien régime must have resulted from the influence of outsiders who openly rejected those traditions. The Enlightenment obviously influenced royal administrators, clergy, and magistrates, as well as Jansenists and Protestants. They all denounced the excesses of the philosophes, but they all absorbed or exploited "philosophic" rhetoric or reasoning in ways and for purposes that deserve more research. Whether or not they assimilated the Enlightenment, however, they themselves made problematic the traditions they all claimed to defend against the philosophes. Their disputes desacralized the monarchy by disrupting the conjunction of religion and politics, discrediting divine ordination, and secularizing citizenship.

The bishops and the parlementaires discredited divine ordination during the conflicts provoked by *Unigenitus*, not by repudiating it in principle but by manipulating it to serve their corporate interests, which they identified with "the public interest." By invoking the standards of orthodoxy and lawfulness to justify their criticism of Louis XV's ecclesiastical and fiscal policies, they tacitly denied the unaccountability of the crown and disclosed the distinction between kingship and kingdom. The magistrates institutionalized their opposition to absolutism by combining Gallicanism with historical and constitutional arguments about the fundamental laws and parlementary registration. These arguments, articulated in the sixteenth and seventeenth centuries and elaborated during the contestations with the clergy in the 1730s and 1750s, outlasted the Jansenist controversies. The Maupeou "revolution" transformed parlementary condemnations of abuses of royal authority—amalgamated with Jansenist contractualism and "philosophic" liberalism—into "patriotic" attacks on divine right and assertions of national sovereignty.

The monarchy had exploited divine right after the civil wars and the Fronde to secure the absolute authority its apologists claimed it needed to settle conflicts and preserve order in the kingdom. The disputes spanning the reign of Louis XV demonstrated the breakdown of this political mission and made divine right politically dysfunctional.

Maupeou wanted respect for royal authority founded upon public awareness of its benefits rather than "the duties of religion," Turgot appealed to "the public interest" in the prefaces to his Six Edicts, and the Keeper of the Seals Barentin described Louis XVI as a "citizen monarch" in his address to the opening session of the Estates-General in 1789. The crown mixed "patriotic" with traditional rhetoric, but it failed to modernize the ideology of absolutism in the last decades of the ancien régime, just as it failed once again to implement fiscal reforms in its last confrontation with the unruly corporate bodies that had already compromised its authority. When Louis XVI forced the Parlement of Paris to register another extension of the *vingtième* in 1787, he reminded the magistrates that "sovereign power belongs to the king alone" and that "he is accountable only to God." When they protested nonetheless that the king must reign "according to the laws" and insisted that taxation required the consent of the nation, chancellor Lamoignon, like chancellor Maupeou, resorted to judicial reorganization. The assembly of the clergy of 1788, invoking the "national interest," not only condemned the crown's latest attempt to tax the "consecrated" property of the Church but also criticized its "arbitrary" mistreatment of the magistrates. The bishops joined their old adversaries in denouncing innovation in the name of what they called the "ancient constitution" and defending privilege against their divinely ordained sovereign.[5]

Absolutism failed in the reform of taxation but prevailed in the reinstatement of toleration. In attempting to tax all of its subjects and in recognizing the natural rights of non-Catholics, the monarchy outlined a more uniform conception of civil status, disentangled from customary privileges and religious conformity. Jansenists, Protestants, and parlementaires all undermined the linking of civil status and religious conformity during the controversies of the eighteenth century. Jansenists subverted it by manipulating it to ensure their access to the sacraments, and Protestants rejected it altogether. Parlementaires contributed to the disengagement of citizenship from Catholicity by

5. René-Nicolas-Charles-Augustin de Maupeou, "Mémoire de Maupeou à Louis XVI," in Jules Flammermont, *Le chancelier Maupeou et les parlements* (Paris, 1883), 603; *Archives parlementaires de 1787 à 1860* . . . (90 vols. thus far; Paris, 1879–), VIII, 2, I, 265; *Les Remontrances*, III, 745; *Archives parlementaires*, I, 373.

protecting Jansenists from deprivation of their sacramental property and tacitly legitimizing marriages "in the wilderness" so as to protect the property rights of Protestants. The magistrates, always ready to denounce "arbitrary" taxes that threatened the property of French citizens, agreed with the anonymous pamphleteer who declared that there was "nothing more sacred in the order of civil things than property."[6] They not only punished crimes against property with increased severity but also stopped punishing crimes like suicide by confiscation of property. The parlementaires, involved in conflicts with the clergy for much of the century, implicitly abdicated their responsibility to enforce many of the laws against religious and moral offenses before the Most Christian King formally renounced his obligation to preserve confessional uniformity in 1787. The parlementary retreat from the traditional jurisprudence of the kingdom, like the royal abrogation of its juridical Catholicity, underscored the impact of decades of disputes about Jansenism and toleration.

6. *Du droit du souverain sur les biensfonds du clergé et des moines et de l'usage qu'il peut faire de ces biens pour le bonheur des citoyens* (Naples, 1770), 113.

Selected Bibliography

The bibliography does not include hundreds of pamphlets, treatises, royal declarations, episcopal mandements, and parlementary decrees consulted in American and Parisian libraries. For references to these printed sources, see the uncompleted *Catalogue de l'histoire de France* (15 vols.; Paris, 1855–1932).

MANUSCRIPTS

Archives Nationales, Paris

Series 29 AP, Volume 3. Roederer papers concerning Jews (1715–87).

Series 257 AP, Volumes 14–19. Correspondence addressed to Etienne-Joseph de La Fare, bishop of Laon (1730s), in Maurepas papers.

Series G8*, Volume 706. "Procès-verbal de l'assemblée générale extraordinaire du clergé de France tenue à Paris au couvent des Grands Augustins en l'année 1788."

Series H, Volume 1639. Protestants (1763–87).

Series H, Volume 3105, dossier 23. Abolition of the poll tax on Alsatian Jews (1784).

Series K, Volumes 695–98. Gilbert de Voisins papers concerning parlements (1715–83).

Series KK, Volume 1326. "Troubles du royaume de France au sujet des édits et déclarations enregistrés aux lits de justice de 1787 et 1788 par le parlement de Paris et ensuite par les autres cours du royaume."

Series 177 Mi, Volumes 74–75 [microfilm of Series 154 AP, Volumes 9–10]. Lamoignon papers concerning the royal commission of 1752.

Series O¹, Volumes 484, 605. Papers of the ministry of the royal household concerning Protestants (1787–88).

Series TT, Volume 435. Memoirs concerning Protestants addressed to Saint-Florentin (1700–48).

Series TT, Volume 436. Analysis of royal legislation against Protestants by the bishop of Nantes (May, 1723).

Series TT, Volumes 437–42. Correspondence concerning Protestants in Languedoc (1741–61).

Series TT, Volume 446. Protestants.

Series TT, Volume 463. Gilbert de Voisins papers concerning Protestants (1765–66).

Series U, Volumes 865, 872. Gilbert de Voisins papers concerning politico-religious disputes (1760s).

Series U, Volume 873. Gilbert de Voisins papers concerning Protestants (1760s).

Series U, Volumes 877. Gilbert de Voisins correspondence.

Bibliothèque de l'Arsénal, Paris

Volumes 2453–58. Marquis d'Argenson collection concerning politico-religious disputes (1731–62).

Volume 3053, folios 276–362. Comte d'Argenson papers concerning the royal commission of 1731.

Bibliothèque de la Société de l'histoire du protestantisme français, Paris

Volume 8. Memoirs on Protestants.

Volumes 304–306. Memoirs, sermons, petitions (1757–90).

Volumes 311–17. Letters addressed to Paul Rabaut (1740–90).

Volumes 328–30. Letters and documents concerning Paul Rabaut and his sons.

Volume 358. Letters addressed to Etienne Chiron.

Volumes 361–66. Court de Gébelin papers.

Volume 367. Rabaut Saint-Etienne letters, memoirs, documents.

Volume 519. Memoirs on Protestants.

Volumes 716–19. Sermons of Paul Rabaut and his sons.

Volumes 816, 923. Memoirs concerning the edict of toleration.

Bibliothèque de Port-Royal, Paris

Lepaige Collection:

Volumes 448–49, 526 bis. Politico-religious disputes (1729–32).

Volume 541. Letters (1755–83).

Volumes 546–47. Politico-religious disputes (1756–58).
Volumes 548–49. Damiens.
Volume 559. Parlements (1764–66).
Volume 562. Assembly of the clergy of 1765.
Volumes 572–74, 576, 578. Politico-religious disputes (1772–78).
Volume 580 ter. Droit public.
Volumes 588–89. Politico-religious disputes (1765–70).

Bibliothèque du Sénat, Paris

Volumes 721–31. Registers of the première chambre des enquêtes of the Parlement of Paris (August 21, 1717–February 3, 1767).

Volume 800, folios 1–100. Durey de Mesnières parlementary journal (January 7, 1749–May 27, 1751).

Volume 800, folios 101–85. Lambert parlementary journal (May 8, 1749–June 8, 1751).

Volume 800, folios 186–248. Rolland d'Erceville parlementary journal (March–September, 1751).

Volume 800, folios 249–388. Novion parlementary journal (September 9, 1752–April 17, 1753).

Volumes 802–806. Brunville parlementary journal (November, 1766–September, 1770).

Bibliothèque Nationale

Clairambault Collection:

Volumes 541, 758. Politico-religious disputes (1730–32).

Fonds Français:

Volumes 6680–87. Siméon-Prosper Hardy, "Mes loisirs ou journal des événements tels qu'ils parviennent à ma connaissance" (1764–89).

Volumes 6822–24. D'Aguesseau correspondence (1715–50).

Volumes 7026–27. Papers of Jean Le Normand, bishop of Evreux.

Volumes 7046–47. Rulhière collection concerning Protestants (1700–87).

Volumes 7565–66, 7570–71, 7573. Durey de Mesnières papers.

Volume 10619. Chrétien–Guillaume de Lamoignon de Malesherbes, "Mémoire sur le mariage des protestants," "Second mémoire sur le mariage des protestants" (1785–86).

Volume 10624. Malesherbes, "Mémoire sur le projet de rendre légitime le mariage des protestants français" (1778).

Volume 10625. Malesherbes, "Mémoire sur le mariage des protestants fait en 1779."

Volume 10627. Malesherbes, "Mémoire sur les affaires de religion" (1776).

Volume 10628. Memoirs concerning Protestants (1757–87).

Volume 10908. Parlementary journal (May 12, 1719–April 2, 1748).

Volume 10909. Parlementary journal (1731–53).

Volume 10986. Armand-Thomas Hue de Miromesnil, "Lettres sur l'état de la magistrature en l'année 1772."

Volumes 13733–35. Pierre-Etienne Regnaud, "Histoire des événements arrivés en France depuis le mois de novembre 1770 concernant les parlements et les changements dans l'administration de la justice et dans les lois du royaume."

Volume 14037. "Affaire du parlement au sujet de l'enregistrement de la déclaration du 24 mars 1751 concernant règlement pour l'administration de l'Hôpital général de Paris."

Volume 14038. Parlementary journal (March 23, 1752–July 30, 1756).

Volume 14039. Nouvelles à la main addressed to the marquis d'Argenson (1750–66).

Volume 20958–59. Parlementary journal (December 30, 1742–November, 1763).

Volumes 23441–58. La Fare papers.

Joly de Fleury Collection:

Volume 84, dossier 858; Volume 97, dossier 934; Volume 99, dossier 954; Volumes 100–101, dossier 960; Volumes 117–18, dossier 1099. Politico-religious disputes (1730–32).

Volume 160, dossier 1488. Royal declaration of April 9, 1736.

Volume 397, dossier 4577. Controversy involving the archbishops of Aix and Arles (1764–65).

Volume 447, dossier 5400. Suicide.

Volume 469, dossier 5762. Suicide.

Volume 472, dossier 5806. Jews.

Volume 1051. Evocations (1656–1784).

Volumes 1476–78. Assemblies of the clergy (1705–88).

Volumes 1479–80. Assembly of the clergy of 1765.

Volumes 1481–83. Politico-religious disputes (1674–1788).

Volumes 1493–1505. Politico-religious disputes (1750s).

Volumes 1570. Ecclesiastical affairs, including the case of Borach Lévi.

Volumes 1648–56. Ecclesiastical fiscal exemptions (1750).

Volumes 1667–72. Protestants.

Volume 1681. Edict of toleration (1787).

Volumes 1687, 1708. Sorbonne (1721–61, 1703–80).

Volumes 2068–73. Damiens.

Volumes 2074–77. Threats against the king (1757–75).

Volumes 2078–2079. Ricard affair.

Volumes 2103–2106. Politico-religious disputes (1750s and 1760s).
Volumes 2206–2207. Marriage.
Volumes 2414–32. Law and administration.
Volume 2476. Guillaume-François Joly de Fleury, "Mémoires historiques."

Nouvelles Acquisitions Françaises:
Volumes 3333–35. Politico-religious disputes (1714–58).
Volume 4715. Thomas, "Eloge de Louis XV."
Volume 8448. Politico-religious disputes (1751–56).
Volume 8496. Barthélemy-Gabriel Rolland d'Erceville, "Histoire des remontrances du 9 avril 1753."
Volume 9511. François Richer d'Aube, "Réflexions sur le gouvernement de France" (1731).

SECONDARY WORKS

Acomb, Frances. *Anglophobia in France, 1763–1789: An Essay in the History of Constitutionalism and Nationalism.* Durham, 1950.

Adams, Francis Geoffrey Waddington. "The Struggle of the French Protestants for Civil Rights, 1750–1789." Ph.D. dissertation, University of Chicago, 1954.

Alatri, Paolo. *Parlements et lutte politique en France au XVIIIe siècle.* Studies on Voltaire and the Eighteenth Century, CLI (1976).

Angeras, P. *L'Edit de 1787 et son application dans la sénéchaussée de Nîmes.* Nîmes, 1925.

Anquez, Léonce. *De l'Etat civil des réformés de France.* Paris, 1868.

Antoine, Michel. *Le Conseil du roi sous le règne de Louis XV.* Geneva, 1970.

———. "Le Discours de la flagéllation (3 mars 1766)." In *Recueil de travaux offerts à M. Clovis Brunel.* 2 vols. Paris, 1955.

Appolis, Emile. "A travers le XVIIIe siècle: Entre jansénistes et constituants, un tiers parti." *Annales,* VI (1951), 154–71.

———. "L'Anticléricalisme dans un diocèse languedocien au XVIIIe siècle." In *Actes du 91e Congrès national des sociétés savantes: Section d'histoire moderne.* 2 vols. Paris, 1969.

Aubry, Gérard. *La Jurisprudence criminelle du Châtelet sous le règne de Louis XVI.* Paris, 1971.

Bailey, Charles R. *French Secondary Education, 1763–1790: The Secularization of the Ex-Jesuit Colleges.* Transactions of the American Philosophical Society, LXVIII, No. 6 (1978).

Baker, Keith Michael. "French Political Thought at the Accession of Louis XVI." *Journal of Modern History,* L (1978), 279–303.

————. "Memory and Practice: Politics and the Representation of the Past in Eighteenth-Century France." *Representations*, XI (1985), 134–65.

————. "On the Problem of the Intellectual Origins of the French Revolution." In *Modern European Intellectual History: Reappraisals and New Perspectives*, edited by Steven Kaplan and Dominick LaCapra. Ithaca, 1982.

————. "A Script for the French Revolution: The Political Consciousness of the Abbé Mably." *Eighteenth-Century Studies*, XIV (1981), 235–63.

————, ed. *The Political Culture of the Old Regime*. Oxford, 1987. Vol. I of Baker, François Furet, and Colin Lucas, eds., *The French Revolution and the Creation of Modern Political Culture*. 3 vols.

Basse, Bernard. *La Constitution de l'ancienne France: Principes et lois fondamentales de la royauté française*. Liancourt, 1973.

Bénabou, Erica-Marie. *La Prostitution et la police des moeurs au XVIIIe siècle*. Paris, 1987.

Bernard, Louis. *The Emerging City: Paris in the Age of Louis XIV*. Durham, 1970.

Bickart, Roger. *Les Parlements et la notion de souveraineté nationale au XVIIIe siècle*. Paris, 1932.

Bien, David. *The Calas Affair: Persecution, Toleration, and Heresy in Eighteenth-Century Toulouse*. Princeton, 1960.

————. "Catholic Magistrates and Protestant Marriages in the French Enlightenment." *French Historical Studies*, II (1962), 405–29.

————. "Religious Persecution in the French Enlightenment." *Church History*, XXX (1961), 325–33.

Bloch, Marc. *Les Rois thaumaturges: Essai sur le caractère surnaturel attribué à la puissance royale, particulièrement en France et en Angleterre*. 2nd ed. Paris, 1961.

Bluche, François. *Les Magistrats du parlement de Paris au XVIIIe siècle*. Paris, 1960.

Blumenkranz, Bernhard, *et al. Histoire des juifs en France*. Toulouse, 1972.

Bonney, Richard. "Absolutism: What's in a Name?" *French History*, I (1987), 93–117.

Bossy, John. *Christianity and the West, 1400–1700*. Oxford, 1985.

————. "The Counter-Reformation and the People of Catholic Europe." *Past & Present*, XLVII (1970), 51–70.

Boutelet, Bernadette. "Etude par sondage de la criminalité dans le bailliage de Pont-de-l'Arche aux XVIIe et XVIIIe siècles." *Annales de Normandie*, XII (1962), 235–62.

Bouwsma, William J. "The Secularization of Society in the Seventeenth Century." In *Proceedings of the Thirteenth International Congress of Historical Sciences*. 5 vols. Moscow, 1970.

Brisset de Morcour, Yves. *La Police séculiaire des dimanches et fêtes dans l'ancienne France.* Paris, 1938.

Bryant, Lawrence. *The King and the City in the Parisian Royal Entry Ceremony: Politics, Ritual, and Art in the Renaissance.* Geneva, 1986.

Cahen, Léon. "La Question de l'état civil à Paris au XVIIIe siècle: Le conflit de 1736." *La Révolution française,* LVII (1909), 193–212.

Cameron, Iaian. *Crime and Repression in the Auvergne and Guyenne, 1720–1793.* Cambridge, England, 1981.

Carcassonne, Elie. *Montesquieu et le problème de la constitution française au XVIIIe siècle.* Paris, 1927.

Castan, Nicole. *Justice et répression en Languedoc à l'époque des lumières.* Paris, 1980.

Censer, Jack, and Jeremy Popkin, ed. *Press and Politics in Pre-Revolutionary France.* Berkeley, 1987.

Certeau, Michel de. "Du système religieux à l'éthique des lumières, XVIIe–XVIIIe siècles: La Formalité des pratiques." *Ricerche di storia sociale e religiosa,* II (1972), 31–94.

Champin, Marie-Madeleine. "La Criminalité dans le bailliage d'Alençon de 1715 à 1745." *Annales de Normandie,* XXII (1972), 47–84.

Chartier, Roger, and Henri-Jean Martin, ed. *Histoire de l'édition française.* 2 vols. Paris, 1983–84.

Chassaigne, Marc. *Le Procès du chevalier de La Barre.* Paris, 1920.

Chastanier, Roger. *Un Aspect des lois relatives aux minorités religieuses: L'État civil des protestants, 1550–1792.* Thèse, Université de Montpellier, 1922.

Chaunu, Pierre. *La Mort à Paris, XVIe, XVIIe, XVIIIe siècles.* Paris, 1978.

Chevallier, Pierre. *Loménie de Brienne et l'ordre monastique, 1766–1789.* 2 vols. Paris, 1959–60.

Church, William F. *Constitutional Thought in Sixteenth-Century France.* Cambridge, Mass., 1941.

———. "The Decline of the French Jurists as Political Theorists, 1660–1789." *French Historical Studies,* V (1967), 1–16.

———. "France." In *National Consciousness, History, and Political Culture in Early Modern Europe,* edited by Orest Ranum. Baltimore, 1975.

———. *Richelieu and Reason of State.* Princeton, 1972.

Cobban, Alfred. "The Parlements of France in the Eighteenth Century." In Cobban, *Aspects of the French Revolution.* New York, 1968.

Cocatre-Zilgien, André. *Les Doctrines politiques des milieux parlementaires dans la seconde moitié du XVIIIe siècle.* Annales de la Faculté de droit et des sciences économiques de Lille, 1963.

Coquerel, Charles. *Histoire des églises du désert chez les protestants de France depuis la fin du règne de Louis XIV jusqu'à la Révolution française.* 2 vols. Paris, 1841.

Cottret, Monique. "Aux Origines du républicanisme janséniste: Le mythe de l'église primitive et le primitivisme des lumières." *Revue d'histoire moderne et contemporaine,* XXXI (1984), 99–115.

Darnton, Robert. *The Literary Underground of the Old Regime.* Cambridge, Mass., 1982.

Dedieu, Joseph. *Histoire politique des protestants français, 1715–1794.* 2 vols. Paris, 1925.

Delumeau, Jean. *Le Catholicisme entre Luther et Voltaire.* Paris, 1971.

———. *Un Chemin de l'histoire: Chrétienté et christianisation.* Paris, 1981.

Deyon, Pierre. *Le Temps des prisons: Essai sur l'histoire de la délinquance et les origines du système pénitentiaire.* Paris, 1975.

Dodge, Guy Howard. *The Political Theory of the Huguenots of the Dispersion with Special Reference to the Thought and Influence of Jurieu.* New York, 1947.

Doolin, Paul Rice. *The Fronde.* Cambridge, Mass., 1935.

Doyle, William O. *The Parlement of Bordeaux and the End of the Old Regime, 1771–1790.* New York, 1974.

———. "The Parlements of France and the Breakdown of the Old Regime." *French Historical Studies,* VI (1970), 415–58.

Dunkley, John. *Gambling: A Social and Moral Problem in France, 1685–1792.* Studies on Voltaire and the Eighteenth Century, CCXXXV (1985).

Echeverria, Durand. *The Maupeou Revolution: A Study in the History of Libertarianism, 1770–1774.* Baton Rouge, 1985.

Egret, Jean. *Louis XV et l'opposition parlementaire, 1715–1774.* Paris, 1970.

———. *Le Parlement de Dauphiné et les affaires publiques dans la deuxième moitié du XVIIIe siècle.* 2 vols. Grenoble, 1942.

———. *La Prérévolution française, 1787–1788.* Paris, 1962.

Ehrard, Jean. "L'Esprit républicain au XVIIIe siècle." In *L'Esprit républicain.* Paris, 1972.

Etlin, Richard. *The Architecture of Death: The Transformation of the Cemetery in Eighteenth-Century France.* Cambridge, Mass., 1984.

Fairchilds, Cissie. *Poverty and Charity in Aix-en-Provence, 1640–1789.* Baltimore, 1976.

Fauchois, Yann. "Jansénisme et politique au XVIIIe siècle: Légitimation de l'état et délégitimation de la monarchie chez G.-N. Maultrot." *Revue d'histoire moderne et contemporaine,* XXXIV (1987), 473–91.

Favre, Robert. *La Mort dans la littérature et la pensée françaises au siècle des lumières.* Lyon, 1978.

Feret, Pierre. *Le Droit divin et la théologie: Aperçu historique sur le pouvoir souverain en général et particulièrement en France.* Paris, 1874.

Feuerwerker, David. *L'Emancipation des juifs en France, de l'ancien régime à la seconde empire.* Paris, 1976.

Figgis, John Neville. *The Divine Right of Kings.* Cambridge, England, 1914.

Flandrin, Jean-Louis. *Familles: Parenté, maison, sexualité dans l'ancienne société.* Paris, 1976.

Fogel, Michèle. "Célébrations de la monarchie et de la guerre." In *La Bataille, l'armée, et la gloire.* Clermont, 1985.

Foisil, Madeleine. "Les Attitudes devant la mort au XVIIIe siècle: Sépultures et suppressions de sépultures dans le cimetière parisien des Saints Innocents." *Revue historique,* No. 510 (1974), 303–30.

Funck-Brentano, Franz. *L'Ancienne France: Le roi.* Paris, 1912.

Furet, François, *et al. Livre et société dans la France du XVIIIe siècle.* 2 vols. Paris, 1965–70.

———. *Penser la Révolution française.* Paris, 1978.

Garnot, Bénoît. "Délits et châtiments en Anjou au XVIIIe siecle." *Annales de Bretagne,* LXXXVIII (1981), 283–304.

Gazier, Augustin-Louis. *Histoire générale du mouvement janséniste depuis ses origines jusqu'à nos jours.* 2 vols. Paris, 1923.

Gegot, Jean-Claude. "Etude par sondage de la criminalité dans le bailliage de Falaise, XVIIe et XVIIIe siècles: Criminalité diffuse ou société criminelle?" *Annales de Normandie,* XVI (1966), 103–64.

Gembecki, Dieter. *Histoire et politique à la fin de l'ancien régime: Jacob-Nicolas Moreau, 1717–1803.* Paris, 1979.

Giesey, Ralph E. *Cérémonial et puissance souveraine: France, XVe–XVIIe siècles.* Paris, 1987.

———. *The Juristic Basis of Dynastic Right to the French Throne.* Transactions of the American Philosophical Society, LI, No. 5 (1961).

———. "Models of Rulership in French Royal Ceremonial." In *Rites of Power: Symbolism, Ritual, and Power Since the Middle Ages,* edited by Sean Wilentz. Philadelphia, 1985.

———. *The Royal Funeral Ceremony in Renaissance France.* Geneva, 1960.

Girault de Coursac, Pierrette. *L'Education d'un roi: Louis XVI.* Paris, 1972.

Glasson, Ernest-Destré. *Le Parlement de Paris: Son rôle politique depuis le règne de Charles VI jusqu'à la Révolution française.* 2 vols. Paris, 1901.

Godard, Philippe. *La Querelle des refus de sacrements, 1730–1765.* Paris, 1937.

Godechot, Jacques. "Nation, patrie, nationalisme, et patriotisme en France au XVIIIe siècle." *Annales historiques de la Révolution française,* XLIII (1971), 481–501.

Goubert, Pierre, and Daniel Roche. *Les Français et l'ancien régime.* 2 vols. Paris, 1984.

Greenbaum, Louis. "The Cure of Body and Soul in the Paris Hospital at the End of the Old Regime." In *Education in the Eighteenth Century,* edited by J. D. Browning. New York, 1974.

————. "Nurses and Doctors in Conflict: Piety and Medicine in the Paris Hôtel-Dieu on the Eve of the French Revolution." *Clio Medica,* XIII (1979), 247–68.

————. "Science, Medicine, Religion: Three Views of Health Care in France on the Eve of the French Revolution." *Studies in Eighteenth-Century Culture,* X (1981), 373–92.

————. *Talleyrand, Statesman-Priest.* Washington, D.C., 1970.

Grieder, Josephine. *Anglomania in France, 1740–1789: Fact, Fiction, and Political Discourse.* Geneva, 1985.

Groethuysen, Bernard. *The Bourgeois: Catholicism vs. Capitalism in Eighteenth-Century France.* Translated by Mary Ilford. London, 1968.

Grosclaude, Pierre. "Comment Malesherbes élabora sa doctrine sur le problème des protestants." *BSHPF,* CIV (1957), 149–72.

————. *Malesherbes, témoin et interprète de son temps.* Paris, 1961.

Gruber, Alain-Charles. *Les Grandes fêtes et leurs décors à l'époque de Louis XVI.* Paris, 1972.

Guicciardi, Jean-Pierre. "Between the Licit and the Illicit: The Sexuality of the King." In *'Tis Nature's Fault: Unauthorized Sexuality During the Enlightenment,* edited by Robert Maccubbin. Cambridge, England, 1987.

Hanley, Sarah. *The Lit de justice of the Kings of France: Constitutional Ideology in Legend, Ritual, and Discourse.* Princeton, 1983.

Hannaway, Owen, and Caroline Hannaway. "La Fermeture du cimetière des Innocents." *XVIIIe siècle,* IX (1977), 181–92.

Hardy, Georges, "L'Anticléricalisme paysan dans un province français avant 1789." *Annales révolutionnaires,* V (1912), 605–24.

————. *Le Cardinal de Fleury et le mouvement janséniste.* Paris, 1925.

Hardy, James. *Judicial Politics in the Old Regime: The Parlement of Paris During the Regency.* Baton Rouge, 1967.

Hatton, Ragnhild, ed. *Louis XIV and Absolutism.* London, 1976.

Haueteur, Anton. *Die Krönungen der französischen Könige im Zeitalter des Absolutismus und in der Restauration.* Zurich, 1975.

Herlaut, Auguste-Philippe. "Un Révolutionnaire en 1758: Le procès de Moriceau de La Motte." *Annales historiques de la Révolution française,* I (1924), 115–34.

Hermann-Mascard, Nicole. *La Censure des livres à Paris à la fin de l'ancien régime, 1750–1789.* Paris, 1968.

Hertzberg, Arthur. *The French Enlightenment and the Jews: The Origins of Modern Antisemitism.* New York, 1968.

Hervé, Jean-Claude. "L'Ordre à Paris au XVIIIe siècle: Les Enseignements du Recueil de règlements de police du commissaire Dupré." *Revue d'histoire moderne et contemporaine,* XXXIV (1987), 185–214.

Hitier, Joseph. *La Doctrine de l'absolutisme.* Paris, 1903.

Hoffman, Philip T. *Church and Community in the Diocese of Lyon, 1500–1789.* New Haven, 1984.

Hudault, Joseph. "Guy-Jean-Baptiste Target et sa contribution à la préparation de l'édit de novembre 1787 sur l'état civil des protestants." Mémoire-diplôme d'études supérieures, Faculté de droit et des sciences économiques, Université de Paris, 1966.

———. "Statut personnel et droit naturel dans l'oeuvre de G.-J.-B. Target." In *Modèles et moyens de la réflexion politique.* 3 vols. Lille, 1977.

Hudson, David Carl. "In Defense of Reform: French Government Propaganda During the Maupeou Crisis." *French Historical Studies,* VIII (1973), 51–76.

———. "Maupeou and the Parlements: A Study in Propaganda and Politics." Ph.D. dissertation, Columbia University, 1967.

———. "The Parlementary Crisis of 1763 and Its Consequences." *Canadian Journal of History,* VII (1972), 97–117.

Hufton, Olwen. *The Poor of Eighteenth-Century France, 1750–1789.* Oxford, 1974.

Hugues, Edmond. *Histoire de la restauration du protestantisme en France au XVIIIe siècle: Antoine Court.* 2 vols. Paris, 1875.

Jackson, Richard A. *Vive le roi! A History of the French Coronation from Charles V to Charles X.* Chapel Hill, 1984.

Joynes, Carroll. "Parlements, Peers, and the *Parti janséniste*: The Refusal of Sacraments and the Revival of the Ancient Constitution in Eighteenth-Century France." *Proceedings of the Eighth Annual Meeting of the Western Society for French History* (1981), 229–38.

Julia, Dominique. "Discipline ecclésiastique et culture paysanne au XVIIIe siècle." In *La Religion populaire.* Paris, 1979.

———. "Le Prêtre au XVIIIe siècle: La théologie et les institutions." *Revue des sciences religieuses,* LVIII (1970), 521–34.

———. "Les Professeurs, l'église, et l'état après l'expulsion des Jésuites." *Historical Reflections/Réflexions historiques,* VII (1980), 459–81.

Kantorowicz, Ernst. *The King's Two Bodies: A Study in Medieval Political Theology.* Princeton, 1966.

Kaplan, Steven Laurence. *Bread, Politics, and Political Economy in the Reign of Louis XV.* 2 vols. Hague, 1976.

Kelly, George Armstrong. "From *Lèse-majesté* to *Lèse-nation*: Treason in

Eighteenth-Century France." *Journal of the History of Ideas*, XLII (1981), 269–86.

Keohane, Nannerl O. *Philosophy and the State in France: The Renaissance to the Enlightenment.* Princeton, 1980.

Kern, Fritz. *Kingship and Law in the Middle Ages.* Oxford, 1939.

Kreiser, B. Robert. *Miracles, Convulsions, and Ecclesiastical Politics in Early Eighteenth-Century Paris.* Princeton, 1978.

Lacour-Gayet, Georges. *L'Education politique de Louis XIV.* Paris, 1898.

Langui, André. "Sentiments d'un juriste à la fin du XVIIIe siècle: Pierre-François Muyart de Vouglans, 1713–1791." *Travaux juridiques et économiques de l'Université de Rennes*, XXV (1964), 177–274.

Le Bras, Gabriel. *Etudes de sociologie religieuse.* 2 vols. Paris, 1955–56.

Lebrun, François. *Les Hommes et la mort en Anjou aux XVIIe et XVIIIe siècles: Essai de démographie et de psychologie historique.* Hague, 1971.

———. *Médicins, saints, et sorciers aux XVIIe et XVIIIe siècles.* Paris, 1983.

———. *La Vie conjugale sous l'ancien régime.* Paris, 1975.

———, ed. *Histoire des catholiques de France du Moyen Age au lendemain de Vatican II.* Toulouse, 1980.

Lecoq, Anne-Marie. "La Symbolique de l'état: Les Images de la monarchie des premiers Valois à Louis XIV." In *Les Lieux de mémoire*, edited by Pierre Nora. 4 vols. Paris, 1984–86.

Lecuir, Jean. "Crime et moralité: Montyon, statisticien du parlement de Paris." *Revue d'histoire moderne et contemporaine*, XXI (1974), 444–93.

Legoff, Jacques. "Reims, ville du sacre." In *Les Lieux de mémoire*, edited by Pierre Nora. 4 vols. Paris, 1984–86.

Lemaire, André. *Les Lois fondamentales de la monarchie française.* Paris, 1907.

Lemaire, Suzanne. *La Commission des réguliers, 1760–1780.* Paris, 1926.

Lemaître, Alain. "Espace sacré et territoire vital au XVIIIe siècle: La Régulation des lieux d'inhumation en Bretagne." *Annales de Bretagne*, CX (1983), 249–59.

Lemoy, Arthur. *Le Parlement de Bretagne et le pouvoir royal au XVIIIe siècle.* Paris, 1909.

Léonard, Emile G. "Les Assemblés du désert: Caractères, adversaires, et conséquences." *BSHPF*, LXXXVII (1938), 470–87.

———. *Histoire ecclésiastique des réformés français au XVIIIe siècle.* Paris, 1940.

———. "Le Problème du culte public et l'église dans le protestantisme au XVIIIe siècle." *Foi et vie*, XXXVIII (1937), 431–57.

———. "Le Problème du mariage civil et les protestants français au XVIIIe siècle." *Revue de théologie et d'action évangélique*, II (1942), 241–99.

Lever, Maurice. *Les Bûchers de Sodome*. Paris, 1985.

Lévy, Edouard. "L'Application de l'édit de 1787." *Revue historique de droit français et étranger*, XXXV (1911), 432–59, 649–78; XXXVIII (1914–15), 230–54.

Ligou, Daniel. "L'Evolution des cimitières." *Archives de sciences sociales des religions*, XXXIX (1975), 61–78.

Lods, Armand. "Les Partisans et les adversaires de l'édit de tolérance: Etude bibliographique et juridique, 1750–1789." *BSHPF*, XXXVI (1882), 551–65, 619–23; XLI (1892), 657–61.

Loeb, Isidore. "Borach Lévi." *Annuaire de la société des études juives*, III (1882), 273–334.

Lottin, Alain. "Les Morts chassés de la cité: Lumières et préjugés, les émeutes à Lille (1779) et à Cambrai (1786) lors du transfert des cimetières." *Revue du Nord*, LX (1978), 73–117.

Lunel, Pierre. "Pouvoir royal et santé publique à la veille de la Révolution: L'Exemple de Roussillon." *Annales du Midi*, LXXXVI (1974), 347–80.

McManners, John. *Death and the Enlightenment: Changing Attitudes to Death Among Christians and Unbelievers in Eighteenth-Century France*. Oxford, 1982.

————. *French Ecclesiastical Society Under the Ancien Régime: A Study of Angers in the Eighteenth Century*. Manchester, 1960.

————. "Jansenism and Politics in the Eighteenth Century." *Studies in Church History*, XII (1975), 253–74.

————. "Tithe in Eighteenth-Century France: A Focus for Rural Anticlericalism." In *History and Society and the Church: Essays in Honor of Owen Chadwick*, edited by Derek Baker and Geoffrey Bet. Cambridge, England, 1985.

Major, J. Russell. *Representative Government in Early Modern France*. New Haven, 1980.

Malino, Frances. "Attitudes Toward Jewish Communal Autonomy in Pre-Revolutionary France." In *Essays in Modern Jewish History: A Tribute to Ben Halpern*, edited by Frances Malino and Phyllis Cohen Alert. Rutherford, 1982.

————. "Les Communautés juives et l'édit de 1787." *BSHPF*, CXXXIV (1988), 311–28.

————. "Competition and Confrontation: The Jews and the Parlement of Metz." In *Mélanges en l'honneur de B. Blumenkranz*. Paris, 1985.

Mandrou, Robert, *et al. Histoire des protestants de France*. Toulouse, 1977.

Margot, Alain. "La Criminalité dans le bailliage de Mamers, 1695–1750." *Annales de Normandie*, XXII (1972), 185–224.

Marion, Marcel. *Machault d'Arnouville: Étude sur l'histoire du contrôle général des finances de 1749 à 1754*. Paris, 1891.

Martin, Daniel. "Clergé et administration face à la débauche au XVIIIe siècle: L'exemple de l'Auvergne." In *Aimer en France, 1760–1860*. 2 vols. Clermont-Ferrand, 1980.

————. "Pratique religieuse et déchristianisation en France au temps des lumières: Etat des recherches récentes." In *Le Sacré: Aspects et manifestations*. Tübingen, 1982.

Martin, David. "Secularization: The Range of Meaning." In Martin, *The Religious and the Secular: Studies in Secularization*. London, 1969.

Maza, Sarah. "Le Tribunal de la nation: Les Mémoires judiciaires et l'opinion publique à la fin de l'ancien régime." *Annales*, XLII (1987), 73–90.

Mazoyer, Louis. "L'Application de l'édit de 1787 dans le Midi de la France." *BSHPF*, LXXIV (1925), 149–76

————. "Essai critique sur l'histoire du protestantisme à la fin du XVIIIe siècle." *BSHPF*, LXXIX (1930), 33–56.

Mer, Louis-Bernard. "Criminalité et répression en Bretagne (appréciation statistique, 1750–1760)." In *Mélanges en l'honneur du doyen Pierre Bouzat*. Paris, 1980.

————. "Réflexions sur la jurisprudence criminelle du parlement de Bretagne pour la seconde moitié du XVIIIe siècle." In *Droit privé et institutions régionales: Etudes offertes à Jean Yver*. Paris, 1976.

Merrick, Jeffrey. "Conscience and Citizenship in Eighteenth-Century France." *Eighteenth-Century Studies*, XXI (1987), 48–71.

————. "The Coronation of Louis XVI: The Waning of Royal Ritual." *Proceedings of the Eighth Annual Meeting of the Western Society for French History* (1981), 191–204.

————. "'Disputes over Words' and Constitutional Conflict in France, 1730–1732." *French Historical Studies*, XIV (1986), 497–520.

————. "Patterns and Prosecution of Suicide in Eighteenth-Century Paris." *Historical Reflections/Réflexions historiques*, XVI (1989), 1–53.

————. "Politics in the Pulpit: Ecclesiastical Discourse on the Death of Louis XV." *History of European Ideas*, VII (1986), 149–60.

————. "Royal Bees: The Gender Politics of the Beehive in Early Modern Europe." *Studies in Eighteenth-Century Culture*, XVIII (1988), 7–37.

Miller, Genevieve. *The Adoption of Inoculation for Smallpox in England and France*. Philadelphia, 1957.

Mogenson, Nels Wayne. "Crimes and Punishments in Eighteenth-Century France: The Example of the pays d'Auge." *Histoire sociale*, XVI (1977), 337–53.

Mousnier, Roland. *L'Assassinat d'Henri IV, 14 mai 1610: Le Problème du tyrannicide et l'affermissement de la monarchie absolue.* Paris, 1964.

————. "Comment les Français du XVIIe siècle voyaient la constitution." *XVIIe siècle,* XXV-XXVI (1955), 9–36.

————. "Les Concepts d'ordres, d'états, de fidelité, et de monarchie absolue en France de la fin du XVe à la fin du XVIIIe siècle." *Revue historique,* No. 502 (1972), 289–312.

————. *Les Institutions de la France sous la monarchie absolue, 1598–1789.* 2 vols. Paris, 1974–80.

————. "La Participation des gouvernés à l'action des gouvernants dans la France des XVIIe et XVIIIe siècles." *Recueils de la Société Jean Bodin,* XXIV (1966), 235–98.

Mousnier, Roland, and Fritz Hartung. "Quelques problèmes concernant la monarchie absolue." In *Relazioni del X Congresso internationale di scienze storiche.* 6 vols. Florence, 1955.

Muchembled, Robert. *Culture populaire et culture des élites dans la France moderne, XVe–XVIIIe siècles.* Paris, 1978.

Muller, Dominique. "Magistrats français et peine de mort au XVIIIe siècle." *XVIIIe siècle,* IV (1972), 79–108.

Murraciole, Marie-Madeleine. "Quelques aperçus sur la criminalité en Haute-Bretagne dans la deuxième moitié du XVIIIe siècle." *Annales de Bretagne,* LXXXVIII (1981), 305–26.

Nau, Paul. "L'Origine des encycliques modernes: Un Épisode de la lutte des évêques et des parlements, 1755–1756." *Revue historique de droit français et étranger,* XXXIV (1956), 225–67.

Norberg, Kathryn. *Rich and Poor in Grenoble, 1660–1814.* Berkeley, 1985.

O'Brien, Charles H. "The Jansenist Campaign for Toleration of Protestants in Eighteenth-Century France." *Journal of the History of Ideas,* XLVI (1985), 523–38.

————. "Jansenists and the Civil Toleration of Protestants in France, 1775–1778: Lepaige, Guidi, and Robert de Saint-Vincent." In *La Tolérance civile,* edited by Roland Crahay. Brussels, 1982.

————. "Jansenists on Civil Toleration in Mid-Eighteenth-Century France." *Theologische Zeitschrift,* XXXVII (1981), 71–93.

Ory, Jean-Marie. "Attitudes laïques devant le monde ecclésiastique en France au XVIIIe siècle." *Revue d'histoire et de philosophie religieuse,* LVIII (1978), 399–424.

Palmer, R. R. "The National Idea in France Before the Revolution." *Journal of the History of Ideas,* I (1940), 95–111.

Pange, Jean de. *Le Roi très-chrétien.* Paris, 1949.

Parguez, Jacques. *La Bulle Unigenitus et le jansénisme politique.* Paris, 1936.

Parker, David. *The Making of French Absolutism.* New York, 1983.

Peré, Georges. *Le Sacre et couronnement des rois de France dans leur rapport avec les lois fondamentales.* Toulouse, 1921.

Péronnet, Michel. "Les Assemblées du clergé et les protestants." *XVIIIe siècle,* XVII (1985), 141–50.

———. "Les Assemblées du clergé sous le règne de Louis XVI." *Annales historiques de la Révolution française,* XXXIV (1962), 8–35.

———. *Les Evêques de l'ancienne France.* 2 vols. Lille, 1977.

———. "Un Exemple d'opposition légale: Les assemblées du clergé de France au dix-huitième siècle." *Parliaments, Estates, and Representation,* VI (1986), 33–42.

———. "Police et religion à la fin du XVIIIe siècle." *Annales historiques de la Révolution française,* XLII (1970), 375–97.

Petrovich, Porphyre [pseud.]. "Recherches sur la criminalité à Paris dans la seconde moitié du XVIIIe siècle." In *Crimes et criminalité en France aux XVIIe et XVIIIe siècles,* edited by André Abbiatéci et al. Paris, 1971.

Piveteau, Cécile. *La Pratique matrimoniale d'après les statuts synodaux du Concile de Trente à la Révolution.* Le Puy, 1957.

Plongeron, Bernard. "Une Image de l'église d'après les *Nouvelles ecclésiastiques.*" *Revue d'histoire de l'église de France,* LIII (1967), 241–68.

———. "Le Procès de la fête à la fin de l'ancien régime." In *Le Christianisme populaire: Les dossiers de l'histoire.* Paris, 1976.

———. *Théologie et politique au siècle des lumières, 1770–1820.* Geneva, 1973.

———. *La Vie quotidienne du clergé français au XVIIIe siècle.* Paris, 1974.

Poland, Burdette C. *French Protestantism and the French Revolution: A Study in Church and State, Thought and Religion, 1685–1815.* Princeton, 1957.

Pontet, Josette. "Morale et ordre public à Bayonne au XVIIIe siècle." *Bulletin de la Société des sciences, lettres, et arts de Bayonne,* CXXX (1974), 127–44.

Portemer, Jean. "Recherches sur l'enseignement du droit public au XVIIIe siècle." *Revue historique du droit français et étranger,* XXXVII (1959), 341–57.

Préclin, Edmond. *Le Jansénisme au XVIIIe siècle et la Constitution civile du clergé: Le Développement du Richérisme, sa propagation dans le bas clergé, 1713–1791.* Paris, 1928.

Quéniart, Jean. *Les Hommes, l'église, et Dieu dans la France du XVIIIe siècle.* Paris, 1978.

Raeff, Marc. "The Well-Ordered Police State and the Development of Modernity in Seventeenth- and Eighteenth-Century Europe: An Attempt at a Comparative Approach." *American Historical Review*, LXXX (1975), 1221–43.

Ranum, Orest. *Artisans of Glory: Writers and Historical Thought in Seventeenth-Century France*. Chapel Hill, 1980.

————. "The French Ritual of Tyrannicide in the Late Sixteenth Century." *Sixteenth-Century Journal*, XI (1980), 63–82.

Regnault, Emile. *Christophe de Beaumont, archevêque de Paris, 1703–1781*. 2 vols. in 1. Paris, 1882.

Reichardt, Rolf, and Eberhard Schmitt, eds. *Handbuch politisch-sozialer Grundbegriffe in Frankreich, 1680–1820*. 10 vols. thus far. Munich, 1985–.

Reinhard, Marcel. *La Légende de Henri IV*. Paris, 1936.

Reinhardt, Steven. "Crime and Royal Justice in Ancien Régime France: Modes of Analysis." *Journal of Interdisciplinary History*, XIII (1983), 437–60.

Rétat, Pierre, *et al. L'Attentat de Damiens: discours sur l'événement au XVIIIe siècle*. Lyon, 1979.

Rey, Michel. "Parisian Homosexuals Create a Lifestyle, 1700–1750: The Police Archives." In *'Tis Nature's Fault: Unauthorized Sexuality during the Enlightenment*, ed. Robert Maccubbin. Cambridge, England, 1987.

————. "Police et sodomie à Paris au XVIIIe siècle: Du péché au désordre." *Revue d'histoire moderne et contemporaine*, XXIX (1982), 13–24.

Richet, Denis. *La France moderne: L'esprit des institutions*. Paris, 1973.

Ricommard, Jean. *La Lieutenance générale de police à Troyes au XVIIIe siècle*. Troyes, 1934.

Rives, Jean. *Dîme et société dans l'archevêché d'Auch au XVIIIe siècle*. Paris, 1976.

Rogister, J. M. J. "The Crisis of 1753 in France and the Debate on the Nature of the Monarchy and the Fundamental Laws." In *Herrschaftsverträge, Wahlkapitulationen, Fundamentalgesetze*, edited by Rudolf Vierhaus. Göttingen, 1977.

————. "Parlementaires, Sovereignty, and Legal Opposition Under Louis XV: An Introduction." *Parliaments, Estates, and Representation*, VI (1986), 25–32.

Rosne, A. [pseud.]. "Une Cause de la décadence de la chaire au XVIIIe siècle: Les Prédicateurs du panégyrique de Saint Louis devant l'Académie française." *Revue du clergé française* (1897), 113–24.

Rothkrug, Lionel. "Icon and Ideology in Religion and Rebellion, 1300–1600: *Bauernfreiheit* and *Religion royale*." In *Religion and Rural Revolt*, edited by Janos Bak and Gerhard Benecke. Manchester, 1984.

———. *Opposition to Louis XIV: The Political and Social Origins of the French Enlightenment.* Princeton, 1965.

Rougier, Louis. "Le Caractère sacré de la royauté en France." In *The Sacral Kingship.* Leiden, 1959.

Rousseaux, André. *La Politique religieuse des rois de France.* Cahiers d'occident, II (1926).

Rowen, Herbert H. *The King's State: Proprietary Dynasticism in Early Modern France.* New Brunswick, 1980.

Ruff, Julius. *Crime, Justice, and Public Order in Old Regime France: The Sénéchaussées of Libourne and Bazas, 1696–1789.* London, 1984.

Rule, John C., ed. *Louis XIV and the Craft of Kingship.* N.p., 1969.

Le Sacre des rois. Paris, 1985.

Sautel, Gérard. *Une Juridiction municipale de police sous l'Ancien Régime: Le Bureau de police d'Aix-en-Provence.* Paris, 1948.

Schramm, Percy Ernst. *Der König von Frankreich: Des Wesen der Monarchie von 9. zum 16. Jahrhundert, ein Kapitel aus der Geschichte des abendlandischen Staates.* 2 vols. Weimar, 1939.

Sedgwick, Alexander. *Jansenism in Seventeenth-Century France: Voices from the Wilderness.* Charlottesville, 1977.

———. "Seventeenth-Century French Jansenism and the Enlightenment." In *Church, State, and Society Under the Bourbon Kings of France,* edited by Richard Golden. Lawrence, 1982.

Shennan, J. H. *Duke of Orleans: Regent of France, 1715–1723.* London, 1979.

———. *The Parlement of Paris.* Ithaca, 1968.

———. "The Political Role of the Parlement of Paris, 1715–1723." *Historical Journal,* VIII (1965), 179–20.

———. "The Political Role of the Parlement of Paris Under Cardinal Fleury." *English Historical Review,* LXXXI (1966), 520–42.

———. "The Political Vocabulary of the Parlement of Paris in the Eighteenth Century." In *Diritto e potere nella storia europea: Atti in onore di Bruno Paradesi.* Florence, 1982.

Shiner, Larry. "The Meanings of Secularization." *Journal for the Scientific Study of Religion,* VI (1967), 202–20.

Stankiewicz, W. J. *Politics and Religion in Seventeenth-Century France: A Study of Political Ideas from the Monarchomachs to Bayle as Reflected in the Toleration Controversy.* Berkeley, 1960.

Stone, Bailey. *The French Parlements and the Crisis of the Ancien Régime.* Chapel Hill, 1986.

———. *The Parlement of Paris, 1774–1789.* Chapel Hill, 1981.

Sueur, Philippe. "Contribution à l'étude des idées politiques des jansénistes français de 1640 à la Révolution française." *Publications de la Faculté de droit et d'économie d'Amiens*, V (1973–74), 5–69.

Swarzfuchs, Simon. "Les Nations juives de France." *XVIIIe siècle*, XIII (1981), 127–36.

Szajkowski, Zosa. *Franco-Judaica: An Analytical Bibliography of Books, Pamphlets, Decrees, Briefs, and Other Printed Documents Pertaining to the Jews in France, 1500–1788*. New York, 1962.

————. *Jews in the Revolutions of 1789, 1830, and 1848*. New York, 1970.

Tackett, Timothy. *Priest and Parish in Eighteenth-Century France: A Social and Political Study of the Curés in the Diocese of Dauphiné, 1750–1791*. Princeton, 1977.

Tarczlo, Théodore. *Sexe et liberté au siècle des lumières*. Paris, 1983.

Tavaneaux, René. *Jansénisme et politique*. Paris, 1965.

Thibaut-Payen, Jacqueline. *Les Morts, l'église, et l'état dans le ressort du parlement de Paris aux XVIIe et XVIIIe siècles*. Paris, 1977.

Thireau, Jean-Louis. *Les Idées politiques de Louis XIV*. Paris, 1973.

Thuau, Etienne. *Raison d'état et pensée politique à l'époque de Richelieu*. Paris, 1966.

Trénard, Louis. "L'Absolutisme éclairé: Le cas français." *Annales historiques de la Révolution française*, LI (1979), 627–46.

Tyvaert, Michel. "L'Image du roi: Légitimité et moralité royales dans les histoires de France au XVIIe siècle." *Revue d'histoire moderne et contemporaine*, XXI (1974), 521–47.

Ulrich, Daniel. "La Répression en Bourgogne au XVIIIe siècle." *Revue historique de droit français et étranger*, L (1972), 398–437.

Valensise, Marina. "Le Sacre du roi: Stratégie symbolique et doctrine politique de la monarchie française." *Annales*, XLI (1986), 543–78.

Van Kley, Dale. "Church, State, and the Ideological Origins of the French Revolution: The Debate over the General Assembly of the Gallican Clergy in 1765." *Journal of Modern History*, LI (1979), 629–66.

————. *The Damiens Affair and the Unraveling of the Ancien Régime, 1750–1770*. Princeton, 1984.

————. "The Estates General as Ecumenical Council: The Constitutionalism of Corporate Consensus and the Parlement's Ruling of September 25, 1788." *Journal of Modern History*, LXI (1989), 1–52.

————. "The Jansenist Constitutional Legacy in the French Pre-Revolution, 1750–1789." *Historical Reflections/Réflexions historiques*, XIII (1986), 393–454.

————. *The Jansenists and the Expulsion of the Jesuits from France, 1757–1765*. New Haven, 1975.

———. "The Refusal of Sacraments Controversy and the Political Crisis of 1756–57." In *Church, State, and Society under the Bourbon Kings of France,* edited by Richard Golden. Lawrence, 1982.

Viguerie, Jean de. "Le Roi et le public: L'Exemple de Louis XV." *Revue historique,* XXXIV (1987), 23–34.

———. "Les Serments du sacre des rois de France, XVIe, XVIIe, et XVIIIe siècles." In *Hommage à Roland Mousnier: Clientèles et fidélités en Europe à l'époque moderne,* edited by Yves Durand. Paris, 1981.

Vovelle, Michel. *Piété baroque et déchristianisation en Provence au XVIIIe siècle.* Paris, 1973.

———. "Le Tournant des mentalités en France, 1750–1789: La sensibilité prérévolutionnaire." *Social History,* II (1977), 605–29.

Watrin, Paul. *La Tradition monarchique d'après l'ancien droit public français.* Paris, 1916.

Weber, Hermann. "Das Sacre Ludwigs XVI. vom 11. Juni 1775 und die Krise des Ancien Regime." In *Vom Ancien Regime zur Französischen Revolution: Forschungen und Perspektiven,* edited by Ernst Hinrichs, Eberhard Schmitt, and Rudolf Vierhaus. Göttingen, 1978.

Williams, Alan. "Patterns of Deviance in Eighteenth-Century Paris." *Proceedings of the Sixth Annual Meeting of the Western Society for French History* (1979), 179–87.

———. *The Police of Paris, 1718–1789.* Baton Rouge, 1979.

Williams, William H. "The Significance of Jansenism in the History of the French Catholic Clergy in the Pre-Revolutionary Era." *Studies in Eighteenth-Century Culture,* VII (1978), 289–306.

Wolff, Louis. *Le Parlement de Provence au XVIIIe siècle.* Aix, 1920.

Woodbridge, John. "La Conspiration du prince de Conti, 1755–1757." *XVIIIe siècle,* XVII (1985), 97–110.

Yardeni, Myriam. "Les Juifs dans la polémique sur la tolérance des protestants à la veille de la Révolution." *Revue des études juives,* CXXXII (1973), 79–93.

Index